Pressing Matters 11 Stuart Weitzman School of Design UPENN 2021–2022

An annual publication
showcasing the work of
our faculty and students

6.5 × 9.5 in.
Published Spring 2023
ORO Editions

Introduction   Winka Dubbeldam

Introduction
Winka Dubbeldam

Thank you for being part of the Weitzman community. I am happy to share that we are fully back to teaching in person at the Department of Architecture this year, after our [innovative] hybrid teaching approach the year before. We have all learned how important our social networks are, and how great a support they can be. We, again, realized how important studio culture is, and how much it enhances the student's learning process.

Education Matters

Over the last few years, we have expanded on our notion of Design-Research—something we have become known for internationally—where advanced computational models meet rigorous research and digital design. Design-Research is initiated as early as in the first year where students begin looking at components and their aggregation, rather than the traditional notion of "columns and slabs." They also practice scheduling their time and budget, and in small teams build a pavilion. This allows them a preview of the architecture practice; to conceptualize, innovate, draw, test, and coordinate design and construction. After the first year, Design-Research is expanded on and studied in different forms, such as working within Philadelphia neighborhoods and understanding diversity. The introduction of "Commons," and how architecture relates to the urban landscape and vice versa, results in urban housing designs. The last year brings this well-rounded study to a close by enlistings students to join specific Design-Research Studios or undertake Independent Thesis Studies. Our third-year studio coordinator and associate professor Ferda Kolatan has commented: "The Design-Research Studio takes on this challenge and explores—through the individual expertise of leading architects in the field—various strategies and speculations that actively shape our environment, present, and future. In this context we view 'Design-Research' as both the indispensable element through which we critically reflect on our world as well as the laboratory where specific and sophisticated design solutions are developed, tested, and applied."

Over the years, we have grown the department in quantity and quality. We added three Masters of Science in Design programs, updated and improved the curriculum, and further developed our diversity, equity, and inclusion by increasing the gender balance and race diversity of our faculty and student poplation. We are proud to be ranked 13th on the **QS World University Subject Rankings for graduate architecture schools [2022]**, and fifth in the USA as the graduate architecture school with the "most hired students." Our fast-growing faculty includes renowned architects, such as, Thom Mayne, Marion Weiss, Wolf Prix, Billie Faircloth, Mette Ramsgaard Thomsen, and many others. After doubling our standing faculty, I would like to take a moment to welcome our recent hires: Rashida Ng joined us as the Presidential Associate Professor with tenure and has taken over as Chair of Undergraduate Architecture this Fall following the inspired leadership of Richard Wesley. We are grateful and excited that Daniela Fabricius and Fernando Lara have joined our standing faculty in History-Theory this year. Billie Faircloth joined us as an Adjunct Professor, with her expertise in leading a transdisciplinary group of professionals leveraging research, design, and problem-solving processes from fields as diverse as environmental management, chemical physics, materials science, and architecture. As a partner at Kieran Timberlake's offices, she brings a critical eye, inquisitive mind, and amazing knowledge to Upenn. Mette Ramsgaard Thomsen was recently appointed as our brand new Cret Chair Professor of Practice [following Thom Mayne]. Mette, an architect with a PhD from the University College London, Bartlett School of Architecture, and currently a Professor, and the Center Director at the Royal Danish Academy Copenhagen, Denmark, will join us this fall. She has piloted special research projects and her focus is on the new digital-material relations that digital technologies bring forth. Advanced computer modeling, digital fabrication, and material specifications, as well as machine learning, are some of the subjects she and her team have investigated. Mette will start at Weitzman with a workshop and talk for the Acadia conference at Weitzman this Fall (October 26–29th) followed by a Design-Research studio in Spring 2023.

Last May we hosted a FestSchrift, with many renowned guests and speakers, in honor of Emiritus Professor, David Leatherbarrow's extensive career and his Association of Collegiate Schools of Architecture Topaz Medal. With the great organization and coordination of the event by Associate Professor, Franca Trubiano, our recently appointed Chair of the Graduate Group, this ensued into a sparkling debate over several days.

Sharing Matters

This Fall we are proud to be hosting Acadia 2022: "Hybrids & Haecceities," a symposium that seeks novel approaches to design and research that dissolve binary conditions and inherent hierarchies in order to embrace new modes of practice. Haecceities describe the qualities or properties of objects that define them as unique. Concurrently, Hybrids are entities with characteristics enhanced by the process of combining two or more elements with different properties. In concert, these terms offer a provocation toward more inclusive and specific forms of computational design. The Conference is organized by our Weitzman faculty: Dr. Masoud Akbarzadeh, Dr. Dorit Aviv, Associate Professor of Practice Hina Jamelle, and Assistant Professor Robert Stuart-Smith. All worked tirelessly to make this a successful event. We are happy it has already attracted international attention and future speakers.

Design Matters

We are excited to announce that we hired Studio Lin to take over from WSDIA to coordinate, define, and design this new *Pressing Matters 11*, our lecture posters, and announcements. Already, our first discussion on WHAT MATTERS inspired all of us to further define our thinking and how to implement that further in education and Weitzman Architecture as a whole. We look forward to continuing this great dialogue with them in the near future. Our goal of diversity, equity, and inclusion is further helped by the fact that the Department of Architecture is part of a multi-disciplinary School of Design and an exceptional research university. We feel that being part of this inspiring whole is what makes us great.

Evolve

On a more personal note, I am happy to announce that this year I will be evolving away [to quote Serena Williams] from my position as Chair of the Department of Architecture. Having already completed 10 years, this will be my last year as Chair of our ever-growing and -innovating Department of Architecture. In that light, we have recently initiated the search for a new Chair, which we hope to complete this year. We are excited for this new opportunity. After my sabbatical, I will return to teaching, and I am looking forward to spending more time on research as Director of the Advanced Research and Innovation Lab (ARI).

This new *Pressing Matters* is only a small glimpse of what is going on in the Department of Architecture. We hope to share with you more in the near future.

— Winka Dubbeldam, Ella Shafer Miller Professor and Chair
   Weitzman Architecture University of Pennsylvania

Introduction Winka Dubbeldam

Summer, Fall 2021

Spring 2022

MSD and PhD Programs 2021–22

Summer, Fall

Summer, Fall

Foundation 500: Summer Design Studio

In this introductory studio for students without an architecture background, students will be introduced to basic aspects of building and building codes, and conventions for architectural representation (scale, notation, and graphic methods). Students will receive an essential introduction to contemporary architectural methods and techniques for drawing, 3D modeling, digital fabrication, and final presentations. Digital tools and techniques will be further expanded from the Digi-Blast Course, and will focus on a broader set of tools in Rhinoceros 3D, Adobe Suite, and V-Ray.

This is the second half of the summer preparatory design studio, taught by Danielle Willems, which follows the Digi-Blast session. Course work will focus on two main projects. The first project is to produce a triptych (2.5D) in correspondence with an abstract sculpture (3D) with discrete parts and spaces related to viewing. The second project is a building proposal with a specific site location in Philadelphia. Both projects are intended to further develop and expand on the modeling techniques, drawing skills and image production established in Digi-Blast.

The Final Project of this studio is to design a Mural Art Gallery and Artist Residency of 2,900 square feet. The design volume will be contained within the row house typology. In addition to the architectural structure each project will incorporate public exterior space. The program of the Gallery/Artist Residency will contain the following: gallery and exhibition spaces, reception, public bathroom, kitchenette, storage, live/work area, private bathroom, and public exterior space. The main focus is on the development of an architectural language of form and space. Descriptive geometry and generative diagrams will be integral to each project. This exciting project will showcase both new and established visual art, and will foster a space for making and creating. The Gallery/Artist Residency will serve as a tectonic and spatial 3D sculpture becoming an iconic billboard, a monument to the city and its local artists.

The site of this Gallery/Artist Residency will be located on the corner of Pine and Hicks. The role of this project is to engage the neighborhood, create a cultural gateway for Mural Arts Philadelphia, and foster interest and exposure for the artist in residence. Capturing the view of pedestrians, creating a sense of wonder in the interior gallery spaces, and rethinking a public street corner are important aspects to consider in the project. In addition each project should explore the intensive properties and qualities of a gallery and exhibition space and the private qualities of an artist residence.

Faculty:

Foundation 500:
Summer Session 2021

Faculty: Larry Mitnick
Teaching Assistants: Keshav Ramaswami & Emily Ying Shaw

The Summer Architectural Studio offers an intensive drawing, modeling, and design experience to candidates for admission to the Graduate Program in Architecture who have not completed the necessary prerequisites or who are required to have additional design experience to qualify for acceptance into the Master of Architecture Program.

The course will develop both analog and digital methods of architectural representation and modeling skills, as well as, visual thinking essential to the formation of the architect. The intent of the drawing component of the course is to familiarize the student with primarily black and white mediums (pencil, charcoal, etc.). Exercises are designed to sharpen the student's ability to see selectively and to transform image to paper through both line and tonal renditions in both analog and digital forms. Exercises will also familiarize the student with basic drafting skills necessary for architectural communication and provide application of computer-aided design programs first introduced through intensive Rhino, V-Ray, and Illustrator tutorials taught in the second part of the course – Digi-Blast 1.

The design components of the course present a rhythm of basic 3D design studies and simple architectural studio investigations addressing the relationship between body, space, and setting. These are intended to build fundamental skills and acquaint the student with the architectural issues of form/space; process/conceptualization; measure/transformation of scale; mapping/surveying the human body; orientation/view and the architectural promenade; simple functional and constructional problems, including sensitivity to context.

Featured Student Work:

Foundation 500:
Protomorphs

Faculty: Danielle Willems
Teaching Assistants: Keshav Ramaswami & Emily Ying Shaw

In this studio students will be introduced to basic aspects of building and building codes, and conventions for architectural representation (scale, notation, and graphic methods). Students will receive an essential introduction to contemporary architectural methods and techniques for drawing, 3D modeling, digital fabrication, and final presentations. Digital tools and techniques will be further expanded from the Digi-Blast Course, and will focus on a broader set of tools in Rhinoceros 3D, Adobe Suite, and V-Ray.

This is the second half of the summer preparatory design studio, which follows the Digi-Blast session. Course work will focus on two main projects. The first project is to produce a triptych (2.5D) in correspondence with an abstract sculpture (3D) with discrete parts and spaces related to viewing. The second project is a building proposal with a specific site location in Philadelphia. Both projects are intended to further develop and expand on the modeling techniques, drawing skills, and image production established in Digi-Blast.

Featured Student Work:

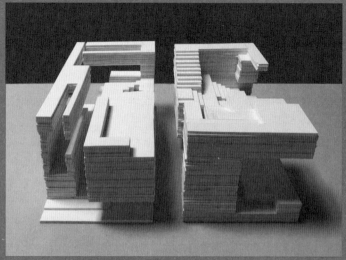

Foundation 500   Larry Mitnick

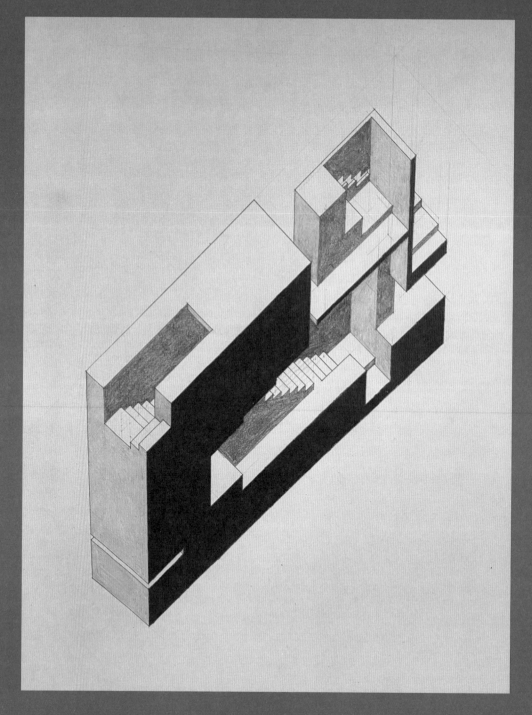

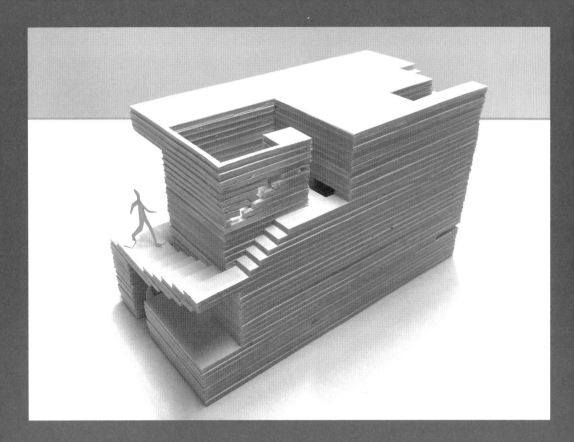

Foundation 500   Larry Mitnick

RUST
Owen Wang

This project is inspired by the process of rust corrosion. The 3D model interprets the push and pull relationship between the original metal as the container and the corroded metal as the out-breaker. It can be read as either the metal container containing the rust or the corrosion that is bulging and deforming the space and form through layering. It parallels how the gallery contains art and artists to define art and to provide shelter, but at the same time the art pieces and the artist are trying to go beyond the gallery's thresh-old. This idea becomes the key concept throughout this project's design. A byproduct of this push and pull is the gradation of permeability produced by both the perforated structure and the bulging of the panels; this process influences the permeable design.

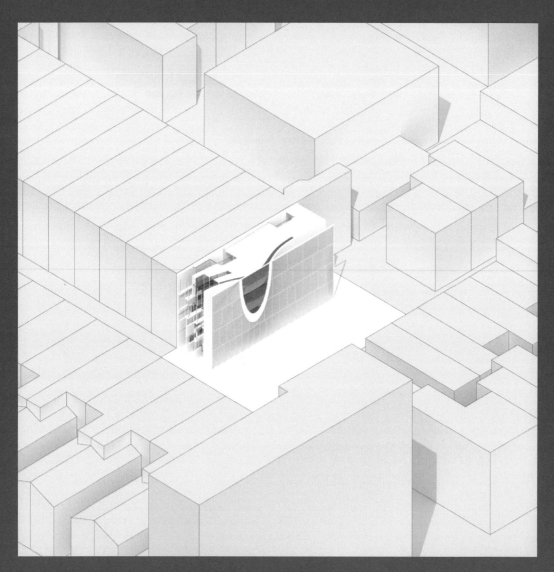

INTO NATURE
Zihan Li

This project started by looking at the artworks of Paul Juno, a Los Angeles multimedia artist who creates oil and agate paintings. At the beginning of the design phase this project looked at the natural rhythms contained in the flow, filution, breaking, and foaming of material processes as they mixed together. Furthermore the design also explores the architectural translation of dissolving, ridges, spatial tunnels, waves, and bubbles.

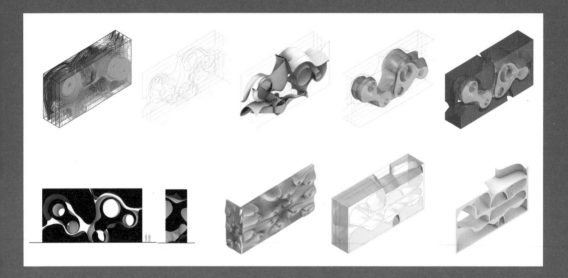

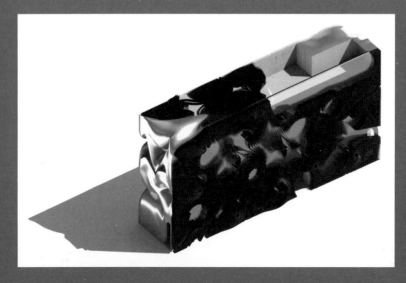

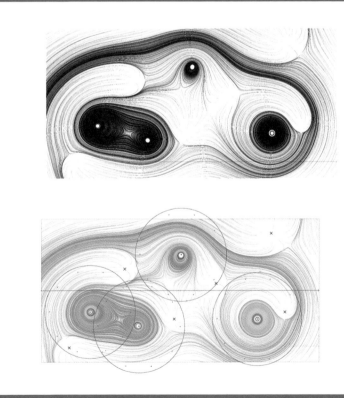

Foundation 500 Danielle Willems

Foundation 501 Studio Overview

Foundation 501: Design Studio I

Coordinator: Danielle Willems

The 501 studio 'Hyperlapse' will explore and re-examine digital techniques in regard to details and tectonics within the architectural world. Our discipline has a long and rich history of architectural details and of our contemporary digital tools' relationship to technology, art, science, material, and structural innovations as well as their implied politics.

The multi-scalar and often infinite zoom, in and out, allows us to design objects, spaces, and forms at the micro to the macro scale in a continuous and fluid method. Architecture as a profession moved toward standardized details at the turn of the 20th century in response to social, economic, and fabrication constraints, but within our contemporary digital design paradigm this becomes fertile space to experiment, explore, and redefine the role of the detail. We will explore digital methods of making and physical material prototypes held together by expanded notions of the architectural detail.

Hyperlapse as a filmic technique will cultivate an architectural position of multiple perspectives at different moments of time. This is the conceptual lens of the studio to which we will speculate on the fundamental and transformative notion of the architectural detail, novel tectonics, digital craft, formal objects, digital material logics, and modes of representations. We live in a time of "Hyperobjects," a term defined by Timothy Morton as

"Hyperobjects, then, are 'hyper' in relation to some other entity, whether they are directly manufactured by humans or not. Hyperobjects have numerous properties in common. They are viscous, which means that they 'stick' to beings that are involved with them. They are nonlocal; in other words, any 'local manifestation' of a hyperobject is not directly the hyperobject. They involve profoundly different temporalities than the human-scale ones we are used to. In particular, some very large hyperobjects, such as planets, have genuinely Gaussian temporality: they generate space-time vortices, due to general relativity. Hyperobjects occupy a high-dimensional phase space that results in their being invisible to humans for stretches of time. And they exhibit their effects interobjectively; that is, they can be detected in a space that consists of interrelationships between aesthetic properties of objects."

This semester the 501 studio will explore the hybrid program of Museum Extension and Public Outdoor Theater. Each studio section critic will present their own take on 'how' the Philadelphia Museum of Art Extension will be decolonized. We will start with closely reading the history of this site and surrounding areas, and the development of "public space" in the form of municipal infrastructures such as the Fairmount Waterworks project. This will give us an opportunity to examine the implied politics of public space and the design language of municipal and institutional buildings.

Faculty:

Foundation 501 Danielle Willems

Foundation 501:
Hybrid Ontological Formations

Faculty: Danielle Willems
Graduate Assistant: Shan Li

Our world is increasingly being understood as an emergent outcome of complexity. Similarly, both analytical and generative tools for the definition of spatial and architectural complex systems have been established within our discipline. It is with these generative tools that this studio re-examines the typology of the Museum. In our current social-political paradigm shift, designers have an important role in questioning the constructed historical narratives and spatial practices of institutions and communities that we engage with. This role translates into crafted speculative architectural spaces and forms that might facilitate a corresponding social change. The studio researched the cultural values and historical significance of specific archaeological and anthropological artifacts through the lens of Decolonization as a spatial and institutional practice. As spatial and institutional practices shift, it has created new opportunities for students to develop alternative models of public spaces, building spaces, and new hybrid programs.

The studio methodology consists of three feedback phases: the generative diagram, prototyping / iterative modeling, and formal/spatial animations. The first exercise starts with the generative diagram phase, which operates as the abstract machine of assembly. The prototyping and iterative modeling phase is a method of rapid and recursive generation of form and materials experiments. The final phase experiments with new mediums of digital representation. The studio interrogated new mediums of contingency through hybrid digital and material experimentation and behavioral systems analysis.

Hybrid Ontological Formations is an investigation into the multi-scalar definition of computational constructs. The focus of this studio is to develop innovative fabrication techniques using composite materials, in order to rethink and re-examine the typology of the museum.

Featured Student Work:

Foundation 501:
Apropos Spatial Organization

Faculty: José Aragüez
Teaching Assistant: Ana Celdrán

This studio looks at the operativity and performativity of 3D tessellation to generate new models of spatial organization in architecture. Specifically, we seek to come up with material ensembles hinging on a combination of a marked level of intricate and expanded three-dimensionality and a productive equilibrium between control and freedom, logic and accident, consistency and anomaly, identity and diversity.

A spatial armature in architecture—such as that propounded in Le Corbusier's Maison Dom-Ino—gives rise to a qualitatively identifiable series of sectors within a bounded volume of space. Further, a given spatial armature transcends the particularities of the final project in which it evolves, whether in terms of materials, program, dimensions, volumetric contours, or any combination of these attributes. In other words, the same spatial armature is capable of extensive differentiation: scalable, and deployable in diverse contexts, it can be made into various dissimilar realizations, though it will not lose its defining identity. A spatial armature is distinct by virtue of its specificities, while its degree of abstraction—relative to a fully fledged, completed realization—makes it generalizable. Any spatial armature embodying a previously unavailable 3D organization extends the bounds of possibility of their conception and realization, and with it those of architectural thinking at large.

Featured Student Work:

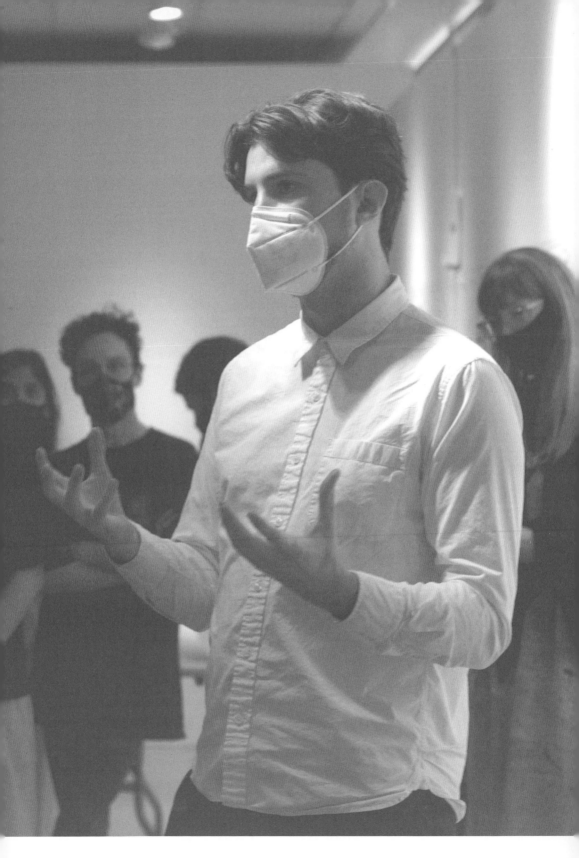

Foundation 501:
All Wrapped Up

Faculty: Dorian Booth
Teaching Assistant: Miguel Matos

The act of wrapping, understood as both a material as well as conceptual process of concealment, is the focus of the projects in the studio. Boats, patio furniture, boxes, or turbines can take on surprising and ambiguous formal qualities through the process of shrink wrapping. Students are asked to reconsider how these properties of shrink wrap can be thoughtfully deployed as a methodology for design at an architectural scale. Three elements—the frame, the membrane, and the concealed mass—will be developed throughout the course of the project using a set of methodologies investigated at a smaller scale through constructed Chambers. The relationship and feedback between these elements, as well as their ability to produce visual illusions and spatial complexity, will be studied through a combination of physical, material-driven studies and digital, physics-based simulations. Explored through an architectural proposal for the extension of the Philadelphia Museum of Art, these techniques can yield unexpected effects and contextual relationships full of contradictory characteristics: seemingly solid volumes give way to hollow shells containing a network of spaces, the collapse and overlay of spaces yield unexpected programmatic adjacencies, familiar forms produce unfamiliar readings, or light structures possess improbable heaviness.

Featured Student Work:

Foundation 501:
The Trojan Decorated Duck,
Architectures For A Post-PMA Future

Faculty: Eduardo Rega Calvo
Teaching Assistant: Reem Abi Samra

Museums like the Philadelphia Museum of Art (PMA), and universities like the one we're in, have been (and still are) key institutions and tools for the advancement of capitalist-colonial modernity. Representations of modernity have shaped empire and capitalist globalization. A western imperialist project for progress and global supremacy, modernity, has been used to erase histories and narratives that might challenge white western supremacy and reveal its crimes while prefiguring alternative futures. The PMA is one of many monuments to modernity; this makes it an excellent site to rehearse spatial imaginations that break the bounds of its capitalist-colonial order, imaginations of futures after-or-post-modernity that are decolonial, anti-capitalist, and ecofeminist. During the semester we'll discuss and collectively imagine futures after-or-post PMA; after its dismantlement; after workers, artists, activists, and communities have taken control over it; after the oligarchs leave. Framed as institutional critiques and in line with this art movement, the various projects of our studio (from containers and pavilions to building extensions) will aim to be politically conscious, critical, and radically imaginative: at once challenging the museum's structures of power and offering visions of rebellious aesthetic spatial strategies.

Featured Student Work:

Foundation 501   Kiki Goti

Foundation 501:
Philadelphia Museum Extension and Waterworks Public Theater

Faculty: Kiki Goti
Teaching Assistant: Anna Lim

The studio investigates the potential of discrete structures to create (inter)active spaces through collaboration and play. Students are asked to explore discrete tectonic systems to produce interactive, playful spaces that engage the public and invite participation. New interfaces and representational tools will help in reimagining participatory processes of design and construction, encouraging the development of intuitive fabrication methods that can respond to the needs of a wider audience.

Although by definition discrete structures consist of identical—or families of identical—units that can be mass produced in a quick and economical manner, the units can be customized through color to create more inclusive and diverse environments. Students explore ideas of colors, textures, and patterns in an effort to design diverse, open-ended systems that stimulate human creativity and imagination.

Through this process, provocative ideas emerge that challenge the way a museum operates as well as the way art is exhibited and experienced. The roles of the "viewer," the "artist," and the "curator" are revised, reimagining more accessible and inclusive processes of creating and displaying art. Narratives of participation and interaction blur the boundaries of public and private space and invite the local community to engage with the museum intuitively.

Featured Student Work:

Foundation 501:
Pipe Dreams

Faculty: Daniel Markiewicz
Teaching Assistant: Kyle Troyer

This semester began with an investigation into the thickened line or the frame as both a conceptual and physical organizing device. Students explored the formal possibilities of pipes and piping techniques both digitally and physically to sculpt volume and to question the role of art museums in today's cultural production. Frame (and framework) acts as both a structural system to which enclosure is applied—spaceframe, balloon frame, A-frame—but also as metaphorical "lens" through which discursive positions are constructed— 'frame of view,' 'frame the argument.' Ultimately, we used this starting point as an approach to design an extension to the Philadelphia Museum of Art, an institution that itself grapples with these concepts when deciding how to "frame" their collection as a whole (conceptually) and in what "frames" individual objects are displayed (physically).

We explored the combination of 2D and 2.5D techniques of composition to arrive at 3D form. Frameworks were developed digitally as well as physically with an investigation into pipe bending, welding, and cold-working mild-steel to accentuate the plasticity of the material. In addition to composition and form, students examined a partial history of the frame, in particular the modernist dichotomy of structure vs. surface. As the semester unfolded and the scale of the problem jumped from installation/display to building/collection students were compelled to articulate their own position for the Philadelphia Museum of Art.

Featured Student Work:

Foundation 501:
Fibrous Architectures

Faculty: Laia Mogas-Soldevila
Teaching Assistant: Nick Houser

The studio focuses on biomorphic design. Specifically, the assembly force flow during natural growth and its potential to inform architectural systems. Packing in tree branches, cacti skeletons, and seed pods executes complex shells and linear elements with simple materials.

In the first material-exploration projects, spools of amorphous fiber form shells with the help of gravity and solidify to describe soft and organic vaulted spaces.

In the final studio project initial logics for space making are driven by directional site phenomena such as fluvial sedimentation, rock erosion, pluvial recollection, wind power, pedestrian motion, or organoleptic experiences. Such multi-scale formative tools take students throughout their personal research unveiling meaning and materialization of flow.

Featured Student Work:

Foundation 501:
Figuring Out the Frame

Faculty: Ryan Palider
Teaching Assistant: Lauren Hunter

The Chamber project was a preamble to a larger conversation we had in the lead up to the design of the museum project. The students weren't asked to translate their chamber projects directly into a museum design, but rather to build upon lessons learned: how objects can make space, how objects can produce novel figuration, and how objects can have multiple readings through the use of materials and graphics. While the chamber dealt with more abstract concepts of form and space making, the museum project looked at more concrete ways in which architecture can engage its context through novel figuration and through the way it makes public space both internally and externally. The studio took the approach that there were three forces that each project needed to address in some way: the city, the museum, and the public. To address how to make a site-specific architecture each student was asked to look critically at the city of Philadelphia to extract an urban or architectural quality to abstract and reappropriate in some way to facilitate a dialog between their project and the site (the park and/or the city as a whole). The studio examined 12 museum examples in terms of how architecture can produce different types of interactions between the public and the galleries it contains. We also discussed how architecture can be more than an object in the landscape and questioned how architecture can extend beyond its physical walls and create and engage with public space around it.

Featured Student Work:

HYBRID ARTIFACTS
Courtney Ward

This project is an exploration and critique of the neoclassic regime imposed by the museum industry and the implication of such on the agency of the artifact. The self-proclaimed aim of the museum is to "fully emerge the visitor into the art" in the sense of creating a surrounding that immerses the visitor into the time period and the aesthetic of the art being displayed. To give the agency back to the object, one must take a non-anthropocentric view of the objects within the container itself, each rendering its own qualities and agency alone, coming together to form a holistic collection. This project understands the objects characterized in terms of their raw geometrical quality. To achieve this the geometry and geological location will combine to create a new container that represents the agency of the objects themselves. This is developed in the formal qualities of things such as the interior pouch, the textures of the walls, and the projected textures within the space. Additionally, the connection to the Fairmount waterworks informs the seams created to separate the space.

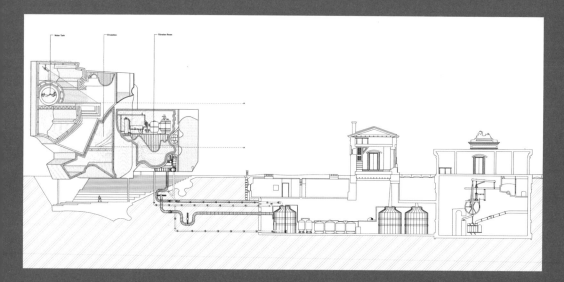

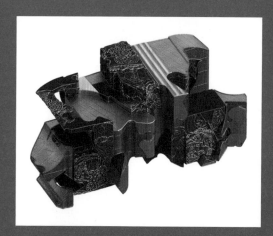

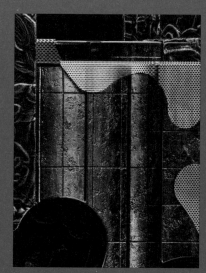

UNVEILED IDENTITY
Daniel Jarabek

Unveiled Identity intends to peel back the façade of the museum typology by recalling the articulation of industrial history and deconstructing the narratives underneath the surface of artistic ownership and display. Through introducing a critical inquiry into the role of the universal museum and its global consequences, the extension proposal to the Philadelphia Museum of Art seeks to erode the western model of privileged artistic consumption that dominates untold narratives. In order to destabilize the unconscious choreography of the user experience embedded within the museum typology, the building utilizes a hyper tectonic construction exploring a grand cantilever form to empower the excessive expression of structure, and therefore, truth. The theatrical celebration of industrial articulation highlights the mechanical, the processional, and the unspoken in service of liberating the art it houses. The structural system operates as fragments slipping into fixed positions along site axes while the program features underground multimedia exhibition space, permanent galleries, and education centers.

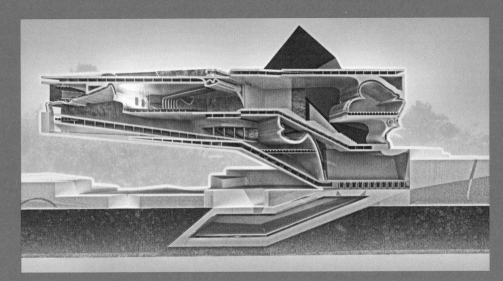

FLOWING POLYHEDRA
Ruifeng (Rose) Wang

The Philadelphia Museum of Art is a 19th-century example of federal-style architecture, which is characterized using architectural orders to emphasize the building's monumentality. This style of architecture was popular during the 19th century. However, this use of architectural orders can also be seen as too strong, as it may not allow for the various communities that the museum serves to fully embrace the space. This is because the museum serves as a cultural hub for the community. The potentials of modular systems and how they can be used to strike a balance between the guiding intention of architectural orders and the freedom of visitors are investigated in this project. The project is focused on the design of a museum. The plan for the expansion of the museum suggests the installation of a path that subverts the conventional architectural order by making use of a continuous 3D tessellation. The project investigates the possibility of producing dynamic circulation while still preserving a certain level of perceptual guidance. This is done by scaling the modules, subtracting from them, and mirroring them. Nevertheless, it opens the possibility of freely exploring the public space, both on the interior and exterior of the building.

WHAT'S IN THE BOX?
Siqi Yao

This project is based on a 3D Infinite Polyhedral consisting of two base units: one with four curved surfaces on the exterior and the other with curves on the interior. The base units are aggregated either edge-to-edge or stacked, and spatial transformations such as extruding and enlarging are applied to create spaces of varying sizes. The curved surfaces are subdivided into building components such as structure, circulation, and furniture. The interior curvature of one of the base units creates an intriguing "mystery box" effect, in which the interior is distinct from the exterior. The building's two major programs, exhibition and community, are distributed vertically. The exhibition section is comprised of mystery-box units connected by narrow bridges, thereby creating a linear narrative and directional exhibition experience. Unlike the exhibition programs, the community rooms are open and adaptable, with operable windows, movable furniture, and partitions. The building has a polycarbonate exterior that leaves room for the imagination. The grid derived from the initial geometry was applied to the design of the site, which included landscape structures and an amphitheater.

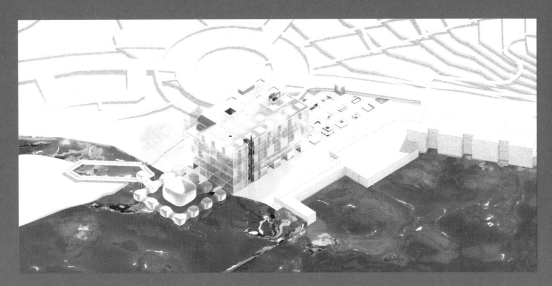

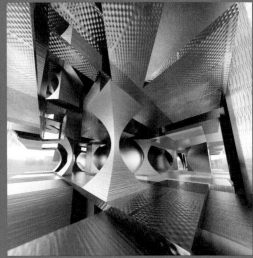

ERODED TENSIONS
Jenna Arndt

The Eroded Tensions proposal is an idea for a site next to the Philadelphia Museum of Art along the Schuylkill River that would rethink the incorporation of water and erosion as a building system and architectural language. By using the river as a dividing line between the historic Museum Mile and the surrounding suburbs, the proposal seeks to reimagine the river's role in the city's urban fabric. By the use of incremental pockets of water purification processes that serve as both educational interactive displays and performative and artistic experiences, the proposal integrates water first as a building system process to be purified and recycled. The architectural interventions at the site's periphery are faithful to the existing urban geometry, while the circulation spine takes on the characteristics of erosion in the organization of climate-controlled and semi-climate-controlled areas and in the aesthetic of excavated surfaces. Within the context of this proposal, conditions are created for the integration of artistic expression, academic study, and leisure pursuits without the presence of any commercial pressure.

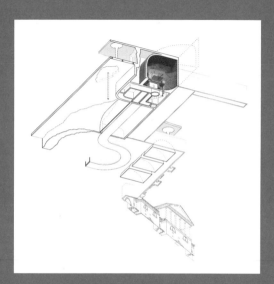

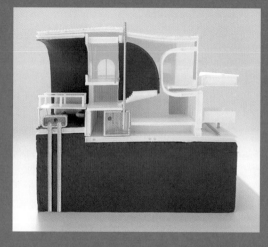

DUPLICITOUS ACCESS
Khang Truong

My study, titled Duplicitous Access, investigates how buildings can manipulate viewers' expectations for how they will interact with works of art and other exhibited objects. Here, display objects appear in view from adjacent programs, but the observer isn't given any guidance on how to interact with the displayed object. An artifact can be viewed from a different location, such as a reading room, the lobby, or even the restroom, even though the actual artifact is located elsewhere. Optical illusions help the viewer find or align the displayed objects, giving the impression that they have been placed there by magic. Illusions of interior spaces can be used in addition to optical illusions to locate hidden items. Illusions, when viewed from a specific vantage point, can visually fuse disparate spatial forms into a single coherent whole, resulting in scenes that collapse multiple spatial readings into a single unified reading that speaks to relationships between, say, an exterior and an interior, or a classroom and a museum gallery. By participating in the illusion, we are able to place the precious items on display somewhere other than a social, cultural, or political pedestal, where they can continue to exist undisturbed.

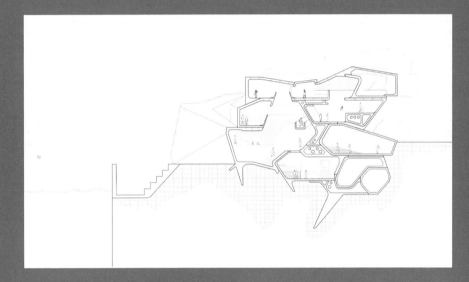

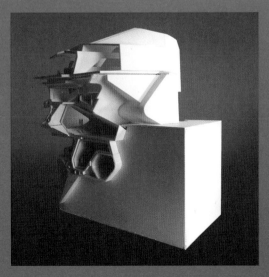

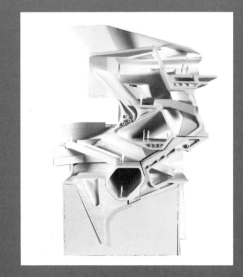

REPATRIATION PHASE 02:
THE VESSELS
Laurel Li

The project is the second phase of a repatriation procedure. It begins with an overall evaluation and critique of the museum's exhibition space layout. Today, the overlapping circulations of the PMA and its western colonial biases confuse visitors and make it simple to overlook or ignore non-western works of art. In addition, the Gallery on the third floor displays a combination of cultural artifacts that is insensitive to the objects and the complexity of their histories. To realize repatriation, the project first establishes a modular mobile architecture entity—"the Vessel"—to store and transport the artifacts to their rightful custodians from whom they were unlawfully removed. It also serves as an exhibition space, a showroom, a canvas for audiovisual projection, etc. In a sense, the material and construction languages of the vessels are also limitless. Second, the project envisions a scenario in which some of the vessels and artifacts are left on site following repatriation, with a design emphasis on the vessels' afterlife.

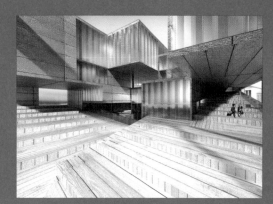

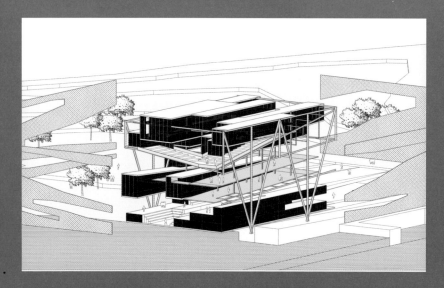

DECENTER, DISTRIBUTE, DEPLOY
Amy Koenig

Artworks are not defined by those in positions of authority, but rather through participation, dialogue, and instruction. Extending the physicality of art and presenting it in a digital space allows for new kinds of encounters and interactions to emerge. Without being limited by what is physically on view, virtual exhibitions can feature a wide variety of works. The museum ceases to be merely a repository for artifacts and instead becomes a venue for the objects themselves to tell their stories. This project explores the potential for a post-PMA future as a deployable and mobile play infrastructure for art and people through a series of arrangements of small architectures. As a result, we can transform any space into a play area or art community center. These architectural beings are sculptures in and of themselves, but they also conceal a hidden function and experience. The new addition serves as a catalyst for a fresh perspective on both art and play.

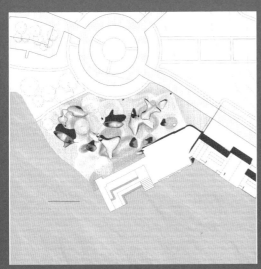

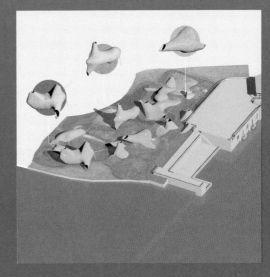

THE WALK
Ruiqi (Riki) Han

The WALK is a proposal for the expansion of the Philadelphia Museum of Art that intends to expand and broaden the public's access to the museum's experience. The museum is designed as a multilayered network of paths that flow organically from the surrounding landscape to the exhibition spaces. By utilizing multiple single elements and assembling them in an additive fashion, a dense but porous system is created that allows fluid circulation and connectivity between indoor and outdoor spaces. There are occasions when multiple paths intersect, cross over, or converge, offering viewers who are wandering through space a variety of unique experiences. The artwork can be viewed from a variety of angles, creating a dynamic, individual relationship between the viewer and the piece. The objective of the project is to design a museum that encourages visitors to stroll through, explore, and wander in the open, public areas.

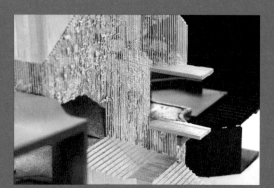

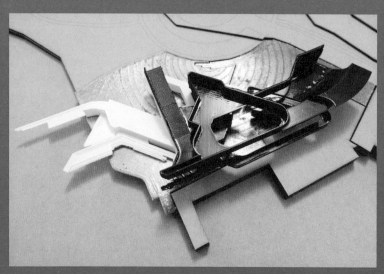

APPERCEPTIVE DISCONTINUITY
Yuanyuan Lin

By introducing elements of disorientation and discontinuity, this project seeks to reconsider how art is displayed and experienced. The building is conceived of as parts of a system rather than as a whole. The separate units house various programs that are linked by public space. There are numerous entrances and paths through the museum. There is no "suggested" route that visitors should take, but each visitor is encouraged to explore the space and find their own unique path through the museum. The solid masses cause areas of compression and decompression, which invite unexpected interactions and events. The goal is to transform the space through spontaneous participation and exploration. The tubing frame, which varies in size and color, adds some differentiation and hierarchy to the spaces while also serving as an abstract guide for visitors. The pattern and texture on the surfaces add to the sense of disorientation and are intended to intrigue visitors visually and haptically.

RECURSIVE FRACTURE
Marjorie Tello Wong

The building is made up of two massive blocks that prevent anyone from seeing the water until they are right up close to it and cross the sleek break. The two masses are composed of disjointed and irregular geometries that complement one another to frame the exterior environment and facilitate the flow of program. The idea of divided masses originated in work done earlier in the semester. Each building serves a different purpose, with the larger building housing exhibition halls and the smaller building housing administrative and instructional spaces. The main cafe is in the basement, which connects the two masses. The copper used for the facade is engraved with design elements taken from the schematic and is held together and stacked by pipes. The overall method of design is iterative, as ideas are borrowed from completed projects and incorporated into the visual representation of the new structure.

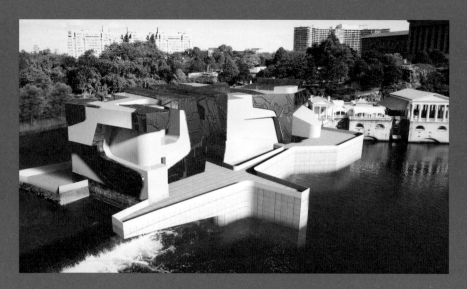

MACHINED EROSION
Leechen Zhu

Located at the intersection of technology and the natural world, the museum seeks to inspire research and development of adaptive strategies in response to changing floodplain elevations and more volatile storm surges. The building's exterior is covered in curved glass channels that are used for active research on coastal ecologies, and the main gallery descends below ground level to bring visitors closer to the water at the lower shoreline. The building was designed to reflect the inseparable bond between land and sea. Water and human ingenuity, which for generations powered Philadelphia from the Fairmount Water Works, are the unyielding sources of inspiration for the museum. It's a novel way to demonstrate the synergy between technological and environmental forces, and how they can be used to spark creative problem-solving and the testing of novel adaptive approaches. The museum is a constant reminder of land and water's inextricable and far-reaching connections to our environment and society.

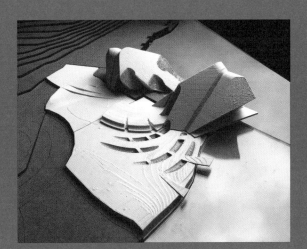

GROWING SPECULATIONS
Sharlene Yulita

This project proposes a novel approach to art curation and engagement at the Philadelphia Museum of Art (PMA) extension. The project's goal is to provide a holistic experience that interacts with society and encourages visitors to view art in a more unified and significant manner. The concept is to exhibit new and old art in conjunction, connected by an "in-between" space that features capsules containing futuristic, not-yet, and what-if art. The proposed extension is intended to generate programmatic and formal tension through the spectator's fluid experience and the growth of the structure. The extension is intended to create a vertical stretch with a density play on the canopy it supports, a horizontal gradation that parallels the scale of the site's rocky hills, and a contrast between the dense canopy and the tenuous columns. The PMA expansion is ultimately a reflection of progress and an ever-changing flow of stories from the past, future, and maybes, where the fourth art is the observer, the minds in which these arts continue to evolve.

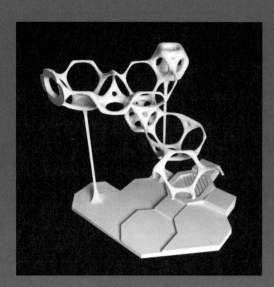

WANDERING
Shaohong Tian

This project is about communication, blending, and free space. It aims to establish a new museum that examines works of art as evidence of the evolution of human civilization from a different perspective than historical participants. The museum's goal is to show America's civilizations as an equal, blending, and inseparable part of human civilization, as well as to express universal emotions for history and respond to the Philadelphia Museum's design needs of decolonization. The project attempts to investigate how to connect different functional areas through visual connections and body perception. The underground museum extends to the ground, allowing visitors to view some exhibits without having to enter the museum. The community activity room has also been extended to the ground level, promoting communication, and broadening the impact of cultural activities. The museum's first floor is lifted and transformed into a public space for citizens, where people, rivers, and natural scenery flow into the structure, creating fantastic light and shadow effects. The permanent exhibition space adopts a non-linear exhibition space, emphasizing the mutual exchange and complimentary and separable state between civilizations.

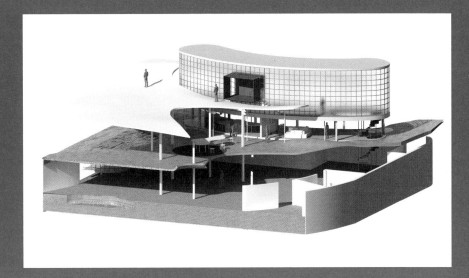

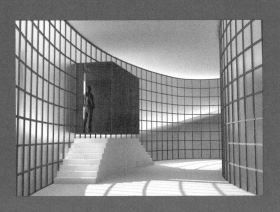

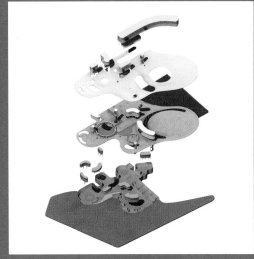

WHOLE IN ONE
Shenyi Zhang

The Whole in One museum project aims to create an open and inviting environment by allowing the public to flow over, under, and through it, as the Schuylkill River does on the site. The building's design incorporates an interlocking system of boxes that overlap and intersect as they span between two grand staircases. The sharp edges of the structure are softened by curvilinear geometries, which creates a series of interconnected gallery spaces with a ramped floor system. On the exterior, the two grand stairs contribute to the formation of a sunken landscape, which, in conjunction with the building's flexible geometries, creates an exterior space with the same characteristics as the interior spaces. The building's design also includes openings in the interlocking boxes, allowing the public to see through the structure from the inside out and the outside in. The geometric system that was used to shape the building and connect the inside and outside spaces visually is built into a perforated graphic that flows against the grain of the project.

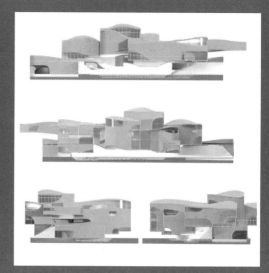

IRIDESCENCE
Francisco Anaya

This project creates an inclusive and welcoming environment that physically imprints freedom of expression through the medium of art. The building is composed of two masses in tension that hug one another, resulting in a series of seams and small openings that serve as peepholes to allow civilians a glimpse of life within the buildings. There is a subterranean mass connecting these masses that houses additional exhibition and education center programs. The facade of the buildings is enveloped by these pipe striations to create new misreadings of the buildings through these figural surfaces that fold along the facade. Through these laminated piped surfaces, people will be able to traverse zones of open space. They serve as a transitional threshold between the exterior and interior and entice individuals to enter. As people approach the building, they will enter through this protruding corner's underskirt. The passage through these interstitial spaces and seams will lead to an expanded spatial condition; this effect will create moments of hierarchy within the museum and frame key public art elements that reside within the intervention.

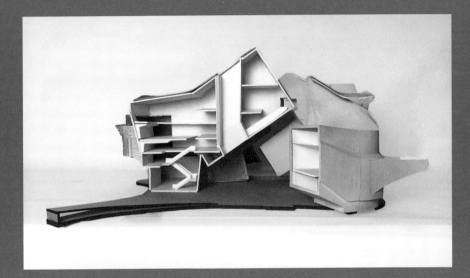

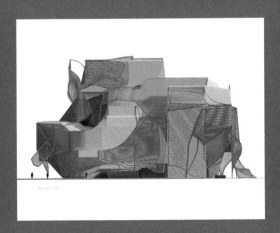

Core 601:
Design Studio III

Coordinator:
Hina Jamelle

The Core 601 Urban Housing Studios define new contemporary modes of living in an urban environment. In a world of increasing demand on existing resources there is newly focused attention on adaptive reuse and the expansion of existing facilities. Each Urban Housing studio section positions the housing project relative to an existing structure. The student proposals will be required to engage with this existing building condition—with one-third of the proposed projects interacting directly with the existing structure while the remaining two-thirds are to be new construction. A goal is to encourage the production of hybrid forms, programs, and architectural conditions that interrogate relationships between new and existing conditions. All Studio Sections develop housing projects of 50,000 square feet on an urban lot with a minimum of two facades. The housing project is designed as a hybrid form of housing/dwelling with a commercial or cultural program that can co-exist with housing. Other key objectives include the study of a building's massing and the physical impact it makes on the city with a highly detailed façade.

Starting with the 2020–21 academic year the Urban Housing and Integration studio's at the University of Pennsylvania

Weitzman School of Design will take as a shared theme Public Common Space. Public Commons has become a term used for shared, equitable access to resources such as air, oceans, and wildlife as well as social creations such as libraries, public spaces, scientific research, etc. Public Common Space for the Second Year Architecture studios will be a catalyst to study the confluence of equity and inclusion through thoughtful inquiry. Each student will engage in architecture's agency to format spaces of equity and proactively develop new modes of ground, landscape, thresholds, and spaces that provide for safe assembly and freedom from harassment.

Across all Urban Housing studios there are three separate event weeks: Plan Week immediately precedes the mid-review and addresses unit design, clear divisions of public and private spaces, building circulation, and preliminary documentation of life safety, egress, and ADA requirements. The Section and Façade Week immediately follows the mid-review and addresses an understanding of vertical and horizontal circulation, building program distribution, façade design, and documentation. Public Common Space Development Week culminates the coordinated weeks with a focus on how to design and develop architectural solutions that address concerns of equity, inclusion, and justice. Public Common Space Week is also supported by a lecture series from key thinkers in the field.

Professional Practice by Phillip Ryan and Environmental Systems by Dorit Aviv are taught concurrently, using the Urban Housing Studio Project as a basis of investigation. Professional Practice bolsters the students' understanding of budgeting, team formation, scheduling, articulating a design vision, and formulating a hypothetical design practice ethos. The Environmental Systems course considers the impact of building designs on the environment and human comfort via three topics: Daylight and Solar Gain, Façade Thermal Performance, and Water and Energy Harvesting.

Faculty:

Core 601   Hina Jamelle

Core 601:
Shifting Hybrids: Adaptive Reuse of the Corbin Building

Faculty: Hina Jamelle
Teaching Assistant: Bingyu Guo

The adaptive reuse of buildings has several advantages over demolition and reconstruction. It can support and benefit local culture, especially in cases where a building is rooted in city or neighborhood identity, history, and culture and offers inspiring spaces. It can be used as a tool for leveraging and streamlining investment, particularly if there is support from vocal community groups. Additionally, new buildings require tremendous amounts of energy and resources to construct. Reuse is often a more environmentally friendly solution, or as a 2005 National Trust for Historic Preservation campaign put it, "the greenest building is the one that is already built."

Despite its many benefits, adaptive reuse projects are often criticized for hastening gentrification. Urban development can displace longtime residents, particularly when it does not include affordable housing. However, repurposing an existing building can act as a catalyst for attracting and retaining a diverse mix of households through unique spaces and structures and can be critical to the character of a neighborhood.

The Corbin Building is a historic office building at the northeast corner of John Street and Broadway in the Financial District of Manhattan in New York City. It was built in 1888–1889 as a speculative development and was designed by Francis H. Kimball in the Romanesque Revival style with French Gothic detailing.

The studio reimagines the beloved venue as the site of a new residential building. Engaging inclusionary housing within the context of adaptive reuse, the project leverages the building's unique historical qualities to ensure and create added property value while procuring additional space through new construction. One-third of the project engages directly with the historic Corbin Building, and the other two-thirds are devoted to newly constructed residential units.

Featured Student Work:

Core 601:
MICRO // MAX: Designs for the Connected Body

Faculty: Gisela Baurmann
Teaching Assistant: Juli Petrillo

The studio proposes an urban housing project and a community justice court on a densely urban site in SoHo, New York. It discusses the notion of comfort in the context of human and non-human habitats, and proposes built environments for various living organisms to flourish in. These environments may spawn interstitial spaces that facilitate novel modes of comfort. MICRO // MAX is invested in matters of social justice while exploring the idea of integrating human housing systems with other ecological processes.

Adaptable living communities, different in range and scale, may operate in parallel and in feedback with one another, spontaneously forming expressions of symbiosis beyond the hierarchical master-servant relations of human/pet, human/décor, or human/nature. The search for such new relations and connections between species and communities opens opportunities to rethink boundaries as defined by normative housing and communal space. It leads to novel cross-species and cross-community interiorized urbanities. Novel ideas of wellness, safety, and responsibility in the context of dense urban living are defined, while primary housing considerations as light, air, and circulation are reexamined through the lens of two species and multiple scales.

Rethinking standard sizes and typologies, as well as assumptions of domestic ease and comfort, will venture to formulate a unique model of luxury: living cross-species, enriched in exuberant contentment through symbiosis and exchange.

Featured Student Work:

Core 601:
LoLux Commons

Faculty: Jonas Coersmeier
Teaching Assistant: Danny Ortega

The design studio LoLux Commons develops hybrid typologies for low-income and luxury housing, and it proposes a new kind of public common space in Brooklyn, New York.

LoLux Commons simultaneously focuses on the two primary growth markets of New York City's real estate: luxury condominiums and affordable housing. It discusses these two extreme segments in context, probes into their interaction, and systematically works out areas of synergy in order to add value for various stakeholders and for the community at large. It finds great potential in bringing together these two housing domains, far greater than what is currently realized in the industry's practice. The city commonly provides incentives such as tax breaks and air rights for developers to include affordable housing units in condominium developments. However, the incentive-driven combination of these two housing types often leads to socially questionable results, namely buildings that in their circulatory structure strictly separate high- and low-income occupants. In contrast, LoLux Commons proposes a housing estate that will foster integration and a new kind of urban encounter for a diverse group of Brooklynites. It promotes urban housing as a space for communication and the place for informal and coincidental encounters. The studio develops a mix of minimal and luxury apartments, and it speculates on how these interactions and communication attributes can be heightened in the specific cultural setting of the Wallabout neighborhood of Brooklyn.

Featured Student Work:

Core 601:
Living Off the Land

Faculty: Scott Erdy
Teaching Assistant: Yuxuan Xiong

Living Off the Land – A Self Sustaining Proposal: We need to develop bold strategies that solve homelessness and hunger simultaneously. "Living off the land" is an architecture invested in self-sustaining food production that provides a viable alternative to over-farming and the development of land that could otherwise be used for carbon sequestration.

Bringing productive farming into population centers would mean fresher food and less pollution-emitting transportation. Concentrating population density and food production in cities allows the rewilding of the surrounding landscape. At the same time, this new paradigm is an opportunity to reinvent the goals of social housing—a model that incorporates food security and shelter.

The program encourages a new paradigm for living that includes agricultural and cultural programs that can co-exist with housing. The hybrid component of the program will focus on culinary arts and food production utilizing Controlled Environment Agriculture (CEA) techniques. Formal arrangements in accumulation and variation of scale of the housing module will be stressed throughout the semester. Students will also develop a theoretical narrative that will inform their hybridized housing program and guide their architectural response to program and site.

Urban growth and suburban sprawl push farmland further from urban centers, requiring a vast network of transportation and distribution that further increases the needed resources and carbon footprint of food production. Reforestation could begin if suburban sprawl and farmland were abandoned and depopulated—leaving the land to its natural processes; allowing it to heal, sequester carbon, and provide breathable air to the planet.

Core 601   Scott Erdy

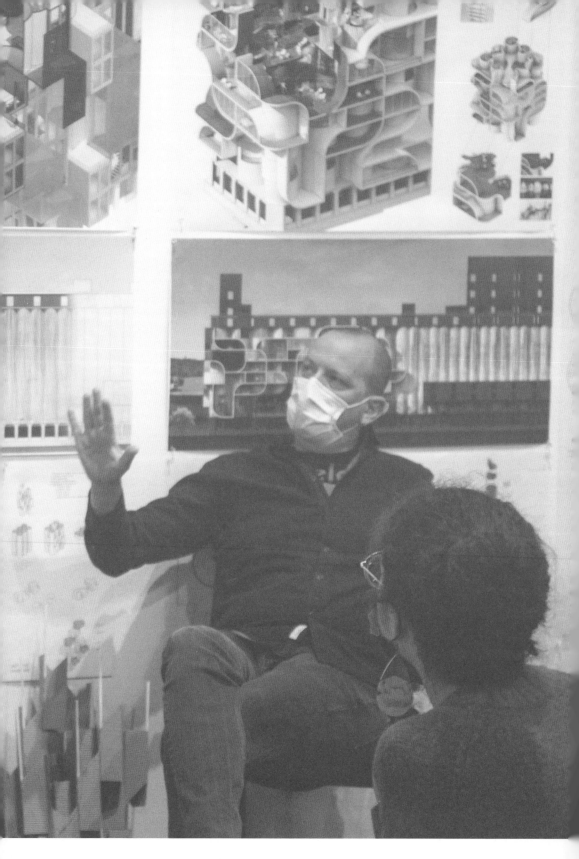

Core 601 Ben Krone

Core 601:
Creative Housing: Red Hook Grain Terminal

Faculty: Ben Krone
Teaching Assistant: Dario Sabidussi

Housing for lower-income groups is an enormous issue nation-wide. Upscale and profitable development often undermines efforts to sanction land use to house families at or below the poverty line. For decades cities have been trying to figure out ways to deal with the issue. Early attempts included failed experiments in large-scale low-income housing developments that led to a host of socioeconomic issues. As cities have evolved these traditionally poor neighborhoods have been endangered by the rapid expansion of market-rate development in neighboring areas. In recent times an assortment of new innovative urban growth policies have been put to the test.

The studio will propose a solution for the relationship between the creative mixed housing and the existing Red Hood Grain Terminal. The initial investigations and proposed housing models will be developed to facilitate the sharing of research across the studio. Finally, these defined elements will be combined and tested in both building and unit form and will have the opportunity to react to the existing structure and the public program.

Featured Student Work:

DISSOLVING CORBIN BUILDING
Zihua Mo

The facade of the historic Corbin Building in New York City is one of the city's most attractive features. The goal of the "dissolving" technique is to preserve the original beauty of the building while updating it to meet the standards for a contemporary residential complex. The balcony and shading elements of the new facade seamlessly integrate with the original, creating a seamless transition between the old and the new.

In this work, we take food to be the common thread. The key element linking the various private dwellings together is the shared kitchen, which can be of varying sizes depending on the needs of the residents. Food also serves to animate the Fulton Center's adjacent underground space and rooftop space, as well as the public common space. Connecting the Corbin Building and the Fulton Center, a food court and rooftop bar bring New Yorkers of all walks of life together.

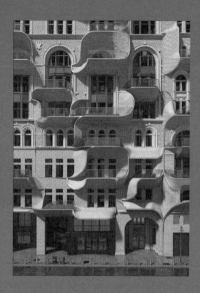

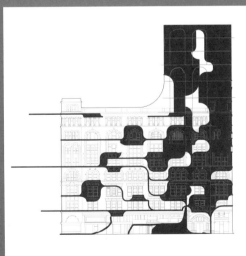

Core 601   Hina Jamelle

SANCTUM FORMATIONS
Monte Reed

Sanctum Formations is an innovative reuse housing project designed to balance the culture of congestion and chaos in Manhattan and offer removal of overstimulation through curated moments in architecture. Manhattan lacks public spaces for free and secular gatherings which provide respite away from overstimulation.

The design is inspired by naturally occurring cavernous and calming formations which also drive the materiality of the building. The core of the design carries levels of curated sensory deprivation spaces, as well as vertical circulation. The new programmed core runs from the top of the housing program down to the large public common sensory deprivation space located beneath street level. The bifurcation and capillary aspect to the project core calms with simplicity and heavy mass on the interior and expresses itself more precisely on the exterior. It's an inversion of the feelings someone may feel while experiencing mental health issues.

Sensory deprivation spaces are distributed throughout the project via the core —giving access to both the residents and the public —to create a proactive mental health and awareness amenity.

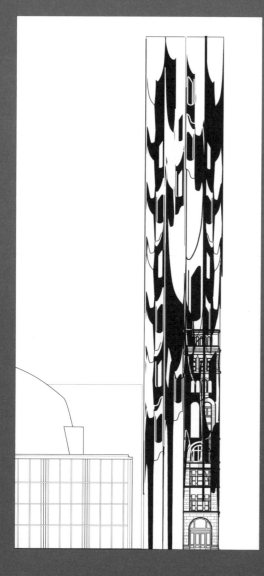

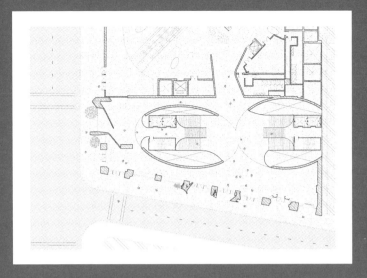

77   Core 601   Hina Jamelle

COVE
Andy Hu

This project aims to reconnect urban dwellers to nature by providing every apartment unit with a terrace and a sky light in a high-density apartment complex in NYC. As you enter your apartment, look up to see the sky or moon through the skylight and down to see the terrace.

The massing responds to the limitations of a terraced tower and the conditions of the site—providing each unit with ample natural light, views of the Hudson, or both.

The massing is divided by the individual units to break its monolithic scale and instead, draw one into the rows of gardens and apartments, each stepped further back from the sidewalk.

In the suspended hallways, one feels a sense of lightness and flight. In the apartments the skylight reminds of the vastness of the sky while the terrace beckons towards earth and soil.

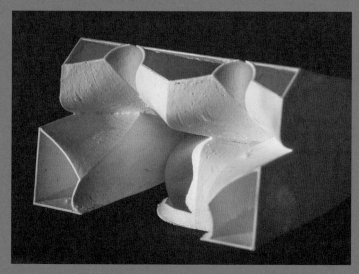

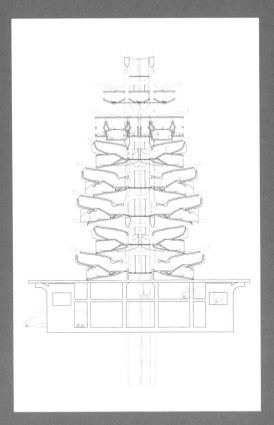

Core 601   Gisela Baurmann

THE FLOWER HOUSE
Kewei Lin

The project is built on the existing UPS building in New York's SOHO neighborhood. It examines the concept of comfort in the context of human and non-human habitats, and it proposes built environments in which various living organisms can thrive. Flowers are the non-human living organism for this project. Flowers require sunlight and fresh air to thrive, so they are mostly found in open and large spaces within the building. The project's goal is to provide its residents with a natural and relaxing environment during their hectic daily lives. Enjoy the natural space by not only seeing but also feeling and smelling it. This project includes the Queens Youth Justice Center in the public common space. The Queens Youth Justice Center strives to keep people out of the criminal justice system and to build vibrant communities. It provides supportive alternatives to incarceration and criminal conviction for those in the system. It works with people both inside and outside of the justice system, offering a variety of supportive services and civic engagement opportunities to people of all ages. Furthermore, it provides leadership training, internships, and opportunities for young people to make a positive contribution to the Queens community.

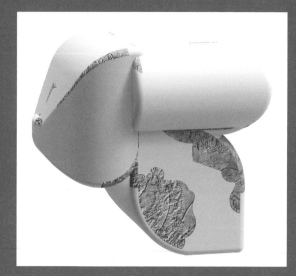
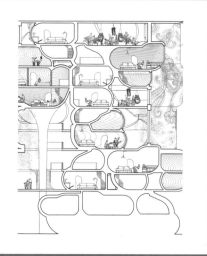

Gisela Baurmann

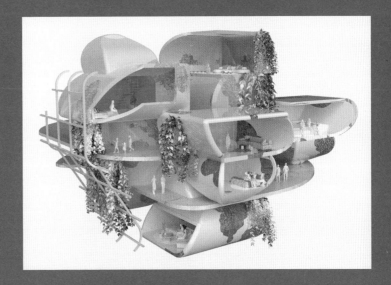

MAXIMUS
Harsana Siva

New York City has been a victim of housing shortage since the early 1980s. By the turn of the century, new buildings were built to accommodate immediate housing needs. Gentrification was an important after-effect of these constructions. Despite providing immediate housing, they divided the communities.

Maximus is situated on an NYCHA housing complex near the Navy Yard and the BQE. Focusing on hyper density as a response to housing demands in the city, Maximus respectfully adapts its form around the site by shifting and orienting itself away from the existing NYCHA housing. It focuses on bringing back a physical and visual connection between two sides of the site, which is currently divided by the BQE. The resulting structure houses a multi-level educational system that also houses a library for not just the adjacent NYCHA building but is designed to provide for the community. The design suggests an immediate connection through the formal expression of the form while also suggesting the eradication of the BQE over time and replacing it with an elevated park. Hence Maximus is designed to reconnect communities while also providing housing for all.

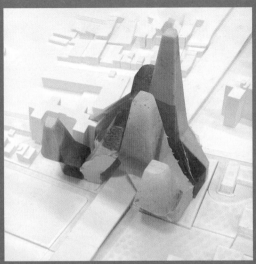

Core 601   Jonas Coersmeier

MEDIA DIPTYCH
Kyle Troyer

The hyper-real resolution of contemporary media obscures the boundaries of simulation and reality. This ambiguous relationship between social media platforms such as Instagram and our physical reality speculates on the subversive capabilities of the image in architecture. Media Diptych explores the confounding of analog media and its digital counterpart as a method of interrogation into today's digital society.

Deep material explorations probe and place the unplanned nature of handicraft into an embedded system of ornamentation within the architectural surface. Through the image of the surface, architecture's mode of reception becomes altered, provisional, and material, fluctuating between transparent and opaque material organizations. What blankets the exterior evolves into a secondary system that is inlaid and distributed throughout the public housing context throughout its interior.

Envelopes form spatial qualities from within to house common spaces that become platforms of media practice to provide a marginalized neighborhood with equal access to today's digital society.

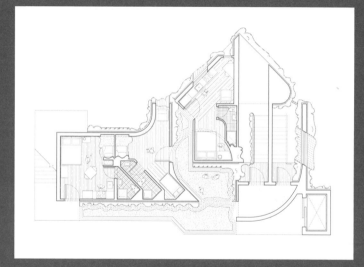

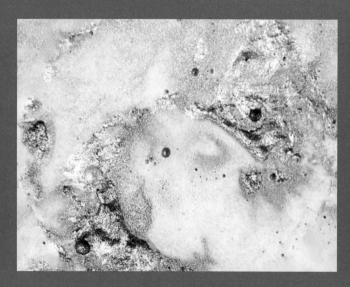

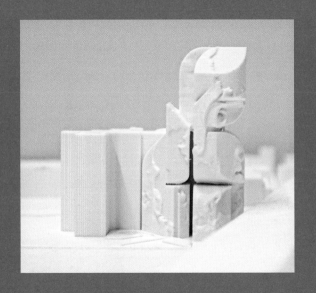

Core 601   Jonas Coersmeier

VERTICAL FOREST–
LIFE IN BETWEEN
Li Yang

"Life in Between" addresses ecological environments, cultural diversity, and food security. This project explores a semi-communal lifestyle in which communal spaces connect and soften urban residents' strict daily routines. This forest creates a green utopia to test a new urban lifestyle. In conventional housing, one unit has all the functional spaces needed for daily life. Controlled environment farming, communication, and transition units will surround it. Reorganized and compacted functional spaces and floating glass cube communal units give the community agency for farming and social interaction. Each single-function pod brings residents together in diverse activity networks. Increased unit quantity and support space like circulation cores and mechanical rooms for assigned residents create the vertical forest. The Vertical Forest introduces a semi-communal lifestyle that blurs private and communal, life and work, solitude, and togetherness. Vertical Forest Tower explores a semi-communal lifestyle in which communal spaces tie up and soften urban residents' daily rhythms. This forest becomes a green utopia to test a new urban lifestyle.

AUTONOMOUS MARKET
Taylor Beck

West Philadelphia's Autonomous Market is a low-income, sustainable urban housing complex. It is both a residence and a vertical farm for the surrounding neighborhood. The complex aims to celebrate the cultural diversity of West Philadelphia by providing micro-climates, greenhouses, and garden spaces that are conducive to the cultivation of a variety of ethnic foods that are representative of the surrounding neighborhoods' populations. Each microclimate garden is connected to a restaurant below it that is operated by the local community, providing them with a space of autonomy, independence, belonging, and culture. In addition, the complex includes a central vertical farm that extends throughout the residential section and serves as a community garden to provide more local produce. Each residential unit has its own private greenhouse unit, and the vertical farm and the journey through it to reach the restaurants at the top of the complex constitute the Autonomous Market's public common space. The complex not only provides the elements necessary to sustain and provide local food to West Philadelphia, but also enables food from various global regions to grow in Philadelphia, bringing the community together to celebrate, embrace, and cherish the diversity of its people.

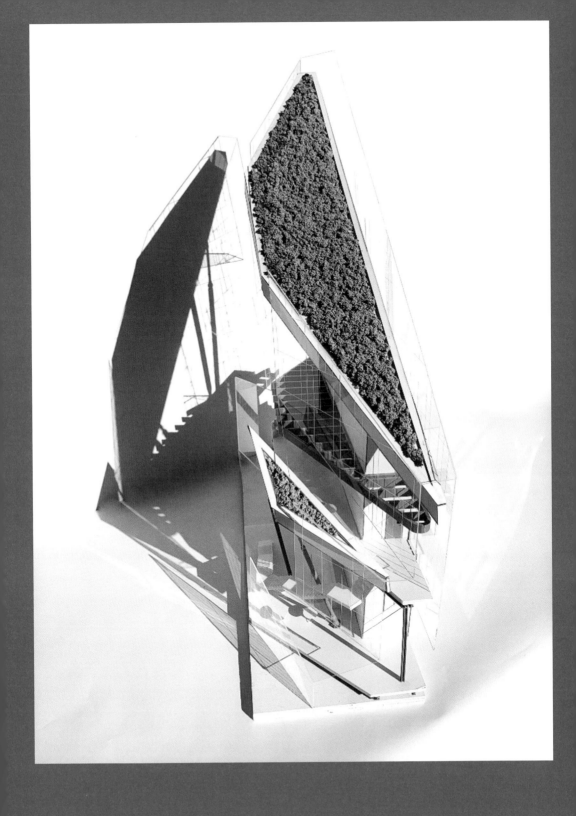

WANDERING ARTIST STUDIO
Jiacheng Huang

The project is in Red Hook, New York, and is focused on providing artists with platforms or studios to create, study, and hold exhibitions. The goal is to attract artists and tourists to gather in the area and provide community residents with a close-up appreciation and participation in artistic creation. The shared space will enrich the community culture and bring new vitality to Red Hook and the surrounding areas. It will not only hold regular exhibitions for wandering artists, but also form a small art trading market, and provide a place for basic aesthetic education for children in the community. The design uses a "ribbon" element to guide the direction of people's activities in the building. It divides public and private spaces, carries the functions of floor-to-ceiling windows and balconies, and connects residential housing and shared space. It allows for residents' free intervention and participation and forms a bridge connecting residents' daily life and artistic activities. It creates a continuous landscape and provides a place for the public to communicate and integrate with each other.

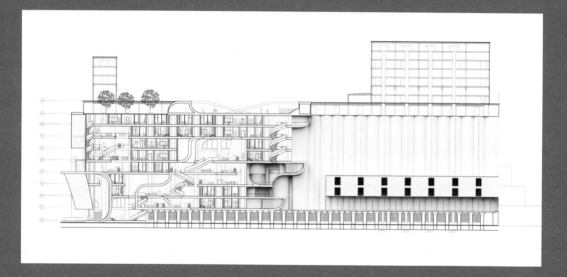

Ben Krone

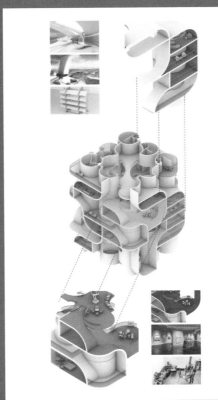

THE LIGHTHOUSE
Nana Ntiriwaa-Berkoh

The project turns an abandoned grain terminal in Red Hook, Brooklyn, New York, into a community performance of life and culture. Using the concept of community gathering as a vehicle to slow the force of gentrification, this building encourages interaction among residents at various stages of life by hosting a variety of mixed apartment types and program spaces. The materiality of the apartment units and community spaces allows for a play between performance and privacy, projecting the activity of the residents as they gather and grow together through light and shadow. Residents can encounter each other visually at times and just have a sense of each other's presence at others due to the transparency of the ETFE façade. Depending on the time of day, this displays moments of gathering, teaching, meeting, and celebrating for those looking towards the Lighthouse to see, much like a curtain revealing life as a performance.

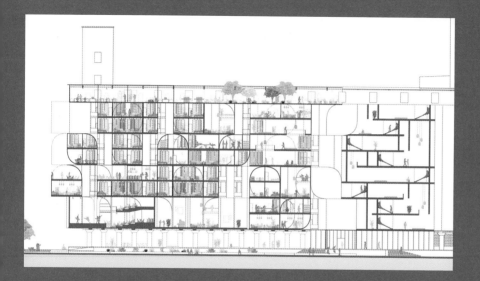

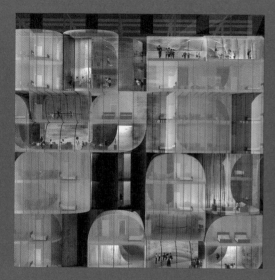

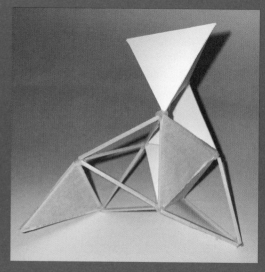

Ben Krone

Core 601   Ben Krone

Advanced 701   Studio Overview

Advanced 701: Design Studio V

Coordinator: Ferda Kolatan

The historical transformations of large cities around the world, from modern metropolises to postindustrial megacities, have radically altered our urban environments and how we live within them. Globally networked markets have produced new economic and political realities leading to unprecedented forms of regulatory frameworks, urban growth, and densification. Infrastructural and technological innovations have changed the ways we build, move, and communicate in the city. Ecological pressures are expanding our understanding of design as an organic and symbiotic endeavor that must consider and include nonhuman actors and agencies. Current crises triggered by infectious disease and social unrest alert us to the dual meaning of the term "city" as both a physical place and a body of citizens. The architecture of the city is always also the staging ground for individual self-expression and collective political action.

These transformations—which are mostly co-dependent— impact profoundly the dynamic material and cultural systems we casually refer to as the city. Known territories dissolve, contradictions thrive, and novel situations emerge. In this constantly shifting urban landscape new opportunities arise, not only for architecture's latest design ambitions (be they pragmatic, experimental, or speculative), but also for a fundamental reexamination of the contemporary city, its meaning and definitions, its politics and aesthetics, its potentials and challenges.

Each studio section of 701 focuses on a design problem in a domestic or international urban area. Research includes travel and detailed study of the specific circumstances of the chosen city and the design problem. While this studio is concerned with the future of cities, it is not an urban design or a planning studio. The projects are chosen to function on a large architectural scale such as mega-building, city-block, infrastructure, park, etc. The future of cities rests on our ability to create robust visions that promote new forms of societal participation, ecological collaboration, technological innovation, and ultimately inspire and excite through exemplary architectural design.

Faculty:

Advanced 701 Ferda Kolatan

Advanced 701:
ICONOCLASH // Infrastructure & Monument

Faculty: Ferda Kolatan
Teaching Assistant: Megan York

In a time when many of our societal values are being examined, challenged, and reordered, questions concerning the meaning of architecture, both as a material artifact and a representational device, become especially pressing. All architecture, no matter how utilitarian, communicate larger ideas through matter. The city is a historical archive where these ideas collect over time and manifest themselves in built form. But as time passes the representational meaning of buildings diminish, change, even reverse, putting them at odds with contemporary needs and desires. This conflict caused by the monumental, iconic quality of buildings is evident in the wild clashes of styles and types in cities but also implicit in the ways we relate to our built environment, how we participate in it, and if we feel inspired or rejected by its architecture.

As the concluding chapter of the New York Trilogy, the studio expands its interest in the architecture of the late Gilded Age – Great Depression era (~1900–1930) to infrastructure. The focus for this semester was the Manhattan Bridge landing area with its entrance portal on the Manhattan side. The starkly contrasting historical, programmatic, and aesthetic qualities represented in the modern structure of the bridge, its Beaux-Arts colonnades and triumphal arch, and the idiosyncratic building stock in neighboring Chinatown are all combined and utilized to conjure up new types of architectural hybrids that promote an urban architecture that embraces difference and contradictions as vital elements for the city and its future.

Featured Student Work:

Advanced 701:
Brooklyn, Buffalo, and Bangladesh
(The Great Climate Migration)

Faculty: Matthijs Bouw

Climate migration is a critical topic of study. Relationships between migration and the climate crisis are manifold and complex. In this studio, we will explore these intersections on a global scale, using three anchoring points: Brooklyn, Buffalo, and Bangladesh.

In Brooklyn, irreversible climate change will result in areas becoming uninhabitable, likely leading to 'retreat' from the coast. Migration away from the coast will, in turn, impact other areas, causing housing stress and displacement but also generating transformational opportunities for both the coastal areas and upland.

Buffalo, NY, at the other side of the Erie Canal, often seen as a possible 'climate haven' because of its ample water resources and temperate climate, has been working hard to attract new people to a city that has shrunk to half its original size, a decline that has exacerbated many other urban stresses. One community that is thriving in Buffalo is the Bangladeshi community that has migrated there mostly from New York City because of the high costs of living.

Bangladesh, in the low-lying delta of three major rivers, is one of the countries most impacted by the climate emergency, with many people on the move, both internally and internationally. As a country that has been living with water for centuries, and that is at frontlines of the climate emergency, it is also at the forefront of understanding its impacts, the power of local adaptation, and in the development of innovative solutions, all of which would greatly benefit the Global North.

Featured Student Work:

Advanced 701   Matthijs Bouw

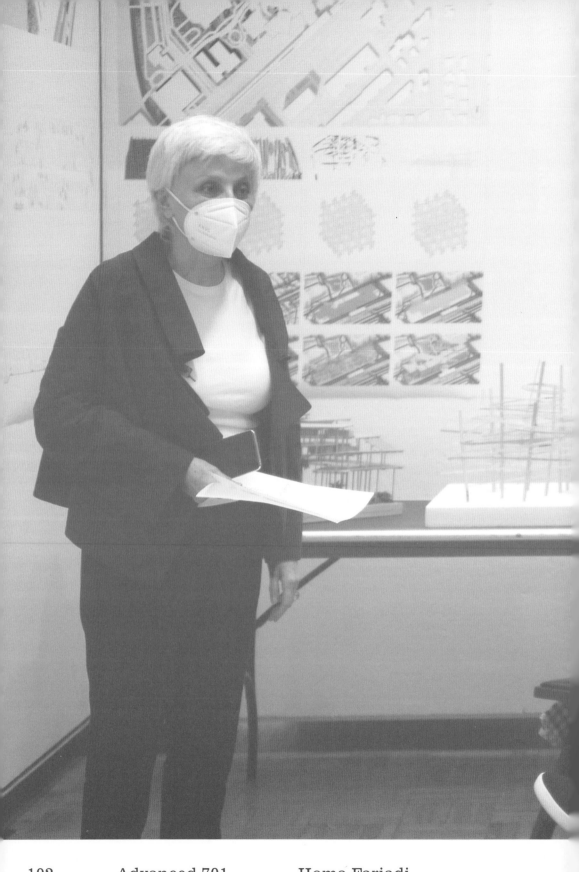

Advanced 701:
Quasi Objects of Architecture:
Atmospheres and Diffused Urbanity

Faculty: Homa Farjadi
Teaching Assistant: Chang Yuan (Max) Hsu

Cities and nature have historically registered their co-dependence in multiple forms through formations of density, design of their open spaces, or through organization of their infrastructure and buildings. This studio will research design potentials of specific modes of space making in the city through considering the architecture of atmospheres.

The post-pandemic city has found renewed reasons to address the co-dependence of the city and nature. Architectural production of atmospheres brings this operational concern to its spatial aesthetics. By considering buildings and nature as quasi objects our studio project will address the direct relation between sensual spatial perception and social agency in the architectural construction of atmospheres.

Featured Student Work:

Advanced 701:
Synthetic Nature, Homuncular Architecture, Worldbuilding

Faculty: Simon Kim
Teaching Assistant: Logan Weaver

This semester, architecture is charged with the city as a Worldbuilding exercise. Worldbuilding is not a recent term but has found its way into our work with the use of active imaginaries, Foucauldian heterotopias, Afrofuturism, and other strategies whereby the vessel of architecture is an agent within a much larger narrative of ground, human, and nonhuman cultures, weathers, and ecosystems. It is more necessary than ever to consider how we are to survive our current late-capitalist state, that Worldbuilding may enter as a measure.

There needs to be a paradigmatic shift in how we sort and measure the environment that Worldbuilding portends. Our humancentric tools and our umwelt, or capacity in how we understand everything, are no longer capable of dealing with the critical manner in how other agents and systems apply their own sovereignties. Essentially, architecture can no longer be seen as an elitist human ark for which our capitalist and supremacist signs and signifiers apply only to our endeavors. This is how we have come to be an unsustainable industry. Architecture, like a body turned inside out, must also afford occupancy for more than just humans. This studio will look at our own nonhuman version of artificial intelligence.

The proposal of the studio is in Los Angeles—specifically DTLA as built environment and Griffith Park / LA river as the not-city.

Featured Student Work:

Advanced 701 Simon Kim

Advanced 701:
There is a Man Cut in Two by a Window

Faculty: Karel Klein
Teaching Assistant: Katarina Marjanovic

Louis Aragon, along with Philippe Soupault and Andre Breton, was one of the founders of Surrealism, a literary, philosophical, and artistic movement which grew out of the preceding Dada movement. Surrealism, as set forth in Andre Breton's 1924 Manifesto, and influenced by Sigmund Freud's theories of the unconscious, sought to emancipate thought, language, and experience from the constraints of rationalism. Paris Peasant (Le Paysan de Paris) is an unconventional text written by Louis Aragon in 1926 and is considered one of the central works of Surrealism.

This studio used Aragon's Paris Peasant as a loose guide for how we engaged the city. Utilizing several AI network types – StyleGANs, sinGANs, style transfer neural networks, etc., we experimented with the ways in which training, and particularly mis-training artificial intelligence produces a kind of image-rich "knowledge" that appears more like an AI subconscious than our familiar, everyday reality. The images that come from this artificial subconscious are oneiric and strange yet have a photographic precision that allows us to see beyond the limits of our own aesthetic reality with great fidelity.

As the Los Angeles Conservancy says it: "the story of Wilshire is the story of Los Angeles." We used Wilshire Boulevard in Los Angeles, CA, this semester as the site for training and revealing the city's subconscious. If we model our observations on Louis Aragon's Paris Peasant, then Los Angeles will be our Paris, and Wilshire Boulevard will be our Passage de L'Opera. Our studio documented Wilshire Boulevard in order to build an artificial intelligence capable of divulging the strange, oneiric aspects of the city of Los Angeles—the subconscious of our AI models mirrored the subconscious of LA.

Advanced 701:
Future of Cities: A Non-Linear Case for a New Type
of Urban Intensification in Irwindale, California

Faculty: Thom Mayne & Ung-Joo Scott Lee

This studio looks at the operativity and performativity of 3D tessellation to generate new models of spatial organization in architecture. Specifically, we seek to come up with material ensembles hinging on a combination of a marked level of intricate and expanded three-dimensionality and a productive equilibrium between control and freedom, logic
and accident, consistency and anomaly, identity and diversity.

A spatial armature in architecture—such as that propounded in Le Corbusier's Maison Dom-Ino—gives rise to a qualitatively identifiable series of sectors within a bounded volume of space. Further, a given spatial armature transcends the particularities of the final project in which it evolves, whether in terms of materials, program, dimensions, volumetric contours, or any combination of these attributes. In other words, the same spatial armature is capable of extensive differentiation: scalable, and deployable in diverse contexts, it can be made into various dissimilar realizations, though it will not lose its defining identity. A spatial armature is distinct by virtue of its specificities, while its degree of abstraction—relative to a fully fledged, completed realization—makes it generalizable. Any spatial armature embodying a previously unavailable 3D organization extends the bounds of possibility of their conception and realization, and with it those of architectural thinking at large.

Featured Student Work:

Advanced 701   Thom Mayne & Ung-Joo Scott Lee

Advanced 701:
Machinic In-Sites

Faculty: Robert Stuart-Smith
Teaching Assistant: David Forero

We are no longer cognizant of the nature of today's built environment or the technologies that enable it. The built environment is a complex, chaotic system, that emerges from the interplay of a multitude of agencies, that are perceived, surveyed, and managed by machine vision and machine learning technologies, of which we have little knowledge or oversight of. Machinic In-Sites explores high-frequency building—a temporary occupancy of the built environment that can be rapidly developed through computer-vision and machine-learning technologies and implemented by additive manufacturing on demand. Operating as a bespoke tailored infill, proposals speculate on community-led entrepreneurialism, challenging established design and development practices through novel forms of autonomous agency and aesthetic effect. The studio's site-situated proposals offer an alternative approach from camouflage or contextualism, instead, exploring haecceities, where their unique characteristics and properties support speculation on how one-off temporal buildings can operate as highly specific bespoke agents within local urban milieus and convey alternative aesthetics.

Featured Student Work:

MONASTERY IN THE RECESSES

Bevy Silanqincuo & Shiyue Liu

Two spatial contexts exist under the Manhattan bridge: to the left is a dense commercial complex that serves as a backdrop for everyday life. The right is only a bridge support that blends in with the busy roadway and booths. These thriving booths and companies across the suitable architectural layout seem to be openly rejecting the waste of space for social success. A Buddhist Temple, an Orthodox Church, a Baptist Church, and others are dispersed around the Greek colonnade, illustrating the need for a spiritually and religiously varied setting. Therefore, the idea transforms the two site footings into a rocky monastery that contrasts with the above-ground structure. Dark, unexpected locations are exquisite monuments. The monastery is nonreligious and focused on reducing routine, comfort, and anxiety. As with many religious pilgrimages, the ascent of the mountain employs scenery and architecture to convey awe and holiness. As part of the excursion, the monks partnered with Chinatown aesthetics, irregular water streams, and rocky subsoil to weaken confidence and test the familiar.

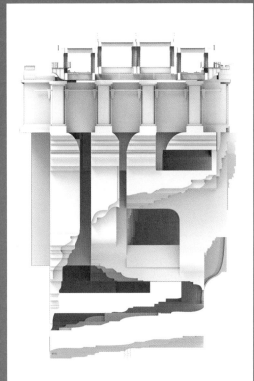

UNDER THE BRIDGE
Yingzhi Chen & Jie Bao

Under the Manhattan Bridge, there is a diving facility that is a component of the project. Reimagining the new emblem created from the hidden structural base and commonplace things involves engaging the ongoing conflict in Chinatown. The Manhattan Bridge once functioned as the quintessential representation of avant-garde architecture and revolutionary technology that represented New York City's rapid expansion in the first half of the 20th century. The proposal intends to revive a new hybrid connection of aesthetic components and thrilling infrastructure, artificial technology, and supposedly natural environs. The former monument of technology has become banal in today's society. Consider the city as a living thing, a body made up of several systems that coexist and even interact while just the outermost layer is visible to the public. The unanticipated diving pool that resulted from the subsurface systems' evolution broke the restrictions established by the bridge to become the new monument and criticism of the city.

Advanced 701 Ferda Kolatan

COMMUNITY CIRCUITRY
Eleanor Garside &
Madeleine Ghillany-Lehar

Community Circuitry is a framework for adaptive energy infrastructure. The neighborhood of Kensington, Brooklyn, is a diverse enclave with a mixed population of mostly white and Asian residents. The neighborhood has been called "Little Bangladesh" in the past, though its proportion of all south Asian residents, especially those from Pakistan, is growing rapidly. With increased climate-induced migration expected from all of South Asia, Kensington can be expected to grow rapidly in the coming decades. Further, Kensington is on relatively high ground and of relatively low density compared with other parts of Brooklyn, which could make it a prime destination for intra-borough and intra-city migration.

As the population expands, the neighborhood's capacity will need to expand in turn. The issue of energy grid capacity is an urgent one; currently, Brooklyn's borough-wide power situation is precarious, and much of the area's electricity comes from coal- and gas-burning power plants. There is an opportunity and a need to densify Kensington in preparation for increased migration, while also expanding its capacity to self-generate clean energy in ways that empower residents. How can we incorporate domesticated energy generation into an expanding community in Brooklyn, with the goal of capacity-building during climate-intensified migration?

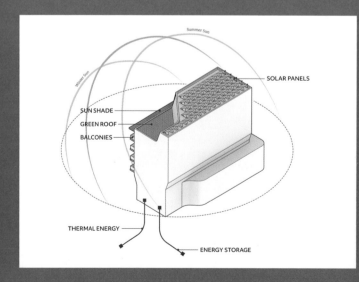

COMMON GROUND
Yasmine McBride &
Yuhan Wang

Climate change exists. Global migration exists. We know climate migrants will multiply globally shortly. Buffalo's population has declined, causing infrastructural, investment, and most crucially economic issues for its residents. Buffalo is becoming a "climate haven," inviting immigrants to boost the economy. Buffalo's population is rising again after 70 years. What happens to rapidly expanding city residents? Developers seize a promising market and engage in profit-making processes that force people out rather than caring for them, resulting in gentrification. Community ownership of property before development allows individuals to maintain and develop in ways that are beneficial to them. As land values rise, they may become landlords in smart, transparent, egalitarian ways. They may create eco-friendly designs. Community land trusts help people reclaim power. This research examines a Buffalo CLT in the Fruit Belt, a mostly Black, historically disinvested region, and imagines its future. Streets become pedestrian-friendly and dwellings become energy-efficient and cheap to build. The Fruit Belt is proof that landowners create beautiful, long-lasting things.

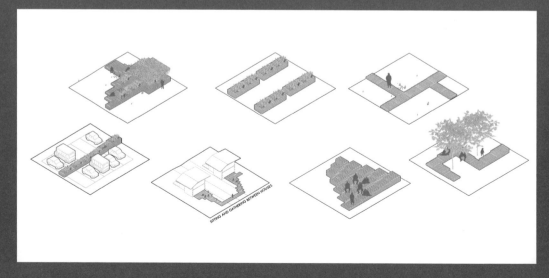

SITTING AND GATHERING BETWEEN HOUSES

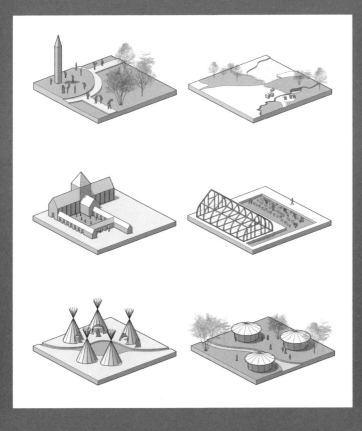

EMBODIED GRID
Eric Fries & Juli Petrillo

The project, which is on Governor's Island, defines a territory that is made up of a number of interconnected grid systems. These systems can be seen both on land and in the water. Nature and the environment, such as currents, wind, and topography, cause deviations from the rational grid. The project is interested in how productive space meets public or recreational space. The grid is made to look like a productive field made up of elements that produce energy and food. Within this productive field are experiential objects like occupied nodes in the tower, gardens, and a series of shadow monoliths. The overall goal of the different systems that work together is to create a spatial arrangement that makes energy and its effect on the systems of the project feel real. So, the project tries to capture how wind, currents, and light can be used to create atmospheres and felt experiences.

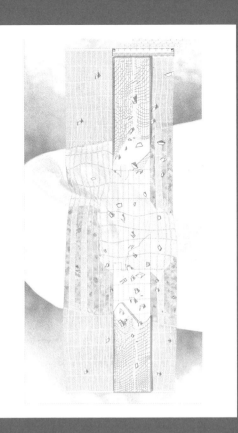

TURBULENT KNOT
Yiyi Luo & Tianchang Chu

Our research began with Quasi-Thing and Anni Alber's Weaving. We chose pain and sight because quasi-things reveal themselves through directing or disturbing the subject's attention. When we studied Anni Albers' spade making, we found the same phenomenon: the spade iterates itself, forming a larger field where the edges of the spade, oriented in different directions, constantly direct and redirect the viewer's visual attention, disturbing and re-constructing eyesight, forming a turbulent field of iterated units. Moving inside the site, we designed an over-all plan approach that encompasses the trajectory of areas with ambiguous environmental conditions, between water and land and air. Trajectories are straight paths of walking, cycling, and sometimes water transportation between destinations. These points create a knot that transforms environmental circumstances in a manufactured palpitating environment and cellular conditioned rooms when approached with uncertain environmental conditions. Amphibious knots are another aspect of our unstable quasi notion with the external environment. The amphibious section drifts, departs, and intersects on the grid. The knot and ship state of the amphibious component transforms the building geometry and the individual sense of horizon, light, and distance.

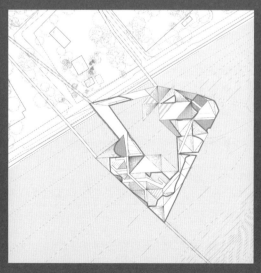

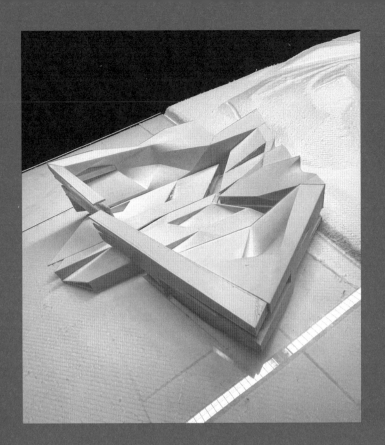

HOMUNCULAR WORLDS
Dario Sabidussi &
Miguel Matos

The Rambler and The Repository possess seemingly opposite qualities and behavioral identities. They exist as independent agents within their respective environments, yet when connected, they rely on each other to create new environmental conditions by processing collected natures that are not only human-centric environments.

Attempting to investigate an architecture that can undo historic extinctions and create new ecosystems, these Homunculi work together in the production of Synthetic Natures. Los Angeles is not only a microcosm of ecologies and human inhabitation but also a uniquely active oil field and tar pit. The homuncular agents burrow their way into the earth in search of fossilized remains of extinct species, slowly becoming a fossilized remain itself. Genome sequencing rooms, behavioral study pods, tar/fossil excavation facilities, and conservation spaces exist within the architecture that lives to find and recreate the species humans have disregarded. This facility leaves the past behind, as historic plant and animal species are released back into the environments in which they once inhabited.

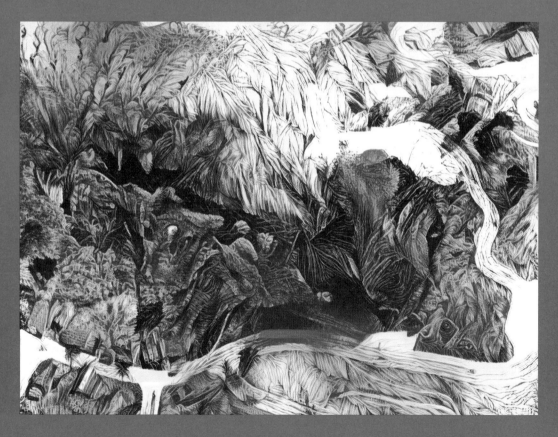

Advanced 701   Simon Kim

SID & NANCY
Nicholas Houser &
Bingyu Guo

Homunculi and characters are potent tools for producing architecture via the interactions and connections they have with each other and their surroundings. This allows for the construction of new worlds on the verge of the Anthropocene and Late Capitalism.

Sid and Nancy are brought into the realm of architectural consequence through the means of public commons outlined with the performance of various stages of toxicity in projected human-centric relationships. This relationship is modeled after the well-known and tragic relationship between the bassist of the Sex Pistols and his partner. These episodic moments, which come close to the sublime but fall short of realizing it, can only ever genuinely take place in a metropolis that is poisonous to itself, and that city is Los Angeles. The Los Angeles Theater on Broadway, the Scholl Canyon Landfill, and Owens Lake are among the locales where our project will replicate the agonisms of attraction, rejection, obsession, and self-centeredness.

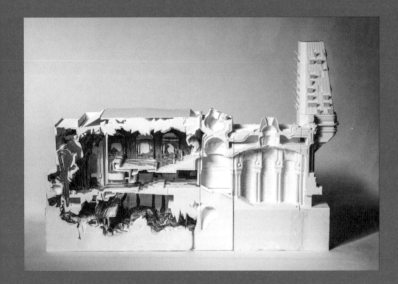

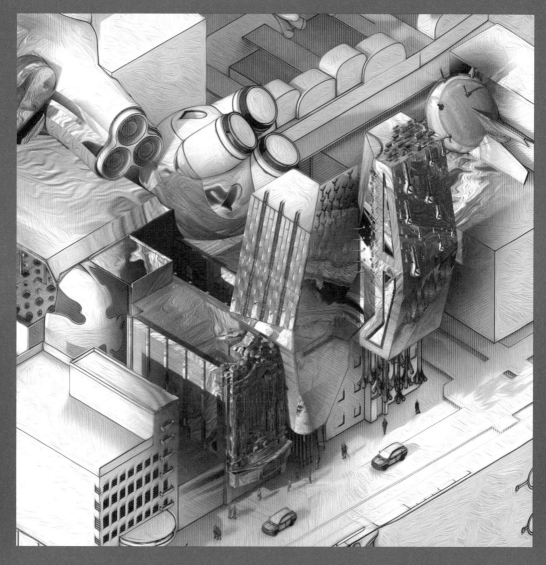

Advanced 701   Simon Kim

AN EXQUISITE ARCHITECTURE
Lisa Knust &
Riley Engelberger

This concept relates to the surrealist "exquisite corpse," where distinct pieces become a whole. Walking along Wilshire Boulevard in Los Angeles inspired these pieces. We were attracted to fire escapes and their powerful shadows produced by plentiful sunshine, ancient steel-framed buildings that show contemporary ads, and basic facades that represent the materiality typically seen along this historic boulevard, all of which make photographs with tones that evoke Los Angeles. The landscape and architectural intervention reflect these trainings. A connected, sutured shape informs the site project the most. The idea blurs normative and surreal by comparing the project to LACMA to the west and the La Brea Tar Pits to the east. Normative moments operate almost as ruins where a structural filigree resulting from AI trainings engages with and sometimes parasitically overtakes. These normative and surreal components reinforce our interest in surrealism doubling and inanimate animation. The parasitic surrealism of the building leaks into the tar pits via landscape seams. These sutured shapes reference the surrounding park and promote wandering as the intervention divides and diverges within the landscape, revealing new locations to explore.

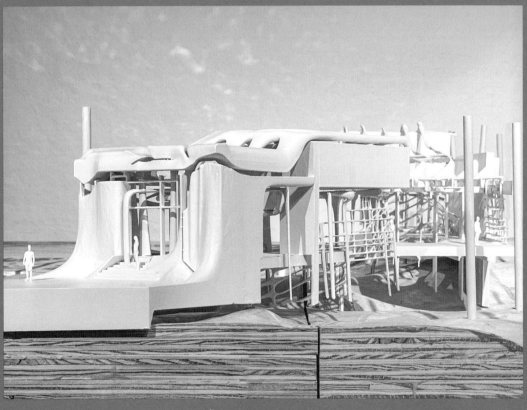

129   Advanced 701   Karel Klein

LA ENCHANTÉE DOPPELGÄNGER
Bashayer Bamohsen

This project employs artificial intelligence and neural networks to produce the irresistible beauty of digital insanity. It tries to examine what Mariana Warner calls "the eerie liminal existence of new kinds of cyber existence." In addition, it examines Architecture's competence and capability to adapt to new forms and configurations of enchantment. This project is concerned with surrealism as a call to re-enchantment, not escape. It aims to re-examine the familiar world in quest of 'the eerie,' extreme strangeness, and the extraordinary. It gives proof that charmed items are neither this nor that. This installation, which is located near the La Brea Tar pit, absorbs the uncanny nature of the pit and hints at the presence of otherworldly entities and pieces. They live in a bizarre, magical limbo underneath the tar's apparent surface. These creatures, dispersed around the metropolis, seek refuge in the psychogeographical hints-guided bits of urban hideouts.

The pieces are designed identically to one another. They create human-accessible places as well as double-spaces that are only accessible to charmed items.

131   Advanced 701   Karel Klein

UPTURNED NAME
Hayoung Nho & Yifan Shi

The urban proposal, Upturned, hypothesizes housing Los Angeles' expected population expansion in 2050 by proposing a new style of urban intensification in Irwindale, California.

Irwindale is proposed as a new adaptable urban core, building on the densification nodes of Downtown Los Angeles, Santa Monica, West Los Angeles, and Long Beach.

The project studies a reversal of the usual urban sector by hosting human density within the pits while the current city grid remains along city, pit, and street-level borders using Irwindale's existing mining pits. A new green public connective tissue unifies and builds on Irwindale's existing natural assets, connecting existing pits, the Santa Fe Dam, nearby townships, and existing infrastructure through an organic, nature-centric figure.

A new lightrail system links the pits inside the green area, and a central transportation hub expands and extends the newly discovered grid while creating distinct city centers at each pit. Different housing typologies, ranging from low-rise to skyscraper, are being developed to house 1.5 million people, the majority of whom will live in parks. This new urban intensification typology is adaptable, allowing it to adapt to unique site and population performance needs, resulting in a new urban development model and typology.

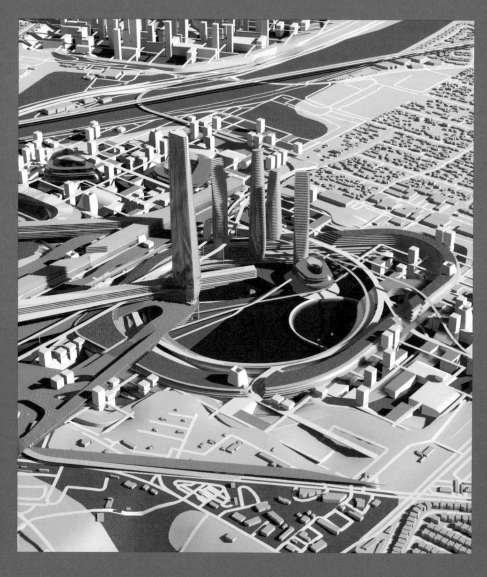

133   Advanced 701   Thom Mayne & Ung-Joo Scott Lee

LAS CANTERAS
Alan Fan

Irwindale is a barren area in the center of the Greater Los Angeles area that is covered with mining quarries all around. Las Canteras, translates to "the quarries"; therefore, the idea is to build towns within the Pits to make up for Los Angeles' ever growing population density.

The approach is to start at a micro-scale with the aim of developing cities one at a time at each individual pit while keeping an overall macro plan in mind. By having parks and houses plateau down to the ground-water lake at the bottom of the pit, which will resemble a typical city plan, an island situation will be produced. The new downtown neighborhoods will be located in the pit's middle. Housing will be erected around the quarry's perimeter, and roadways and public transit will be constructed all around it. The ring and the center of the building are connected by a cross-shaped connecting corridor.

Advanced 701   Thom Mayne & Ung-Joo Scott Lee

RECURSIVE INFILLS
Anna Lim & Danny Ortega

Recursive Infills is a research-oriented maker space and gallery space addition that will be located between the Philadelphia Charter Arts School and the future Phase II Expansion of the Rail Park. It was designed as a custom-tailored solution to the existing artistic community that is located in the surrounding area. Metal, cloth, a fiber-optic composite, and a dual-extruder system of 3D printers are some of the materials that will be used during the on-site fabrication of this project, which is planned in chunks and layers. Studies conducted using a Generative Artificial Network (GAN) centered on recyclable commodities, artwork, fabrics, and basic geometric shapes that were tailored to the location provided the inspiration for the design. The end product is a mishmash of formal and material qualities, as well as an odd color palette, which is meant to emphasize the reused nature of the construction. The goal of the research project known as Recursive Infills is to conduct an in-depth analysis of the possibility for recycling and trash management in Philadelphia to work more closely together in order to reuse construction materials within a system that has the capacity to go on forever.

Advanced 701   Robert Stuart-Smith

HILLING
Yulun Liu & Dongqi Chen

Philadelphia, like many other cities, is experiencing a significant mental disease problem. A location of art and abandoned industrial land in Callowhill (Spring Garden Street, Philadelphia) is implanted with a fitted infill artificial nature, a space for physical and emotional respite. The project "Hilling" is a 3D-printed temporary building that houses mental-health and wellness activities that use Eco-art therapy techniques.

Eco-art therapy is a pioneering approach to promoting mental health via the production of artwork through the observation and appreciation of environment. With the use of machine learning, such as AI perceptions and styleGAN generation, the project is developed as a new synthetic form of nature to serve as a neighborhood attraction that may aid in the treatment of mental illness. The building forms were generated using a styleGAN design approach that included natural characteristics into the design massing, which helped turn the abandoned area into a new constellation of programs including art studios, galleries, and schools. The ambiguous position between nature and architecture makes it unique. As nature, it is occupiable and conquerable, yet as building, it reveals inhabitable areas with mystifying, unnatural qualities that give visitors a place to ponder and find urban relief.

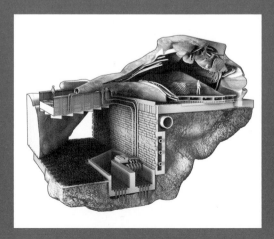

Required Courses

ARCH 511
History and Theory I
Faculty: Joan Ockman

Between the opening of the Crystal Palace in London and the construction of Lever House in New York City 100 years later, a culture of architecture calling itself "modern" emerged. This historical overview places the evolution of architecture from the middle of the 19th century through World War II into global perspective, taking into account not just transformations in building practice and architectural aesthetics, but the broader socioeconomic, political, technological, environmental, and intellectual background that shaped it. We trace architecture's changing modes of production and reception, its disciplinary and institutional renovations, the debates that animated it, and, not least, its complex geographies. Going well beyond iconic buildings and canonical "isms," we pose the following questions: In what ways did architecture respond to, participate in, and mediate the unprecedented experiences of modernizing societies? How did urban and environmental crises, cataclysmic wars, and technological advances affect architects' understanding and design of built space? How, in turn, did new buildings and projects reflect societies' self-image and their aspirations to become modern? What can architecture's manifestations over the course of this century tell us about the meaning of modernity itself? In attempting to answer these questions, we take note of shifting historiographic paradigms and reflect on the genealogical relationship and relevance of this formative period to contemporary architectural practice and thought.

The course aims to foster a strong understanding and appreciation of architectural history and of history in general. Lectures are organized both chronologically and thematically. The weekly lectures are augmented by focused discussions in the recitation sessions and by readings from a rich array of primary and secondary sources. ARCH 511 is the first half of a two-part sequence continuing in Spring 2021 with ARCH 512, which picks up the narrative of modern architecture in the mid-20th century.

ARCH 521
Visual Studies I
Faculty: Nate Hume, Miroslava Brooks, Brian DeLuna, & Olivia Vien

The coursework of Visual Studies will introduce a range of new tools, skills, and strategies useful for the

The 2020 Summer Olympics are held in Tokyo, Japan after a year-long delay due to the COVID-19 pandemic.

Egyptian authorities finally release the *Ever Given* after it blocked the Suez Canal, a major international trade route for six days in March.

development and representation of design work. Drawing and modeling strategies will be investigated for ways in which they can generate ideas and forms rather than be used solely as production tools. Control and the ability to model in an intentional manner will be highlighted. Likewise, drawing exercises will stress the construction of content over the acceptance of digital defaults in order to more accurately represent a project's ideas. Documents will be produced that strive to build on and question drawing conventions in order to more precisely convey the unique character of each project. The workflow will embrace a range of software to open up possibilities to achieve intended results and resist constraint of a single program's abilities. The course will be separated into three phases, each focusing on a different set of topics related to the work in studio. These phases will be in a sequential consolidation of techniques and methods. Each exercise must therefore be complete before progressing to the next. The exercises will have specific requirements and be presented by the students, as well as submitted for grading, before the next exercise is introduced.

ARCH 531
Construction I
Faculty: Philip Ryan

This is the first of two courses explaining Construction Technology. This course will introduce the student to the relationship of design and construction in the creation of buildings. The early lectures will trace the evolution and innovation of construction technique throughout history. It will then be followed by a primer describing how design and

the act of drawing establishes a vocabulary that architects use to describe the construction of buildings. This will look at how conceptual design and communicating intent aid in the creation of a great building. The remainder of the semester will build a "light-scale" building from the ground up, examining the fundamental material and construction concepts related to construction starting with excavation and ending with interior finishes. The labs will complement the lectures with site visits and more focused lessons.

ARCH 535
Structures I
Faculty: Masoud Akbarzadeh & Richard Farley

Fundamental structural principles of systems, elements, and materials are related to the study of morphology of structure. Methods are taught to develop skills, knowledge, and intuition for the application of structures to architectural design, including form finding. The students pursue structural optimization in subsequent seminars and design studios, carrying out into the profession.

The ARCH 535 course introduces structural principles, morphology, form-finding, and material science, complemented with digital analysis techniques that are verified with standard calculation techniques for selecting and sizing structural elements, with particular consideration for physical dimensions, span, materiality, and construction determinants.

Lectures provide a study of skeletal behavior and experiencing structural principles. The analysis and design of cables, trusses, beams, columns, and frames are covered, as well as an investigation of the properties

of structural materials. Homework exercises and labs demonstrate the relation of structural configuration and efficiency in the design of architectural structures.

ARCH 611
History and Theory III
Rebellious Architecture:
Social Movements
for Spatial Justice
Faculty: Eduardo Rega Calvo

A shortened version of the elective seminar introduced last fall, Rebellious Architecture is an introductory survey-like 611 module that lays out theoretical tools to explore a rebellious mode of practice for architecture, one that acknowledges its relations to the structures of power, and stands in solidarity with movements for justice and liberation. In readings and conversations (often departing from architectural scholarship), we learn about architecture's entanglements with the social and political processes that produce space, and expand on key concepts like the rebel, refusal, and spatial justice. It introduces to the roots of structural injustice (capitalism, colonialism, racism, and patriarchy), and their inscription in space and architecture; and learns from across social movements for justice (autonomist, feminist, decolonial, and post-capitalist) as they refuse the status-quo and construct other, more equitable worlds.

ARCH 611
History and Theory III
New York as "Perfect Model":
The City According to Lewis
Mumford, Robert Moses,
Jane Jacobs, & Rem Koolhaas
Faculty: Joan Ockman

"New York is the perfect model of a city," stated Lewis Mumford, "not the model of a perfect city." As the largest

city in the country, historically characterized by its
density, its population
diversity and disparities of
wealth, its cultural dyna-
mism, and its geographic
peculiarities as an island
archipelago, New York has
long been an incubator for
urban complexity and experimentation. This course
counterposes the ideas of
four important and radically
different thinkers whose
urban perspectives and
practices were shaped by
their experiences of and
responses to 20th-century
New York: Lewis Mumford
(1895–1990), Robert Moses
(1888–1981), Jane Jacobs
(1916–2006), and Rem
Koolhaas (1944–). Set up
as a four-part argument or
debate, the course frames
their respective ideas and
careers in terms of the
following themes: "ecological
city," "infrastructural city,"
"everyday city," and "spectacle city." By contrasting and
critically reflecting on
Mumford's environmental
humanism, Moses's large-
scale housing and highway
projects, Jacobs's community
activism, and Koolhaas's
celebration of the urban
imaginary, we address larger
social, political, and environmental issues, including
power, agency, gender, race,
diversity, and nature in the
city. In carefully placing each
figure within their historical
context, we also trace the
evolution of New York's
built and physical environment over the course of the
last 100 years. Selections
from classic texts like
Mumford's *Culture of Cities*,
Robert Caro's *The Power
Broker*, Jacobs's *The Death
and Life of Great American
Cities*, and Koolhaas's
Delirious New York will be
read in light of recent
critical reassessments
and contemporary urban
problematics.

ARCH 611
History and Theory III
Architecture from
Antiquity to Futurity:
Global Origin Stories
Faculty: Matthew Miller

The architectural "object" or
"work"—prototypically seen
as a building for dwelling
—existed as a practice prior
to the earliest known writings
in Western empires (i.e.,
Vitrius in 15 BCE). Yet, few
engage deeply with the events
and contextual forces that
gave form and foundation to
the two centuries of the
architectural profession:
a practice that has become
both more specialized and
more diffuse among many
actors in the design world. In
this course, we will be continually asking, "What is the real
origin story of architecture?"
through various eras and
actors. The goal is to help
learners deploy two cultural
concepts—"sociogenesis" (the
emergence of a structure of
cultural meanings as a social
phenomena) and "synchronicity"—to excavate and tell a
counter-humanist interna-
tionalist story of architecture
as a multipolar, multi-faceted
prism of urbanism. All told,
we will be able to come away
from this course better able
to do five things: 1) Frame
architecture as both a spec-
tacularized formal expression
of imperial/elite values and an
overlooked ode to everyday
people's needs—regionally,
representationally, abstractly;
2) See architecture's vernacu-
larity while also appreciating
"synchronicity and intercon-
nectivity" beyond globalization; 3) Embed decolonial
notions of "counter-human-
ism" to foster curiosity in the
architectural history and
theory of marginalized
"genres" of peoples—women,
minorities, enslaved, indigent,
revolutionaries—who con-
struct in three dimensions;
4) Develop comfort with

architectural storytelling and
writing as a habit as much as
an artform itself; 5) Foster a
sense of reflection and wonder
about how one's own position
affects their approach to
architecture in relation to
one's peers.

ARCH 621
Visual Studies III
Faculty: Nate Hume, Miroslava
Brooks, Brian DeLuna, &
Michael Zimmerman

The final of the Visual Studies
half-credit courses. Drawings
are explored as visual reposi-
tories of data from which
information can be gleaned,
geometries tested, designs
refined and transmitted.
Salient strengths of various
digital media programs are
identified and developed
through assignments that
address the specific intentions and challenges of the
design studio project.

ARCH 631
D3 Design Detail +
Data + Delivery
Faculty: Dr. Franca Trubiano

A study of the active integration of various building
systems in exemplary architectural projects. To deepen
students' understanding of
the process of building, the
course compares the process
of design and construction in
buildings of similar type.
The course brings forward
the nature of the relationship
between architectural design
and engineering systems,
and highlights the crucial
communication skills required
by both the architect and
the engineer.

ARCH 633
Environmental Systems I
Faculty: Dorit Aviv

OBJECTIVES: 1) To under-
stand architecture and
building systems in the
context of environmental

forces, natural processes of the earth, and the laws of thermodynamics. 2) To consider the impact of building design on the environment and on human comfort.

ARCH 699
Structures / Architectural Technology / Technology Lab
Faculty: Mohamad Alkhayer

The structural simulation component of the course is designed to help architecture students think visually about structural performance. It helps one assess the structural implications of morphological and geometric design decisions. Students are introduced to structural modeling, its terminologies, and components. Simulation software (VisualAnalysis) is introduced to visualize the structural behavior of a building and to gain instant feedback related to structural components' geometries and properties.

ARCH 771
Professional Practice II
Faculty: Philip Ryan

ARCH 771 is the second of a two-course sequence that discusses the issues and processes involved in running a professional architectural practice and designing buildings in the contemporary construction environment.

ARCH 771 will build on the knowledge of the Project process gained in Arch 672 to examine the way in which an office is "designed" to facilitate the execution of design and construction. Issues of finance, liability, ethics, and the codes that overlay atop the design and construction industry will be discussed.

The lectures will draw connections between the student's studio design knowledge to date and the instructor's experience in practice including local building examples and guest lectures by relevant professionals. Guests from within the field of architecture and construction (and outside frequently) will supplement the semester lectures.

Electives

ARCH 711
Topics in Arch Theory I:
Modern Arch. in Japan—
Culture, Place, Tectonic
Faculty: Ariel Genadt

This seminar explores the diversity of forms and meanings that architecture took on in Japan since its industrialization in the 19th century. Through this lens, it poses wider questions on the capacity of construction, materials, and their assembly to express and represent cultural, aesthetic, climatic, and social concerns. Rather than an exhaustive survey, the course demonstrates salient topics in Japan's recent architectural history, as a mirror of parallel practices in the world. It examines drawings, images, texts, and films about architects whose work and words were emblematic of these topics, including: the role of technology in construction and cultural expression;

tensions between tradition and creation; resistance, weakness, and resilience in face of environmental forces; tectonic expression in relation to place; and the concepts of dematerialization and abstraction in architectural expression.

ARCH 719
Archigram and Its Legacy
Faculty: Annette Fierro

Acknowledging the ubiquitous proliferation of "Hi-Tech" architecture in contemporary London, this research seminar examines the scope of technology as it emerges and re-emerges in the work of various architects currently dominating the city. This scope includes the last strains of post-war urbanism that spawned a legacy of radical architecture directly contributing to the Hi-Tech; a particular focus of the course will be the

contributing and contrasting influence provided by the counter-cultural groups of the '60s—Archigram, Superstudio, the Metabolists, and others. Using the premise of Archigram's idea of infrastructure, both literal and of event, the course will attempt to discover relational networks between works of the present day (Rogers, Foster, Grimshaw, etc.). As this work practices upon and within public space, an understanding of the contribution of technology to urban theatricality will evolve, which is relevant to contemporary spheres of technological design practices. Students will be required to produce and present a term research paper.

ARCH 721
Designing Smart Objects
Faculty: Assaf Eshet

Today's children enjoy a wide array of play experiences,

The UN Environment Programme announces that leaded petrol in road vehicles is phased out globally, a hundred years after its introduction.

El Salvador becomes the first country in the world to accept Bitcoin as an official currency.

with stories, learning, characters, and games that exist as
physical stand-alone objects
or toys enhanced with electronics or software. In this
course, students will explore
the domain of play and
learning in order to develop
original proposals for new
product experiences that are
at once tangible, immersive,
and dynamic. They will
conduct research into education and psychology while
also gaining hands-on exposure to new product manifestations in a variety of forms,
both physical and digital.
Students will be challenged
to work in teams to explore
concepts, share research,
and build prototypes of their
experiences in the form of
static objects that may have
accompanying electronic
devices or software. Final
design proposals will consider
future distribution models
for product experiences such
as 3D printing, virtual reality,
and software/hardware
integration. Instruction
will be part seminar and
part workshop, providing
research guidance and
encouraging connections will
subject-matter experts
throughout the Penn campus.

ARCH 724
Technology in Design:
Immersive Kinematics /
Physical Computing:
Body As Site
Faculty: Simon Kim

The aim of this course is
to understand the new
medium of architecture
within the format of a
research seminar. The subject
matter of new media is to be
examined and placed in a
disciplinary trajectory of
building design and construction technology that adapts
to material and digital
discoveries. We will also build
prototypes with the new
media, and establish a
disciplinary knowledge for

ourselves. The seminar is
interested in testing the
architecture-machine relationship, moving away from
architecture that looks like
machines into architecture
that behaves like machines:
an intelligence (based on the
conceptual premise of a
project and in the design of a
system), as part of a process
(related to the generative
real of architecture) and
as the object itself and its
embedded intelligence.

ARCH 725
Design Thinking
Faculty: Sarah Rottenberg

Creating new product con-
cepts was once a specialized
pursuit exclusively performed
by design professionals in
isolation from the rest of an
organization. Today's products are developed in a
holistic process involving a
collaboration among many
disciplines. Design thinking
—incorporating processes,
approaches, and working
methods from traditional
designers' toolkits—has
become a way of generating
innovative ideas to challenging problems and refining
those ideas. Rapid prototyping techniques, affordable
and accessible prototyping
platforms, and an iterative
mindset have enabled people
to more reliably translate
those ideas into imple-
mentable solutions. In this
course, students will be
exposed to these practices
and learn how to engage
in a human-centered
design process.

ARCH 727
Industrial Design I
Faculty: Chris Murray &
Ed Mitchell

This course provides an
introduction to the ideas and
techniques of Industrial
Design,which operates
alongside Engineering and

Marketing as the design
component of Integrated
Product Development.
The course is intended for
students from engineering,
design, or business with an
interest in multi-disciplinary,
needs-based product design
methods. It will follow a
workshop model, combining
weekly lectures on industrial
design history, processes,
tools, and the profession,
with a progressive set of
studio-based design projects.

ARCH 731
Experiments in Structure
Faculty:
Mohamad Al Khayer

This course studies the
relationships between
geometric space and those
structural systems that
amplify tension. Experiments
using the hand (touch and
force) in coordination with
the eye (sight and geometry)
will be done during the
construction and observa-
tion of physical models.
Verbal, mathematical, and
computer models are secondary to the reality of the
physical model. However
these models will be used to
give dimension and document
the experiments. Team
reports will serve as interim
and final examinations. In
typology, masonry structures
in compression (e.g., vault
and dome) correlate with
"Classical" space, and steel
or reinforced concrete
structures in flexure (e.g.,
frame, slab, and column) with
"Modernist" space. We seek
the spatial correlations to
tensile systems of both
textiles (woven or braided
fabrics where both warp and
weft are tensile), and baskets
(where the warp is tensile
and the weft is compressive).
In addition to the experiments, we will examine
Le Ricolais' structural
models held by the Architectural Archives.

ARCH 732
Technology Designated Daylighting
Faculty: Janki Vyas, LEED AP BD_C, & O+M

This course aims to introduce fundamental daylighting concepts and tools to analyze daylighting design. The wide range of topics to be studied includes site planning, building envelope and shading optimization, passive solar design, daylight delivery methods, daylight analysis structure and results interpretation, and a brief daylighting and lighting design integration.

ARCH 732
Technology Designated Material and Structural Intelligence
Faculty: Sameer Kumar & Florian Meier

The semester-long project will involve a gradual development of architectural ideas that are intimately informed by and centered on knowledge of Structure and Materiality. Employing both physical and digital simulations, the students will synthesize knowledge acquired in previous courses in structures, materials, and construction methods to develop architectural solutions within a carefully selected set of determinants.

ARCH 732
Technology Designated Geometric Structural Design
Faculty: Masoud Akbarzadeh

Geometric structural design provides a comprehensive introduction to novel geometric methods of structural design based on 2D and 3D graphical statics. The primary emphasis of the course will be on developing a general understanding of the relationship between structural forms in equilibrium and the geometric representation of their internal and external forces. This link is the main apparatus for designing provocative structural forms using only geometric techniques rather than complicated algebraic/numerical methods. Moreover, special consideration will be given to materialization of the structural geometry and the proper fabrication techniques to construct the complex geometry of the structure.

Note that this course is based on ongoing research in the field of 3D graphical statics, and therefore provides students with the opportunity to directly contribute to the current research in geometric methods of structural design. Familiarity with a parametric software is required, and code-writing ability is an asset. Particular attention will be given to structural model making and careful structural drawings. The outcomes of the course will become a primary collection of Polyhedral Structures Laboratory. Also, a unique summer research fellowship will be available for highly motivated students to build a one-to- one scale structural prototype based on the forms developed in the class.

ARCH 732
Technology Designated Matter, Making, and Testing: Designing with Next Generation Precast Concrete
Faculty: Richard Garber

This seminar will focus on precast concrete and specifically its materiality—how it is manufactured and the logistics of its assembly—and its cultural effects through both traditional uses within the urban environment as well as new approaches to building typologies such as housing. Through a strategic partnership with Northeast Precast (NEP), based in Millville, NJ, students enrolled in the seminar will gain access to places where precast concrete is made, formed, and put into action. In addition to readings and case studies via traditional seminar delivery, students will have access to Northeast Precast's state-of-the-art facility where they will learn about the precast-concrete manufacturing process and produce panel prototypes for wall assemblies that respond to structural, thermal, and water-proofing performance. Students will develop a delivery workflow utilizing digital tools to communicate with and transmit panel, assembly, and formwork concepts to NEP staff, fostering a collaboration opportunity for students that is not regularly experienced in architecture school.

Northeast Precast is our industry partner on a four-year grant awarded by the Precast/ Prestressed Concrete Institute (PCI) totaling about $330K in financial and in-kind support.

ARCH 737
Semi-Fictitious Realms
Faculty: Jeffrey Anderson

This course will study the evolutionary advancements made that now allow us to fully inhabit digital worlds through Virtual Reality. Using the Unity Video Game Engine, students will generate immersive, photo-realistic models of unbuilt architectural works and explore digital/physical interactivity. These models will be designed to have compatibility with both 6-DOF and 3-DOF Virtual Reality equipment as well as flythrough-style experiences for keyboard and mouse using various web-hosting platforms. From the terraces of Paul Rudolph's Lower Manhattan Expressway to Boullée's

Cenotaph for Newton, the goal of this course is to breathe new life into places and spaces that have, until this time, never been built or occupied.

ARCH 739
New Approaches to an Architecture of Health
Faculty: Mikael Avery

Health care is taking on a new role in our society—refocusing from episodic care for those who are ill or symptomatic to providing life-long care geared towards maintaining wellness. These changes are evident across numerous areas of design, from wearable technologies that track and analyze to large-scale building initiatives that aim to create healthier environments and improve lives through strategic planning initiatives.

A concrete, physical representation of this paradigm shift can be found within the hospital building itself and in the new manner in which hospitals are looking to serve their patients and care for their clinicians. Simultaneously both public and private spaces, hospitals are complex systems in which sickness, health, hospitality, technology, emergency, and community share space and compete for resource. In order to frame our present-day understanding of the role of architecture (and design) in fostering health for individuals and within communities, this seminar will begin with an exploration of the historical and contemporary perspectives on the role of the architect and built environment on health.

ARCH 741
Arch Design Innovation
Faculty: Ali Rahim

This design seminar will explore cultural progression, digital design techniques,

and aesthetics that yield contemporary architecture details that contribute to Architectural Design Innovation. Innovation is not merely change. Innovation is effective precisely to the degree that it inflects culture. The longevity of any innovation is directly related to its ability to sustain and continually encourage its effect; innovation is change that people find useful or meaningful. Architecture design innovation is dependent on design techniques that form the pivot between culture and its progression. Design techniques affect the technical that influences technology and as technology improves it progresses culture and techniques are reinvented to continue cultural progression. As techniques change so does culture and as culture changes so do the aesthetics.

ARCH 743
Form and Algorithm
Faculty: Ezio Blasetti

We will develop the potential beyond finite forms of explicit and parametric modeling towards non-linear algorithmic processes, and seek novel patterns of organization, structure, and articulation as architectural expressions within the emergent properties of feedback loops and rule-based systems. This seminar will accommodate both introductory and advanced levels. No previous scripting experience is necessary. It will consist of a series of introductory sessions, obligatory intensive workshops and lectures followed by suggested readings, and will gradually focus on individual projects. Students will be encouraged to investigate the limits of algorithmic design both in theory and practice through a scripting environment.

ARCH 761
Introduction to Real Estate Development
Faculty: Richard Garber

The course introduces students to the participants and components to the development process, as well as specific development strategies and design tools for engaging them. Design in this sense is not simply a vision, or a concept utilized for obtaining approvals; it is understood as an encompassing set of procedures that both allows for and ensures that goals are being met at all stages of a project, from early conception through the approval process and building construction. Students will learn how to engage municipal land-use laws and regulations, produce strategies for geometric development based on land- use and environmental constraints, and use simulation to perform value-adding operations to a development proposal. Through lectures and exercises, students will have the opportunity to analyze a building and the redevelopment procedures surrounding it, and develop a geometric response and then parse data from that model to drive a series of documents relating to project cost, funding, and schedule. These documents will be analyzed against a variety of construction means and funding models so a time—and cost—effective basis that meets design intentions can be developed.

ARCH 765
Project Management
Faculty: Charles Capaldi

An introduction to construction management, project management, and various construction project delivery systems. In the study of construction delivery systems, we will examine the players, relationships, and the advantages and disadvantages of different contractual and practical relationships, both on the construction site and at the tops of the various "paper piles." Exercises and lectures will focus on developing perspectives into the various roles, needs, and expectations of the many parties involved in a construction project and the management skills and techniques that help to bring a project to a successful conclusion.

ARCH 768
Real Estate Development
Faculty: Alan Feldman

This course evaluates "ground-up" development as well as re-hab, re-development, and acquisition investments. We examine raw and developed land and the similarities and differences of traditional real estate product types including office, R&D, retail, warehouses, single-family and multi-family residential, mixed use, and land, as well as "specialty" uses like golf courses, assisted living, and fractional-share ownership. Emphasis is on concise analysis and decision making. We discuss topics including market analysis, site acquisition, due diligence, zoning, entitlements, approvals, site planning, building design, construction, financing, leasing, and ongoing management and disposition. Special topics like workouts and running a development company are also discussed. Course lessons apply to all markets but the class discusses U.S. markets only. Throughout the course, we focus on risk management and leadership issues. Numerous guest lecturers who are leaders in the real estate industry participate in the learning process.

ARCH 811
Theories of Architecture:
Constructing a Settler
Colonial History of
American Architecture
Faculty: Charles Davis

This course develops a settler colonial history of "American Architecture" that establishes a racial critique of the social, ethical, and technical elements of the built environment. Key texts from Settler Colonial Theory, American Studies, Critical Race Theory, and Whiteness Studies provide the intellectual basis for reinterpreting architectural case studies and texts across time, from the late-19th to the early-21st century. Students will work in groups to mine local and digital archives to reinterpret canonical case studies of American architecture, as well as to recover the lost contributions of people of color.

After being installed in the Sierra Pacific Synod of the Evangelical Lutheran Church in America, Rev. Dr. Megan Rohrer becomes the first openly transgender and non-binary Bishop in any major Christian denomination.

SpaceX launches Inspiration4, the first all-civilian spaceflight, carrying a four-person crew on a three-day orbit of the Earth.

Sep 2021

		01	02	03	04
05	06	07	08	09	10	11
12	13	14	(15)	16	17	18
19	20	21	22	23	24	25
26	(27)	28	29	30	31

Sep 15: Book Launch for *Strange Objects, New Solids and Massive Things* and lecture by Winka Dubbeldam

The Department of Architecture presents a book launch for *Strange Objects, New Solids and Massive Things* (Actar 2021) with a welcome and lecture by Miller Professor and Chair of Architecture, Winka Dubbeldam.

Strange Objects, New Solids and Massive Things explores the work of Archi-Tectonics, the award-winning architecture firm founded by Dubbeldam in 1994, in light of a paradigm shift in contemporary design enabled by advances in technology and design conceptualization. Examining the architectural object and the process of its emergence and production, the book demonstrates in great detail how the firm's unique design methodology of research, optimization,

and construction innovation leads to original, characteristic designs. Rather than a traditional monograph, the book, as manual, was conceived itself as a Strange Object reflecting the non-standard way the firm's projects come into being. WSDIA's iconic layout is intended as a "below the surface" manual or taxonomy of the firm's work, considering each project according to its particular formal and performative characteristics, thus establishing overarching areas of research and narratives but also the singular nature of the design process and its final outcome. With more than 600 images and graphics, *Strange Objects* traces the past 15 years of innovative multidisciplinary work produced by

Archi-Tectonics through 10 case studies that explore process, experimentation, and production—including the upcoming Asian Games 2022 park and stadiums, reaching completion. With essays by Winka Dubbeldam, Manuel Delanda, and Jonathan Jackson, along with a lengthy interview between Dubbeldam and Zack Saunders, the book celebrates the potential of the Strange Object and its capacity to generate new forms and meanings. Reconceiving how the architectural object is produced and experienced changes the very concept of objectivity and meaning of architecture.

Sep 22: Felecia Davis: Seams: Crafting an Architecture
The Jeffrey Fine, C'76, MArch'78 and Andrea Katz Lecture

The path that one walks as a Black architect or designer has many seams, or places that one improvises and stitches together to make a story, or really understand where one is in the world and how to make sense of things that cannot under any circumstances make any sense and never did. There are many gaps and lacunae that are bridged by these seams. Working along these gaps constructs a place of creativity, and ways of making that integrate fragments from the past but in fact also project a future. [I] will present prior and current works in computational textiles or textiles that use sensors or microcontrollers or simply the natural properties of the textile itself to communicate some information to people. These projects are examples of work along a seam.

Felecia Davis' work in computational textiles questions how we live. She re-imagines how we might use textiles in our daily lives and in architecture. Computational textiles are textiles that are responsive to cues in the environment using sensors and microcontrollers or textiles that use the changeable properties of the material itself to communicate information to people. In architecture these responsive textiles used in lightweight shelters are transforming how we communicate, socialize, and use space. Davis is interested in developing computational methods and design in relation to specific bodies in specific places engaging specific social, cultural, and political constructions. Davis is an Associate Professor at the Stuckeman Center for Design Computing in the School of Architecture and Landscape Architecture at Pennsylvania State University and is the director of SOFT-LAB @ PSU. This lab is dedicated to developing soft computational materials and textiles and is for the use of Penn State students and faculty, industry, and community partners engaged in collaborative research and projects. The point of the lab is to establish a culture of hands-on making and thinking through computational materials and the lab links together research, teaching, and practice.

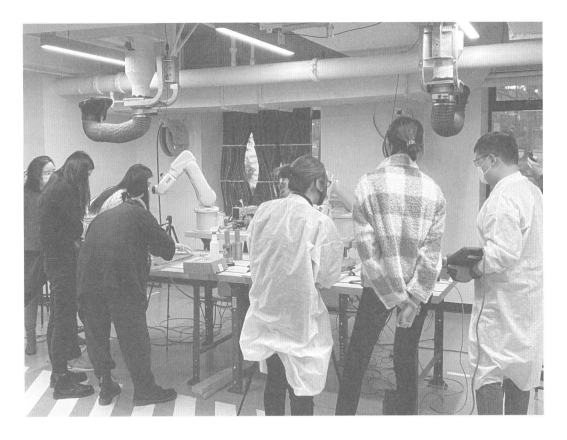

Sep 27: Architecture and Robotics: New Modes of Practice and Pedagogy

Robert Stuart-Smith in conversation with Ezio Blasetti, Winka Dubbeldam, Billie Faircloth Evangelos Kotsioris, Nathan King, Jose-Luis García del Castilloy López, Andrew Saunders.

Last year, the Weitzman School of Design launched a new MSD program—the Master of Science in Design: Robotics and Autonomous Systems (MSD-RAS), and completed the new ARI Robotics Lab, bringing industrial robots into the heart of the Weitzman School's Meyerson Hall. These exciting developments not only offer unique opportunities for students to gain knowledge and skills in advanced state of the art technologies, they also provide a means to critically and creatively question the role of the architect in the face of increasing automation in the construction and design industries. In the early years of what is now described as Industry 4.0, many sectors of our economy are shifting from mass production and automation to leaner modes of on-demand, autonomous manufacturing, promising not only more user engagement, but also creating unprecedented levels of consumption and waste. With robotics, 3D printing, AI, IOT, and Machine Learning technologies already impacting many aspects of our lives, how can we empower Penn's graduates to operate with greater agency in a fast-evolving Posthuman world? What opportunities are there within design research at Penn to address issues such as social and economic inequality, or climate change? How does creative engagement with autonomous systems impact design authorship or aesthetics? With a return to in-person teaching on campus, the Weitzman School of Design is excited to share recent work of the MSD-RAS program, and brainstorm together on UPenn's next steps in robotics.

Sep 29: G. Huljich and M. Spina in Conversation with F. Kolatan: *Mute Icons and Other Dichotomies of the Real in Architecture*

Georgina Huljich and Marcelo Spina (PATTERNS), and Ferda Kolatan (Associate Professor of Architecture, Weitzman; Co-Founder, SU11) will discuss topics relevant to PATTERNS' recently released book *Mute Icons*. A book signing will follow with the authors.

Part-history, part-theory, and part-monographic atlas, *Mute Icons* aims to construct a viable alternative to the icon's cliché and exhausted form of communication, positing one that is decidedly introverted and withdrawn. Developing a language and a sensibility for discovering simultaneous, contradictory, and even unexpected readings of architectural form, PATTERNS's new book, *Mute Icons*, aims to carve out a

niche in contemporary culture and history by suggesting that far from being a crowd-pleaser, architecture can persist within society as a constructive cultural and social irritant.

Born and raised in Rosario, Argentina, Marcelo Spina and Georgina Huljich are both renowned architects and distinguished educators. Together, they lead the Los Angeles-based and award-winning architectural practice PATTERNS, which they founded in 2002 as a speculative platform to explore an increasingly global design culture. Their work reveals a rigorous and progressive approach to projects and buildings across materials, scales, agendas, and geographies, insisting on the cultural and social relevance

of architectural form, contemporary aesthetics and emerging technologies. Their books include *PATTERNS: Embedded*, the studio's first monograph published in 2010 by Shanghai-based ACDCU and *Mute Icons and Other Dichotomies of the Real in Architecture* recently released by ACTAR Press. Marcelo Spina is a Design Faculty at SCI-Arc and Georgina Huljich is an Associate Professor at UCLA AUD. They are also visiting professors at the Weitzman School of Design.

Vincent van Gogh's newly discovered *Worn Out* is shown at the Van Gogh Museum in Amsterdam for the first time.

NASA's Lucy takes off on a mission to explore never-before-seen Trojan asteroids.

News

Sep 2021: Weitzman to Honor MASS Design Group and the City of Minneapolis

Weitzman has recognized two organizations who have embraced design as a vehicle for a healthier, more sustainable, and more equitable environment. MASS Design Group, the nonprofit firm based in Boston and Kigali, Rwanda, will receive the 2021 Kanter Tritsch Medal in Architecture, and the City of Minneapolis will receive the 2021 Witte-Sakamoto Family Medal in City and Regional Planning for Minneapolis 2040, a comprehensive plan to guide the city's growth. They were presented at a November 18 public celebration at the Kleinman Center for Energy Policy.

The Kanter Tritsch Medal in Architecture was established in 2017 through a gift from Penn alumna Lori Kanter Tritsch (MArch'85) and her partner and fellow Penn alumnus William P. Lauder. The Medal honors an architect or firm that has changed the course of design history, with a particular focus on the areas of energy conservation, environmental quality, and/or diversity.

The Witte-Sakamoto Family Medal in City and Regional Planning was established by William Witte (C'73, MCP'75), an alumnus of the Weitzman School and member of the Board of Advisors at Weitzman, and his wife, Keiko Sakamoto, Esq. to recognize a firm, team, or professional for an exemplary plan that advances plan making in at least four of the following areas: social equity, environmental quality, design, public health, mobility, housing affordability, and economic development.

Oct 2021: *Under Pressure: Essays on Urban Housing* by Hina Jamelle, Weitzman Architecture

Last fall Jamelle moderated a panel discussion and launch for the book with Ayata (UCLA, Young and Ayata), Erdy (Weitzman, Erdy McHenry), Pearson (Architectural Record), Phillips (Weitzman, ISA Architects), and Mogas-Soldevila. Weitzman on *Under Pressure: Essays on Urban Housing* (Routledge, 2021), edited by Hina Jamelle, senior lecturer and director of urban housing, gathers and contextualizes recent conversations on urban housing through a design lens. The book traces its origins to a conference organized by Jamelle in 2016 at Weitzman, and includes work produced in graduate architecture urban housing studios at Weitzman Architecture alongside illustrated essays by leading professionals.

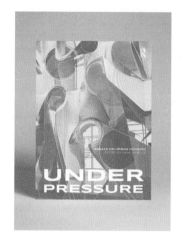

    The book has four frameworks for analyzing and acting upon the pressures affecting urban housing: Learning from History, Changing Domesticities, Housing Finance and Policy, and Design and Material Innovation. A number of Weitzman faculty contributed essays to *Under Pressure*, including Scott Erdy, , Laia Mogas-Soldevila, Hina Jamelle, and Brian Phillips. The studies suggest new formal identities for housing design, elevating the typology's status through careful, highly articulated designs created by students from Weitzman's Department of Architecture that serve to contextualize and highlight the most relevant and provocative issues in each project.

Nov 2021: Rashida Ng Appointed Presidential Associate Professor at Weitzman Architecture

In Spring 2022 Rashida Ng joined the standing faculty in the Department of Architecture as an Associate Professor and succeeded Richard Wesley, Adjunct Professor of Architecture, as Chair of Undergraduate Architecture. In addition, she will hold the appointment of Presidential Associate Professor through June of 2027. Presidential Professorships are five-year chairs awarded by University of Pennsylvania President Amy Gutmann to exceptional scholars who have the potential to advance faculty eminence through diversity across the University.

    Professor Ng is a nationally respected leader in reforming architectural education and served as president of the Association of Collegiate Schools of Architecture, where she was on the Board of Directors from 2015 until the Summer of 2021. She has been on the faculty at the Tyler School of Art and Architecture at Temple University since 2005, where she is an Associate Professor and served as Chair of the Architecture and Environmental Design Department until the Summer of 2021.

    Ng has recently turned her attention to the intersection of racial and environmental justice in architecture. This work provides actionable approaches for climate mitigation, while considering intersections with social infrastructures and restorative justice.

Dec 2021: Weitzman Architecture Faculty Honored at AIA PA 2021 Architectural Excellence Awards

Five faculty members and alumni of the Department of Architecture were honored last month by the Pennsylvania chapter of the AIA with a 2021 Architectural Excellence Award. Among the firms from across Pennsylvania recognized for excellence in design, contributions to the profession of architecture, and commitment to the quality of the built environment were Erdy McHenry Architecture, ISA, DIGSAU, and KieranTimberlake, which are led by instructors or graduates of the Weitzman School.

KieranTimberlake, led by alumni Stephen Kieran (MArch'76) and James Timberlake (MArch'77) received the Medal of Distinction, the highest honor given by AIA PA. They also received a Merit Award for their design of Jeff and Judy Henley Hall, University of California Santa Barbara.

The Silver Medal went to Erdy McHenry Architecture for Anderson Hall. Located on Temple University's campus, Anderson Hall features a grand glass atrium, creating a new gateway into the academic building.

ISA, which is led by alum and Lecturer Brian Phillips (MArch'96), received an Honor Award for the project 22 South 40th Street. ISA's Oxford Green was also recognized with a Merit Award.

Dec 2021: PhD Candidate Wins 'Building and Environment' 2021 Best Paper Award

Nancy Ma, a candidate for the PhD in Architecture affiliated with the Center for Environmental Building & Design, has won the Building and Environment 2021 Best Paper Award. One of three papers awarded among 4,500 submissions, "Adaptive behavior and different thermal experiences of real people: A Bayesian neural network approach to thermal preference prediction and classification" was co-authored by Liang Chen and Jian Hu with faculty advisors Professors Paris Perdikaris, SEAS, and William Braham, Weitzman, and published in *Building and Environment Vol. 198* in July of 2021.

The paper documents an original Bayesian neural network (BNN) algorithm to tackle the problem of high uncertainty in the prediction and classification of building occupants' thermal preferences. The research of Ma, Chen, and Hu offers insight into quantifying human-building interaction during architectural design as well as making a positive impact on building energy consumption and occupant wellness in the indoor environment. Building and Environment is an international journal that publishes original research papers and review articles related to building science, urban physics, and human interaction with the indoor and outdoor built environment.

Spring

Foundation 502 Studio Overview

Foundation 502: Design Studio II

Coordinator: Annette Fierro

The second design semester of the first year follows the introduction in the previous semester of properties of objects and lessons of artifacts, conveyed through basic tools and technical skills. In Architecture 502, these foundational precepts are situated and challenged within the plethora of external contingencies that architecture must answer. The semester preoccupies itself with concepts of site, taking students through analytical and speculative methodologies through which the complexities of an urban site are understood, conveyed, and mobilized. The semester also introduces students to the aspirations of program, assigning a large, multifaceted program for students to implement, but also asking students to write for themselves an addition to that program, imparting the effect that program, as a dimension of human activity, has to embod architectural form. The final component of Architecture 502 is a historical precedent, a figure or seminal idea or reading, chosen yearly for its ability to reflect on a contemporary issue; this year's, for example, is Colin Rowe and Fred Koetter's Collage City, which interrogates and reflects upon the increasing use of graphic techniques of collage that have reappeared in advanced design pedagogies. This topic is taken up in conjunction with the history/theory curriculum of the first year.

This year's program is an urban market, placed in Philadelphia district characterized as a failed urban-renewal site of the 1970s, now contested between two identities: the first as a traditional part of Philadelphia's Chinatown, the second as part of a quickly gentrifying arts and residential loft district. Running next to the site is a much-anticipated park development on a disused section of elevated rail—a project that is at the center of the neighborhood's cultural strife. The first intention of the urban market is to explore the potential of this program as a social condenser, overlapping and accommodating the intersection of different agencies and agendas: historically the urban market functioned as the agora, the center of social and civic life, as well as the commercial center of every city and town. While urban markets still function in this capacity to varying degrees around the world, the urban market in the United States can be traced through a series of diminishments. In contemporary America, the cultural centrality of the traditional market has long been suspended, but its traces continue in different forms, scales, and disposition to city morphology. This typology is open to reconsidering: a market is transparent to its local and regional constituency, a market acts as a potent translator of the needs and conditions of site, a mobilizer of economic past and future terms.

Faculty:

Foundation 502   Studio Overview

Foundation 502   Annette Fierro

Foundation 502:
Future Sutures

Faculty: Annette Fierro
Teaching Assistant: Juli Petrillo

The identity of the city has always been co-dependent on its representation: from early fantastical maps, to factually surveyed aerial perspectives, to Nolli diagrams of positives and voids, and collages done by early "post-modernists." The latter took on collage as an acknowledgement of the existing city, a rebellious gesture positioned against the autonomous, scientifically ordered modernist city. Here inclusions of photographic evidence of the city represented its ungraspable messiness, its resistance to being taken over and rationalized by over-arching entities. This studio takes as its site of production the capacity of collage: to identify by existing matter outside of drawn representation, to depict ephemera of simultaneity, to incorporate multiple levels of information impossible to convey otherwise. With the many transformative possibilities made available by the original technique, and its digital extensions, the attributes of a given physical site at different scales can be refigured in multiple meaningful ways. What does it mean to graphically characterize and then to follow through the implications of photographic description? What new dynamic conditions can be mobilized when taking conventional 2D collage and finding new ways to express 3D relationships? What does it mean to find and nurture disjunction through graphical method which takes on the additional consequences of social, physical, and economic domains? These techniques will be mined to reimagine how they lie tangential to critical investigation, and then to utilize overlay, morph, collision, to locate, newly figured edge or set of points, which will be the loci for finding and releasing the tension of the site. This, our methodology for finding and releasing the tension of the site through the alchemy of the tool.

Featured Student Work:

Foundation 502:
Slipping Loops

Faculty: Gisela Baurmann
Teaching Assistant: Michaela Dawe

Colorful, minimal, liminal, ephemeral, transitory, mysterious ... going to the markets always promises a treasure hunt. One never knows what to expect, what riches to unearth. Markets are big playgrounds of discovery and can hide all kinds of unexpected treasures. They bear opportunity for fabricators and vendors of all skill, practical, and social provenance to display their goods, make a living, and become part of a community.

The studio enhances the connections, minimalism, adaptability, and efficiency that by definition constitute market organizations. Enticing about the site are its ruptures, its inconsistencies, and scalar as well as programmatic jumps. Exciting also are the site's dynamics, the bubbling energy, and self-directed liveliness that exist.

The studio walks a tightrope between continuity and rupture when developing the new market project. Finding programmatic alliances, existing programs on and around the site give opportunity to align through the new proposed programs. Existing initiatives, such as manufacturing spaces and local infrastructures, are strengthened, while allowing the ruptures and discrepancies that define the site now to continue to exist side by side.

Crochet stitches are analyzed in their spatial and structural capacities and subsequently transformed to acquire radically new space-making and material qualities. Through the continuity of a single line, crochet serves as a conceptual method of organization to develop highly connective program proposals and rich spatial geometries.

Slip-cast models explore modular volumetric opportunities within the urban field of the Buttonwood site and the programmatic agenda developed by each student.

Featured Student Work:

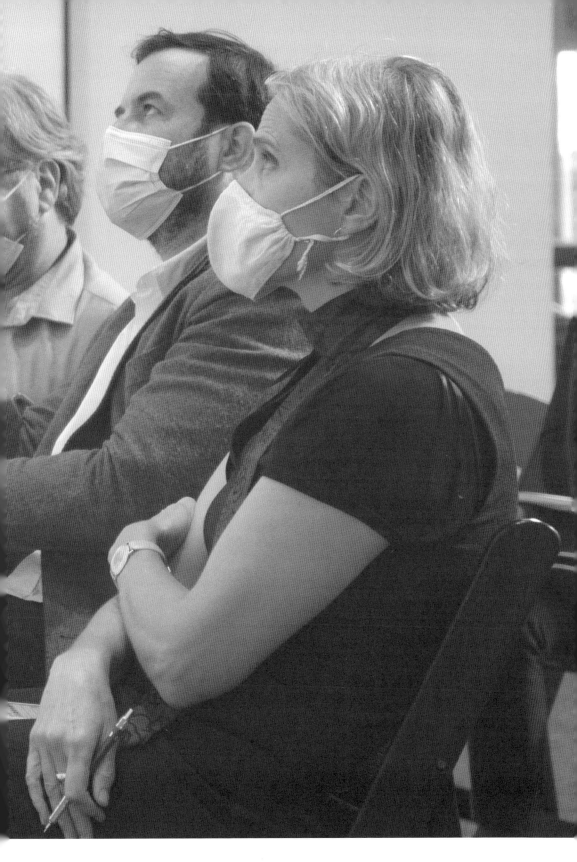

Foundation 502 Gisela Baurmann

Foundation 502:
HyperObjects - Cybermaterial Hybrids

Faculty: Ezio Blasetti
Teaching Assistant: Mingyang (June) Yuan

The project this semester will be the design of a hybrid market building program in Philadelphia's Callowhill neighborhood. The project will be concerned with the relationship of the city and architecture, generative formation, and social dynamics. We approach computational design as a generative framework for urban morphology and as an embodied infrastructure within the city itself. As such, beyond the correlation of simulation, this studio positions different mediums onto a flat ontology and mines the collateral effects of the synchronicities and divergences between them. We seek novel forms of organization, structure, and articulation as architectural expressions within the emergent properties of data and algorithmic design.

The studio will research and generate a multi-dimensional terrain of data, which will attempt to capture and compress the various infrastructural, environmental, and architectural parameters of the site. This abstract construction will be our conceptual and literal site of intervention. Design will operate as a feedback tool of navigation and adaptation. Students will research and create multi-dimensional representations of the metropolitan area of Philadelphia and the Callowhill neighborhood. Our attempt will be to map spatial and temporal patterns and speculate on the potential urban future infrastructure that would allow for real-time sensing and processing its data. The Urban Market is itself a hyperobject that operates on a multiplicity of dimensions with different ways and degrees of access.

Featured Student Work:

Foundation 502:
Automatic Assembly

Faculty: Kevin Cannon
Teaching Assistant: Ana Celdran

Our studio focused on how the introduction of a new form transforms place. The primary directive of our studio was to make meaningful engagement and exchange with the site. Through an initial series of analytical collages or maps, students were asked to develop and illustrate an idea of place. What each designer sees and interprets from the site is of significant ontological interest and establishes how their projects will participate and situate themselves on the site in a meaningful way. Collage was then used pictorially to illustrate key foundational moments of interaction with the site. These served to illustrate initial conceptual project ideas and perhaps gestures.

The act of making architecture is seen as transformative. Architecture in this way is seen as an act of addition; urban form is understood to be full of signifiers that reveal opportunities for the transformation of meaning through the addition of new built form. Students were asked to consider their building as part of some larger whole and each component of program a character within the larger story. The students were asked to consider what it means to assemble materials and program in a way that communicates an inherent meaning and experience.

Featured Student Work:

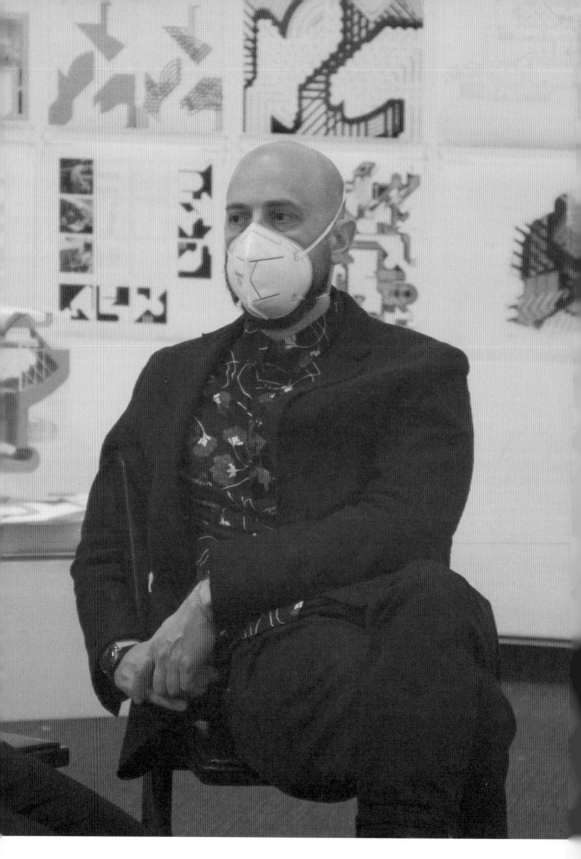

Foundation 502   Brian DeLuna

Foundation 502:
Spolia Agency

Faculty: Brian DeLuna
Teaching Assistant: Harsana Siva

Cities have been a source of fascination for architects throughout history, and studied as agents of power, production, economy, environment, and safety. In recent years, there has been a paradigm shift to reconfigure and overlay existing urban systems and agencies between public space, housing, commercial, industrial, and infrastructure to address climate change, rapid urbanization, and social inequality.

This Studio will begin with multiple modes of researching and cataloging of selected cities through graphic and symbolic representation. The first exercises will study cartography, texture, data, projection, and topographic types of mapping. We will research and explore how to layer different, various elements and results of the cultural, social, topographic, and the built environment. This Studio will include historic precedents from the Baroque to the Contemporary. The goal of the Studio will be to utilize new and existing explorations of cities to produce original architectural scenarios (prototypes) that will lead to new visual and spatial relationships.

Featured Student Work:

Foundation 502:
Futurecurrent: The Emergent City

Faculty: Vanessa Keith
Teaching Assistant: Bingyu Guo

This studio will push the boundaries of existing paradigms to envision new models for life on this planet rooted in practices that are both ancient and cutting edge. We will be working at the intersection of the urban and architectural scales to develop visionary proposals for the site in the present day, as well as generations into an imagined utopian future. We will be referencing Cyber-, Steam-, and especially Solar-punk art, music, and literature for inspiration, as well as utopian and alternative strategies for creating equitable and environmentally sound future socio-political ecologies.

Our site, located in Philadelphia's Callowhill, or Chinatown North, neighborhood, sits at the intersection of North 10th and Buttonwood Streets, and is characterized by striking changes in density and scale, gentrification, and the scar of past urban renewal bisecting what used to be a continuous neighborhood. Our work will be centered on the design of an urban market and supporting public and community programs connected to the Rail Park. We will also be considering smaller interventions in the surrounding urban fabric that, along with our project as centerpiece, intend to create a series of shifts that alter the urban landscape for the better. It is understood that even a small or seemingly insubstantial event may touch off a series of larger transformations, as well as the reverse. Indeed, Michael Sorkin urged that, as designers, we should be "ready for an explosion of fresh forms, inspired by the democratic roots of the critique of modernist urbanism, by a deeply ecological sensibility, by a fond embrace of the pluralist character of our culture, and by a critical incorporation of the new and inescapably transformative technologies of electronic adjacency" (Sorkin, *Some Assembly Required*, 4).

Featured Student Work:

Foundation 502   Vanessa Keith

Foundation 502:
The Fox and Productive Tensions

Faculty: Jacqueline Martinez
Teaching Assistant: Monte Reed

"The fox knows many things, but the hedgehog knows one big thing."
— Archilochus

Situated within the critique of urbanism, there lies a base dichotomy between two schools of thought known as the Fox and the Hedgehog, dating back to the Greek poet Archilochus and expanded upon by the philosopher Isaiah Berlin addressed in "Collage City" by Colin Rowe and Fred Koetter. The basic position is the difference between a singular, universal organizing principle—the monumental hero approach—understood as the Hedgehog; and the Fox representing multiplicity, the tangential and sometimes contradictory stimulus colliding at once. The critique of the Hedgehog as an approach to urbanism, for our purposes, is the top-down, single-author object-ness in the sense that it has been asserted on the city, controlled, and authored by someone other than you, the populous. The Fox approach on the other hand, is innately more inclusive due to the conglomeration of the many, the aggregate of the heterogeneous elements that contribute to a dynamic whole, as there appears to be multiple authors through multiple timescales, operating in a dynamic state; it is not static, not complete; you the populous are invited to participate and are welcomed to the growth. We will be taking on the role of the Fox and exploring this entropic dynamic state, the heterogeneous collage, burrowing into the realm of the multiple—the delicious collisions, the intersections, the tensions, playing with our complex context in Callowhill and the public market as the iconic composite of the private and public collaged together.

Featured Student Work:

Foundation 502:
How Bazaar

Faculty: Ryan Palider
Teaching Assistant: Lauren Hunter

The Bazaar conjures up images of a bustling urban space filled with a kaleidoscopic array of sights, sounds, and aromas. These types of spaces have played an important role in shaping the cities they occupy. The title is meant to be misinterpreted to conjure up images of the juxtaposition of the elements that one can experience. The diverse mixture of objects, experiences, and people that one encounters at a market illustrates how collage is already embedded in the DNA of markets, making it an ideal technique to use to make transformations to this typology.

We began by thinking about the project from the inside out. The collages produced by the students aren't meant to be conceptual diagrams of the types of interactions the students want their architecture to produce between the site, neighborhood, and the city. The collages the students produced were instrumental in clarifying their thinking about the type of market they want to design.

Featured Student Work:

WASTELAND
Francisco Anaya

The proposed project is a model for community-based trash management that aims to shift away from traditional methods. The intervention acts as a recycling center where trash is collected, processed, and subdivided based on its material makeup. The goal is to reuse these materials as building materials for the market or convert them into products for sale. The market members will refurbish and resell these recycled materials. The facades of the market will be in a constant state of change as trash gets refurbished. The public will be able to observe the process of recycling trash, which is transformed into an artisanal movement. As time passes and trash builds up, the market will change along with it, creating new layers of ornamentation and program. This creates a model for the community to be in charge of managing their trash which will remove the current management for trash which is detrimental to our society.

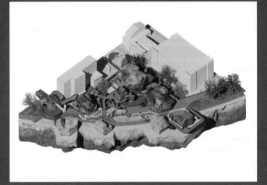

HETERO(STASIS)
Danny Jarabek

Humanity reached a tipping point in 2020. Human-made anthropogenic mass out-weighed natural biomass on Earth. To correct these wrongs, we must accept material friction and rethink space as a vehicle for solutions to recalculate anthropogenic mass and biomass.

Hetero(STASIS) uses technology not to exploit and overwhelm environmental circumstances but to raise them to the top for public perception and awareness.

Poor environmental wellness in North Chinatown affects emotional, physical, and social health. The project symbolizes this suppressed and harmful interaction between the community and its surroundings.

The project organizes a self-sustaining operational network with a net-positive carbon footprint using local manufacturing waste, carbon dioxide, water, user-delivered biomaterial, and glass recyclables to produce microalgae biofuel.

Hydroponic algae pods grow algae for biofuel and electrical energy to power the site and local industry. The technology harvests algae and recycles glass printed by robotic arms around the site to build and aggregate glass tubes for photo-bio-reactive distribution of organic biomaterial relevant to site microclimatic conditions at a specified date and time. Thus, customized technology performs climatic data by its physical self-sufficiency.

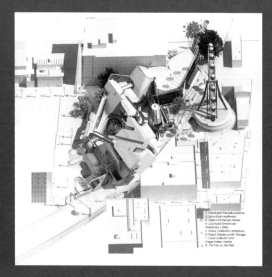

TANGLED-UP
Yan (Jennifer) Zeng

Tangled-up is a project that uses crochet stitches as a tool for organizing space and developing architectural logic. It aims to create a ceramics studio, educational maker space, night market, and exhibition space, all while analyzing the relationships between arts, culinary, and commerce in the neighborhood. The project is made of various connected pods with sector footprints and features a translucent branch-like walkway on roof level that directs people to each program within the market, engaging multi-dimensional interaction with the rail park, the street, and the underground. The project is more like an extension of nature and life, which is organic, perceptual, and full of emotion. The focus of this market is greenery and handicraft. The walkway on top and behind each structure protects the vendors from the sun and rain. At the same time, it helps to define the perimeter of the market in the landscape, attracting the passers-by with its translucency and openness to the stalls of ceramics, handicrafts, plants, flowers, and foods and bar. All of the programs are braced by metal steel structures that seem to be part of the branch of the walkway, connecting them as part of the system.

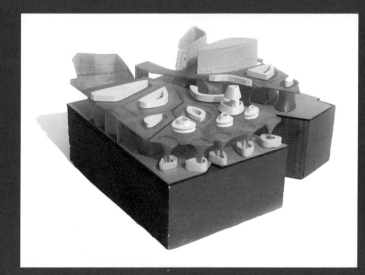

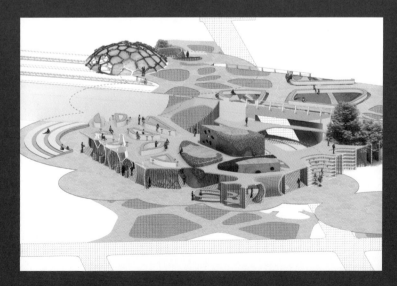

SALVAGER
Sharlene Yulita

Callowhill is a growing neighborhood that is trying to grow beyond the industrial waste and outside developers that are blocking its way. Here comes a Salvager, a person who looks for potential in hard or ordinary things. The Salvager wants to put the pieces of Callowhill back together in a way that is both sustainable and forward-thinking, creating an ecosystem for neighborhood outreach. The self-driving carts work with the community to pick up things that people have thrown away around the neighborhood. These items will then be processed and turned into new, sustainable building materials. The carts have more than one use because they can be used to collect, deliver, and sell goods at the market. So, the market is always changing, and local businesses can park anywhere in the neighborhood and sometimes even outside of it. The Salvager's main goal is to give people a chance to meet each other and get to know each other, so that differences between new and old residents of the community can be resolved.

STEAM CYBERPUNK
Hei Wai (Valerie) Tse

Technology has shaped civilization throughout history. Technology has shaped the built environment and lifestyle in different times. Blockchain is a technology with many applications. Blockchain non-fungible tokens (NFTs) provide digital items a concrete worth and scarcity comparable to limited resources, despite their association with concurrency. The NFT market doubled to $17 billion from 2019 to 2021. Growth challenges market typology assumptions.

Steam Cyberpunk explores how NFTs and computing might be used to develop a building typology that seamlessly blends physical and virtual realities. Viewing digital art in a real venue grounds the NFT experience and provides a focus for economic activity, education, and connecting Philadelphia's growing NFT community with local, national, and worldwide works and artists.

The architectural typology draws on the site's industrial heritage, notably Philadelphia's 33-mile-long network of subterranean steam pipes, to create areas for 3D hologram manufacturing and distribution for digital art.

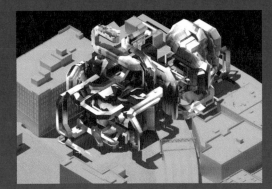

RAIL PARK
Bohan Lang

The Rail Park in Philadelphia's Callowhill neighborhood is one of several instances of abandoned human products, especially abandoned infrastructure. However, the term 'abandoned architecture' is paradoxical since it is not really abandoned; rather, it is abandoned relative to people, not plants and animals. Similarly, wild plants seem disorderly to us yet are highly ordered to themselves.

The market is a hyper object that functions on a multiplicity of dimensions in varied ways and degrees of access, but the fact that the abandoned component of a market adds a further layer of dimension is essential to our project. Consequently, I introduce the plant market, embracing the wild and establishing a hybrid state in which humans and animals use the site at various times and on different scales. We are identical to these wild plants: in the beginning, people occupy the majority of the area, while the wild only begins to grow on top of the structural grid; at the end, there will be no humans, but just wild plants.

ABOVE THE RAIL / BEYOND THE BOUNDARY
Siqi Yao

The abandoned viaduct in Philadelphia is an invisible but harsh boundary. One cannot obtain a clear picture of it because it is currently hidden behind the junk-yards, branches, and fences. However, one can clearly sense its presence because it divides the Callowhill neighborhood into two architectural territories: a vibrant artistic one to the west and a dilapidated one to the east. Communities are the foundations of a dynamic and interconnected network that position cities to thrive. Therefore, they must be connected, resilient, healthy, and motivative. The design goal is to connect the two territories and reactivate the spirit of the neighborhood. To approach that, an aggregation of 'bridges' shaped by the existing grids is placed above, under, beside, and on the viaduct. They will act as extensions of the existing facilities on both sides of the viaduct, bridging over the invisible boundary.

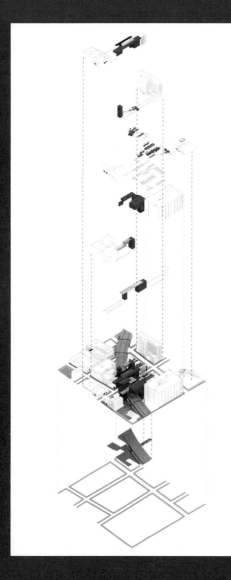

SWOOP DU SOLEIL
Jessica Wong

The junction of the numerous identities and histories of the Callowhill/North Chinatown area are reimagined in a new marketplace inspired by the roots of one of Philadelphia's first circuses and prior links to industrialization. The marketplace has a performance area, public garden, café, and artist spaces woven and draped in a sea of scaffolding generated from the radial tangencies of the viaduct and the junction of N. 10th Street below. The sweeping ribbons inside the space frame depict the fluidity of circus movement, and each ribbon functions as a different performer in the development of a new community attraction that draws on its historical tales to create a rejuvenated identity for the area. Individual interests and curiosity determine the uniqueness of the individual's experience in this fabrication of space. Each kind of program in the development has multi-modal access and circulation, resulting in bigger program pieces and smaller pockets of assembly. Through performance and celebration, the user's trip seeks to strengthen community cohesion and dismantle controversies around the neighborhood's distinct identity.

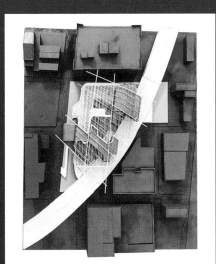

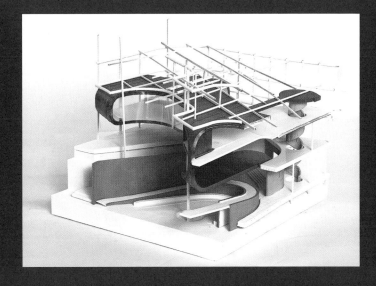

||: RHYTHM REMIX
RE-MARKET :||
Ruifeng (Rose) Wang

Hip hop has significant roots in Philadelphia, from music to subculture to architecture. "Remix is reconstruction, break-dance is shape, and rap is construction and voice," according to Hip Hop architectural philosophy. Hip hop expresses the tensions in Callowhill's diverse community and shows creative spatial design.

The market seeks to reconcile massiveness, lightness, openness, and proximity.

The market design is sampling and layering charming clips or parts from the city's industrial heritage, great architecture, and colorful graffiti over abandoned lots to create a refreshing mix for visitors to explore.

Architecture is like hip hop music. While attentively traversing the market, one could feel the vitality from the varied activities grid by grid. Hip hop artists are teaching and painting on panels distributed around the grids, while thrift stores on the wheel are selling old clothes and art amid the people.

Community members share ideas face-to-face at the market.

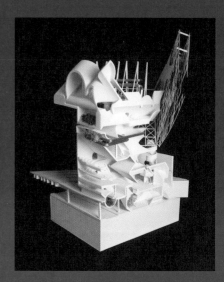

ARTWORK & AGENCY
Alexandra Viscusi

This studio started with study and mapping of many areas of the city, with a concentration on murals and other forms of public art. We visited the location of our plans in Callowhill, Philadelphia, which was located next to a defunct rail park. Using mapping methodologies and grids, both of which were objectives of the studio, we were entrusted with designing a structure that could accommodate two programs, one of which was a required market.

This idea intends to combine a farmer's market with public art in Callowhill. Using the grid as an object, natural light may enter different rooms while opening the building's structure to achieve a balance between the inside, outside, and in-between. By minimizing the size of the structure on the ground floor, the site stays open for the outdoor farmer's market to take over; this also allows the landscaping of the site to provide a much-needed greenspace in this urban location.

The public art initiative gives the Callowhill community the ability to express themselves and retake control of their voices and area. This facility is intended to serve both as a place to produce art and as a venue for the presentation of art.

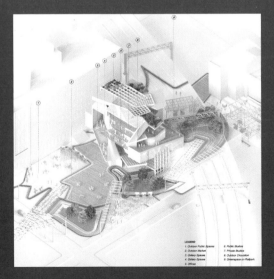

DAWN
Daniel Lutze

The Dawn is a new marketplace and urban typology located in Philadelphia's Callowhill/Chinatown neighborhood. Inspired by the layers of history ingrained into the nearby facades, the marketplace takes the form of a rock that has been smoothed out by flowing water over the course of centuries. The building skin is an array of planters with growing moss and vines, photovoltaic panels, and white UHPGC panels to regulate heat load and light distribution. The layout of the landscape follows a similar formal motif, and its curves play gently with both the shape of the marketplace and the curve of the Reading Railroad tracks. On the inside, the marketplace houses a large market hall with space for several vendors of different kinds, a restaurant kitchen with register window to the street, multiple studio spaces for artists, and offices to house the Philadelphia Chinatown Development Corporation's community gardening program. Using this new space, the PCDC would be able to turn parts of the site landscaping, as well as new landscape plots on the railroad tracks, into community gardens, and help not only educate community members about community gardening but provide them with plots for their own sustainable food growth.

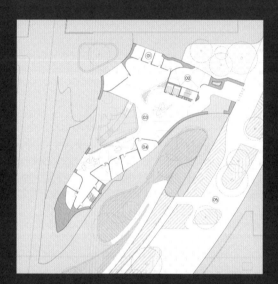

DISSOLUTION
Amy Koenig

Based on studies of the works of painters Gordon Cheung and Zhou Fan, whose work focuses on the passage of time and the mark a brush makes, I decided to investigate the site's weathering in further detail. Due to the site's uneven erosion, certain areas are more historically rich than others. Collages created by AI have brought attention to the dynamic erosion of space and time. There are certain places where the history is starting to fade away at the hands of erosion, while other places are seeing dramatic changes. The study of "spacetime" defines an occurrence that may have both spatial and temporal characteristics. When applied to the market, these concepts of space and time merge to produce settings that preserve relics of the past. I used a digital assemblage to experiment with this concept visually, playing with shapes to get a variety of spatial effects. The market's outward appearance is gradually becoming contradictory because of widespread subtractive movements. The building's materiality deteriorates, and its facade grows as living concrete as time passes, bringing it closer to a solar punk future.

CALLOWHILL EFFLORESCENCE
Gyo Sun Hwang

The project uses the principles of erosion and the expansion of wild nature as a natural phenomenon to design a space that can redefine and rejuvenate the Callowhill area. The project is inspired by the erosion of industrial structures and the wild nature growing over them, resulting in an organic blending of materials and redefining of the elements into a new property. The blending use of excavated spaces, newly added structures, and the viaduct's negative space allows the blending of different elements and redefining of the abandoned structure. This process of dematerialization and neutralization, and loss of characters and colors, allows the materials to be responsive to other materials; even though some losses of characteristics are done, the resulting blend of multiple elements generates a new characteristic. The symbiotic relationship between erosion and wild nature is also an essential aspect of the nature that is applied to the project; erosion process provides the space and nutrition back to nature and the cycle repeats as organic materials erode again. This is expressed through many subverting moments in the design and structure, playing with both the negative and positive spaces derived from erosion process.

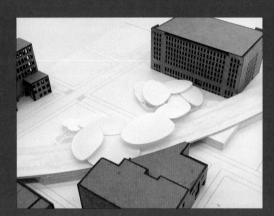

THE MIXED WORLD
Ming Chen

Callowhill is the consequence of a battle between wild nature and industry, particularly for the viaduct on the site. The viaduct in its current state is a symbol of the clash between the wilderness and industrialization. What will happen after that? Is there a Mixed and Balanced Moment in the middle? The Mixed World draws on the insights learned from other components (wilderness, industry, seed library...) or mastering tectonic systems.

The construction systems have been identified as the Rhizomatic system (branching system) and Packing system from the investigation of the Wild Nature and Industry revolution to the material form transition. The Rhizomatic system serves as the fundamental backbone of the whole structure, and the Packing system is the primary approach for dividing the functional space. The two tectonic systems act independently and collide on this spot. Aside from the basic systems, the key programs are a market space and a

seed library. With this neighborhood and core idea in mind, the seed library was brought into this location as a catalyst for drawing people and facilitating collisions between the Wilderness and the human world.

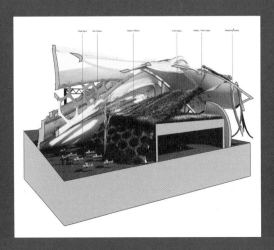

THE REMEDIAL MEMORY
Shenyi Zhang

The Remedial Memory initiative seeks to revitalize Callowhill by linking it to its rich past via the creation of a market and community center. Callowhill was America's first Chinatown and major immigration hub. In the 1960s, urban renewal efforts like the Vine Street expressway destroyed Callowhill's industrial dominance and separated Chinatown, inhibiting its growth. The market and community center will link Chinatown and Callowhill and create a lively neighborhood. Three levels of open public space will foster a new collective experience; an undulating landscape with gathering spaces, play spaces, and a performance space; a new urban public space with a performance stage, a food court, and a swimming pool; and an urban farm that grows a variety of produce for the market and local restaurants. The project's materiality is inspired by local artists' representation of Callowhill, and it will be cloaked by a metallic louver double layer to abstract the figures' hue, allowing users to establish their own relationship to it. Remedial Memory creates the Callowhill market and community center from pieces, creating an urban experience that acknowledges the past while looking to the future.

URBAN CONDENSER
Ying Chen

The Callowhill Market is influenced by research on the connection between the Callowhill area and its environs. Callowhill, a neighborhood in Philadelphia, is on the edge of a rebirth, thanks to the influx of artists and the proliferation of restaurants in the area. Meanwhile, pedestrianizing the viaduct railway would help Callowhill link with neighboring communities, which in turn will encourage a variety of cultural organizations and social activities to take place there. Through a series of scenario collages, depicting tales of three sorts of possible visitors' varying activities on the site from morning to evening, the site's promised energetic linkages that flow through and across the many programs will offer a broad range of urban experiences. Rather from being discrete events within a community, programming and cultural events are instead woven together to form a seamless whole. The architecture will be fused into a spatially and aesthetically rich environment by bringing together overlapping programs and intersecting forms. This market serves as an urban condenser, bringing together a variety of cultural and urban activities to provide a lively amenity for the surrounding community and the city at large.

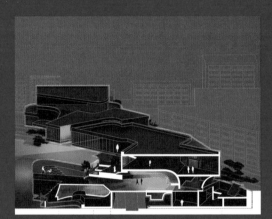

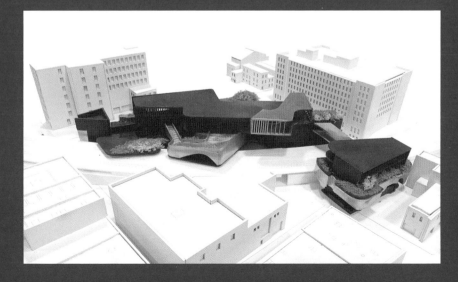

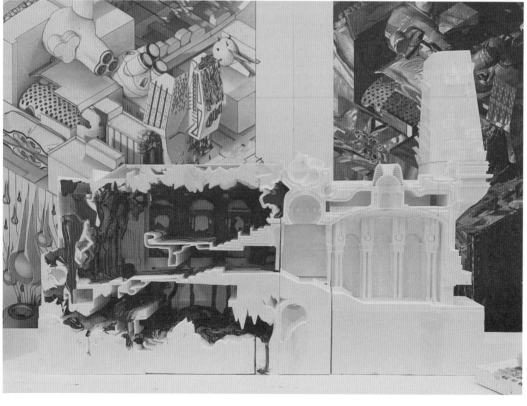

Core 602:
Design Studio IV

Coordinator:
Simon Kim

The fourth semester core studio is integrative: an architectural practice where design teams and construction consultants are focused on an urban site in the production of a large, multi-use building. In this segment of the curriculum, what has been taught in the prior three semesters in Structures, Environmental Systems, Professional Practice, Visual Studies, Building Construction as well as History and Theories are brought to focus in this studio.

While these courses are comprehensive, they also provide a technical and standardized base upon which polemics and challenges of cultural expression, context, energy, iconicity are further developed within each studio as directed by its instructor. These means and methods are made functional by placing students in small design teams, with repeated meetings with specialists and consultants from the allied disciplines as organized by each instructor. These consultants have ranged from Arup, Buro Happold, Front Inc, Foster and Partners, and Walter P. Moore.

As well as meetings with their consultants in each studio section, there are two studio-wide exercises – Structures Week and Envelope Week. These assignments are a continuation of the shared studio exercises from ARCH601 – Section Week and Plan Week – and are considered necessary in the education of an architect before progressing into Option Studios and the professional realm.

The goals of Structure Week – early in the semester - is to develop and demonstrate a feasible and projective structural system in digital finite element analyses (FEA), and in its calculations. These structures are tested in physical models and prototypes. Drawings of materials, sizing, and connections are also submitted. The second shared exercise of Cladding Week expands upon Structures Week with developed sections, elevations, and details for the cladding system as defined: single or double facade, masonry, cavity wall, insitu, or shell. This is done shortly before final presentations as schemes become advanced.

Furthermore, ARCH602 continued the polemic of Public Commons, introduced in ARCH601 housing studio. Public Commons has become a term used for shared, equitable access to resources such as air, oceans and wildlife as well as to social creations such as libraries, public spaces, scientific research, and technology.

Faculty:

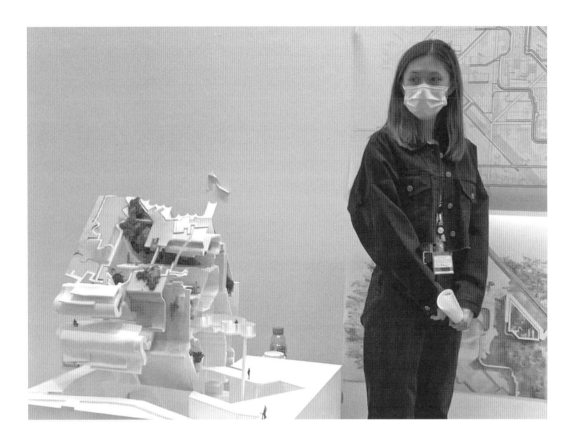

Core 602:
CUBOIDS and CYLINDS:
The multi-span and the thick envelope

Faculty: Simon Kim
Teaching Assistant: Diego Ramirez
Client: Billy Dufala (RAIR Philadelphia)
Consultants: Erik Verboon, Gustav Fagerstrom, & Stan Su

Architecture at this moment can be examined afresh to the sociopolitics and ecological pressures of the Anthropocene. Rather than remain complicit with late capitalism or bound to western European ideologies, our discipline of shaping cities, private, and public spaces should be freed to pursue difference and diversity. Other narratives, other worldviews may be enfolded in the work of structural, mechanical, tectonic systems that come together to produce buildings.

This studio embraces the theme of Public Commons and equity. Public Commons has become a term used for shared, equitable access of all communities to natural resources such as air, oceans, and wildlife as well as to social creations such as libraries, public spaces, technology, and scientific research. We will work on architecture as fictive narratives and futurisms, towards architecture and site in interaction with history and technology.

We will be working with the artist Billy Dufala and his recycling program, RAIR Philadelphia (Recycled Artist in Residency or rairphilly.org) on their Metal Bank Super Fund site. Positioning an expanded recycled arts program on the newly acquired superfund site elevates RAIR's mission as a dynamic hybrid ecosystem generating a dialogue between the manufactured waste stream and restorative natural ecologies through art and public engagement.

Featured Student Work:

Core 602:
Playscapes

Faculty: Miroslava Brooks
Teaching Assistant: Veronica Rosado

This studio, titled Playscapes, posits that spaces in-between are equally as important as spaces within. The seemingly innocent function of a playground has the potential to reclaim public space as a creative laboratory for learning and experiencing our physical world, and in doing so helps strengthen and rebuild social bonds. We explored how play can open up novel ways of thinking about ecology, community, and public space, looking at two different ideas of play and space-making: one —based on Isamu Noguchi's playground proposals—is about ground modulation, subtle shifts in topography, gradients, openness, and continuity; the other—based on Aldo van Eyck's urban playgrounds—is about repetitive elements, barriers, and obstacles that one climbs over and passes through.

With these in mind, students were tasked with designing a new public hybrid of exterior/interior playgrounds and a child-care/community center located in Stamford, Connecticut, along the Mill River. Of particular interest was the development of a porous aggregated building typology and its relationship to the ground. The plan was the primary modus operandi, though equally important was the development of tectonics and materiality. In fact, as an integrative fourth-semester studio within the core curriculum of the M.Arch I program, careful consideration was given to the integration of all aspects of architecture —its volume, structure, envelope, circulation, contexts, environment, and landscape strategies. Ultimately, the hope was for the students to formulate their own critical position and research agenda through an integrated design of a building and its surrounding public space, and in doing so outline the bases for one's own architectural project.

Featured Student Work:

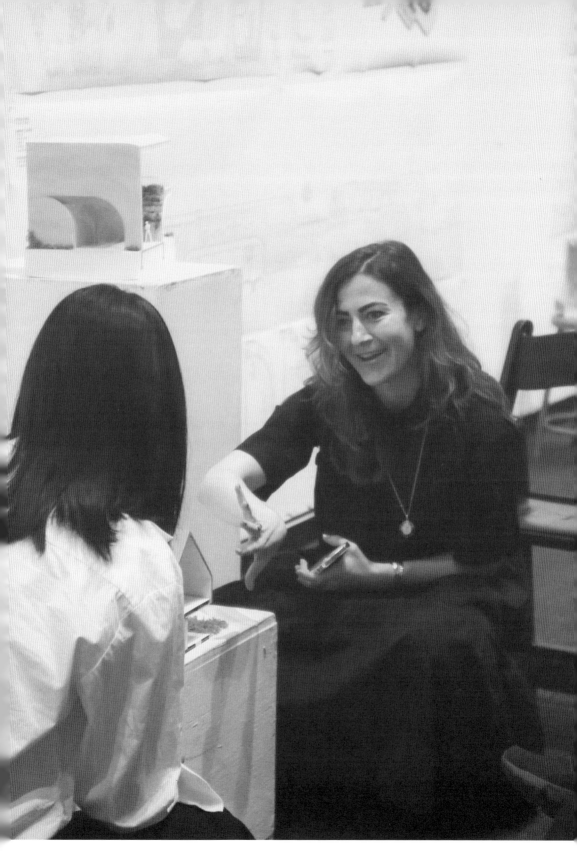

Core 602   Miroslava Brooks

Core 602:
Envelope Stuffing

Faculty: Nate Hume
Teaching Assistant: Miguel Matos
Engineer & Façade Consultants: Eddy Roberts,
    Jamison Guest, & Michael Tortella

The studio was interested in looking at the envelope as an inhabitable mediator bringing the exterior in and interior out. These liminal zones have the potential to house public spaces that resist traditional solutions such as static ground-floor lobbies or inert atriums but instead forge dynamic zones laminated, embedded, and suspended in the envelope. The buildings looked to produce new relationships between volumes and enclosure through understanding them as an ensemble of things and denying the reading of a single mass and wrapper. The stuffing engaged the expanding palette of building materials that break down the traditional distinction between the natural and the artificial. Composite materials hold multiple properties of the raw and the processed, not only questioning what is natural but also producing new natures and aesthetic effects. The hybridization of these materials is formed through several means including laminating, embedding, and compressing organic and inorganic matter.

    To explore these notions the studio designed a headquarters for a food center dealing with shortages and surpluses. These ranged from companies combating depleted food sources through alternative products to organizations developing food from waste. As more of the planet becomes inhospitable for farming and urban populations continue to rapidly expand, there is intense need for new means of producing food whether it is through artificial lab-grown items or natural foods produced in new ways. This project will investigate the ramifications of these developments on material form.

Featured Student Work:

Core 602:
Decadence & Degradation

Faculty: Daniel Markiewicz
Teaching Assistant: Umar Mahmood
Façade Consultant: Vishwadeep Deo
Structural Consultant: Erich Oswald

In this studio, we designed a Bath House. We engaged with concepts of the picturesque as described by Yve-Alain Bois in "A Picturesque Stroll around Clara-Clara," as well as the relationship between cultural excess and formal erosion, or in other words: decadence and degradation. We examined the problematic historical role of the public restroom and aimed to propose forward-looking public space projects. While the weight of these concepts were available to students to either pursue or resist, each group was charged with developing a building for construction, with real-world fabrication details in mind.

We began our Bath House explorations with an examination of the picturesque, which is most commonly associated with the 18th- and early-19th-century discussion of pictorial values of architecture and its relationship to landscape. Yve-Alain Bois engages with the picturesque through the work and discourse of the sculptor Richard Serra. Specifically, he cites Serra's own working method as particularly appropriate for the picturesque due to the artist's resistance to orthographic plan drawing. As described by Bois, Serra's preference for the elevation, as opposed to the plan, is a characteristic inherent to the picturesque movement, which with rolling landscapes is itself "a struggle against the reduction 'of all terrains to the flatness of a sheet of paper.'" This studio however loved the plan. And we refuted the positions of Bois, Serra, and others by using the plan to engage with central notions of the picturesque, with inclusive public space planning and with contemporary bath house design.

Featured Student Work:

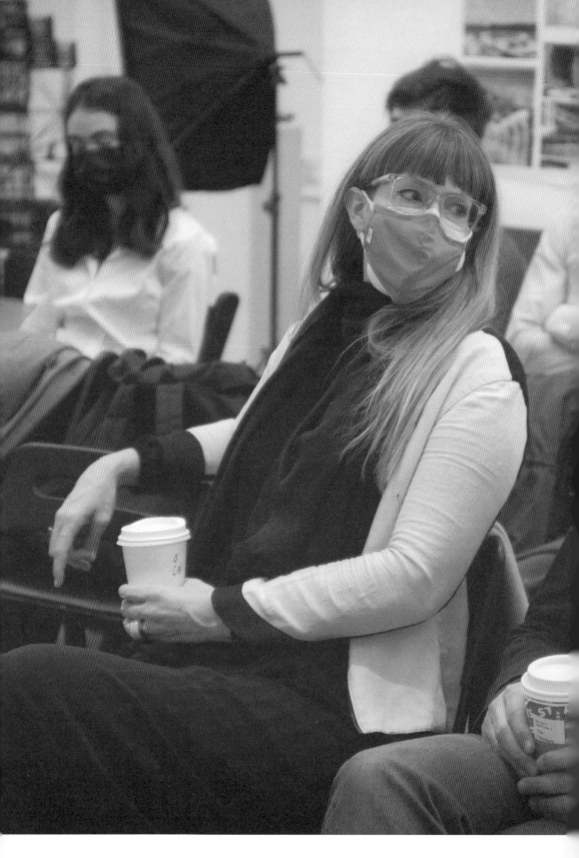

Core 602:
Monolithic, Machine Hybrids

Faculty: Danielle Willems
Teaching Assistant: Shan Li

Monolithic, Machinic Hybrids perceives architectural formation as part of a larger, self-organizing, adapting, material process. Our studio will start with reconsidering the Cenotaph—being both "Monolithic" and ancient, these impressive vessels of void—as a generative point of departure to re-conceptualize a new type of artifice in relation to the typology of the Data Center. While engaging in the production of ontological architectural axioms through the generative capacities of algorithms, one focus will be the relationship between computation and machine learning. "To solve a problem on a computer, we need an algorithm. An algorithm is a sequence of instruction that is carried out to transform the input to output—Machine learning, a type of artificial intelligence that enables computers to learn from large data sets, is the basis of numerous developments from speech recognition to driverless cars." Conceptually, the Data Center and Museum will operate as a platform to explore post-human and machinic architectural space.

Featured Student Work:

CUBOIDS AND CYLINDS
Francesca Dong &
Emma McMonigal

The Delaware River is Philadelphia's water supply and cargo lifeline. As the sixth-most polluted river in the US, it raises issues about water fairness and accessibility for Philadelphians of all socioeconomic classes. The city's growing population requires sustainable and ethical water purification. Hydrolic Machina redefines water as a public commons resource and spectacle in all its forms to solve water inequalities. Our idea engages the public in Philadelphia's water supply process from harvesting through decontamination, filtration, and fermentation. We're creating a hybrid environment that blends art and ecology with the site's industrial character after examining the Metal Bank Superfund Site and recycling factory. The Facility promotes water fairness in Philadelphia's sociopolitical and ecological fabric. The hyper-industrialized Hydrolic Machina will preserve, develop, and reinvent Philadelphia's aquatic environment to achieve water justice for the city's residents. Hydrolic Machina redefines water as a human right and a resource for everybody to alleviate water disparity. This project filters polluted rainfall and river water as it flows through the building. This will teach and engage the public about Philadelphia's water supply.

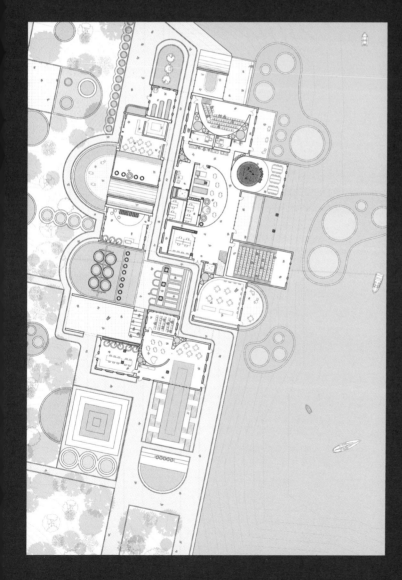

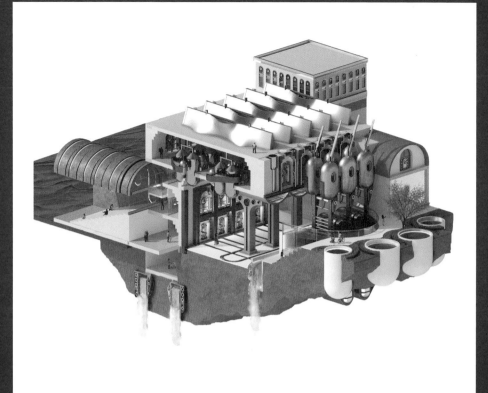

CUBOIDS AND CYLINDS
Lixue Cheng & Zihua Mo

The Philadelphia Superfund Site Metal Bank is next to Interstate 95 and the Delaware River. It seems to be a piece of green land near the lake, but it is really an industrial center for waste recycling, which may deceive visitors. Walking along the river's bank at the spot seems to be a tranquil embrace of nature. It is a wildness where people may stumble across a dead deer after a short stroll, yet it is also an artificial area with poisonous dirt and mechanical sounds.

A goal of the project is to preserve the site's original vibe whilst creating a new project there. The conversion vibe between nature and human-made would be translated into the context of a splashing landscape and a pile of rocks with synthetic details and human activity programs, resulting in a human playground and a feasible architecture that encourages individuals to reconsider the meaning of trash.

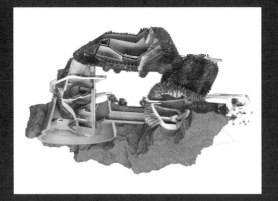

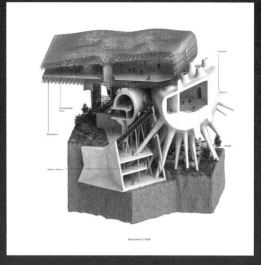

VILLAGIO
Joao Freitas &
Christelle Salloum

Our idea of play was inspired by our cultural backgrounds and upbringing. Both Lebanon and Brazil associate play with streets and places nestled between buildings that were not necessarily designed for that purpose. Nevertheless, we were also interested in the way landscape photography serves as a tool to position natural elements that start to frame each other, encapsulating the subject matter.

We translated these ideas into porous aggregation clusters of 30-foot-high conic modules that resulted in the creation of a village-inspired architecture in the urban context of Stamford, Connecticut. On the outside, the treatment of the facade combines a gradient pink limestone material with strategically placed seams of metal, visually tying the buildings together. The coloration chosen for the building is transferred onto the ground and creates seamless connections between the building and the landscape.

On the inside, varying skylight sizes create different lighting conditions within the interior spaces. This is another way we utilized a main architectural element to frame nature within a space and allow the variation of natural light conditions to animate the architecture.

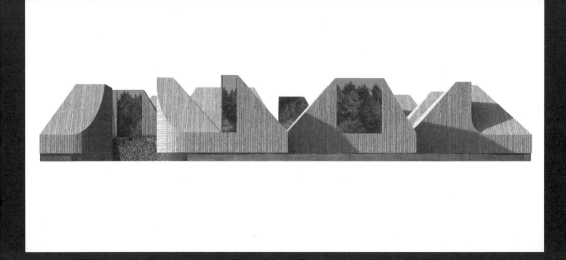

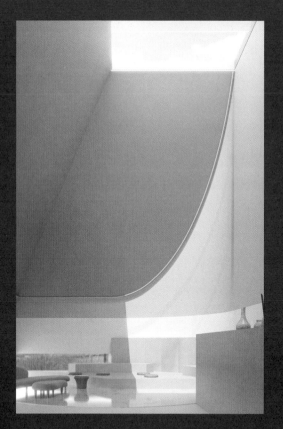

CURIOUS GORGE
Emily Shaw & Jun Lee

Sited in Mill River Park, the project reacts to and builds upon the distinct ecological rehabilitations of the larger area. River tributaries and bioswales are integrated into design infrastructures, providing spaces that facilitate a constant negotiation and dialogue with the natural environment and native ecology.

Play is examined through a lens of tactility and exploration across ages, using spaces of tension and whimsy to incite the natural curiosity of the community and engage them in the local ecology. Material properties and spatial thresholds integrate these ideas by behaving in unexpected, reactive ways. Wood slatting and brick coursing break from normative canons in response to the geometry of the building and spill outside the footprint. Waterways weave through the site and invade interior and exterior volumes, influencing both circulation and programming, to provide a constant state of spatial dialogue and blur the delineations of program and site.

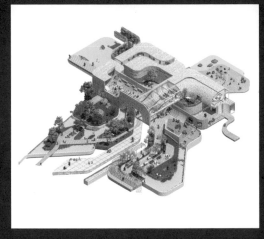

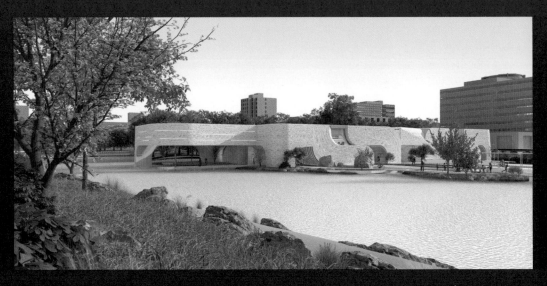

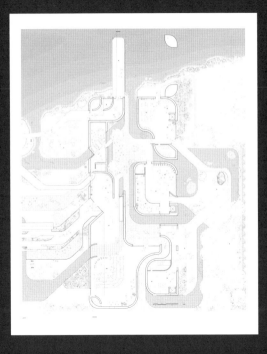

PASTURES & PURLIEUS
Monte Reed & Kyle Troyer

Architecture's dichotomic relationship with the countryside has long alienated the involvement of traditional and humble material systems within the discipline. Focusing on the polemics of the hyper-sterile and the ultra-rustic, the project probes the future projection of the cultured meat industry through the intervention of both contemporary and historical models of building methods and materials in an effort to combine unlike systems into a hybrid venture. Situated between wilderness and domestication, the ambiguous mystique of the purlieu shears through a series of silo-esque volumes, questioning the relationship between human habitation and laboratory space. Thatching as a traditional building method is challenged through its manipulation, perversion, and exaggeration, as it stuffs envelopes and creates thick, billowed forms. The envelope is further interrogated through the filtering of unconditioned space, allowing the exterior environment deep within the building.

Core 602 Nate Hume

LIMINAL SPACE
Rhea Nayar & Cherie Wan

The idea that there is space that is beyond a limit or a threshold that has been established is what is meant by the term "liminality." The new food and innovation center wants to investigate what this unknown place looks like and how it can liberate the public from the preset "street" that links us in a prescribed fashion. The program for the building considers how food waste can be converted into fertilizer that runs through the entire building, from the roof to the basement, creating a sustainable feedback loop. In addition, the program makes use of this as an opportunity to increase the variety of produce that is available and its accessibility by bringing fruits that are native to Asia to a new hub that is being established in Philadelphia. It is possible for pedestrians to wander on metal sidewalks that support the development of fruit and plant life. This makes it possible for the interaction between the general public and the many levels of building systems to become more entwined.

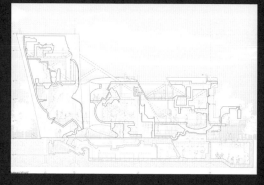

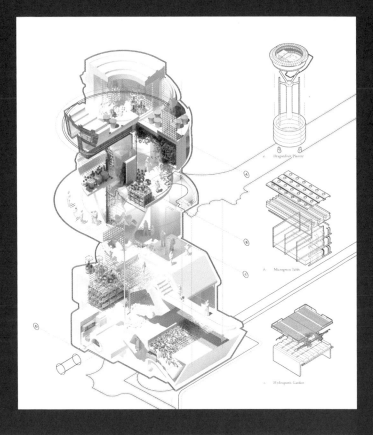

a. Dragonfruit Planter

b. Microgreen Table

c. Hydroponic Garden

EXPOSÉ
Michaela Dawe &
Yasmin Goulding

Our project is designed to showcase the interaction between the natural and man-made elements. The plan of the project is influenced by the organization of the city and the materials used are inspired by the native environment. The ambiance is created by considering how humans might interact with the bare environment in different stages of undress. In our design, we have considered the opposing approaches of traditional French and English garden organization. While the French approach is characterized by imposing order and geometry on the natural environment, the English approach is focused on mimicking nature and working with it instead of against it. The project is in a wild parkland nestled within a larger urban grid, and we have aimed to incorporate both these attitudes in our design. We have used the interactions of existing bedrock and built stone-paneled walls to create spaces that vary in intimacy. This allows our guests to find a place where they feel comfortable and at peace, regardless of their level of undress.

FLOWED GEODE
Michael Ting, Hanyan Chen, & Jingwen Wu

"The eroding qualities of water"

The project features a series of interconnected pools, each with their own distinct characteristics and individual features. The design aims to provide a variety of pools and spaces, allowing visitors to choose their preferred pool and the ability to flow between them. The pools are designed to address the prompts of the bathhouse program as well as the ideas of gender/sex fluidity alongside the ruinous and the picturesque. To achieve this, the project breaks away from traditional ideas of an "ideal" form and instead focuses on providing a wide variety of pools and spaces. The materiality of the pools also introduces "imperfect" features like weathering and moss, along with "welcoming" features like trees and plants in between gaps. This approach doesn't impose an ideal mindset; instead, it enables the possibility of many mindsets. This allows visitors to flow between these mindsets via the connectivity of the pools, providing an inclusive and open experience.

Daniel Markiewicz

DATA DROP
Han Gao & Jiacheng Huang

The project lies on the Anable Basin in Long Island City, New York, across the east river from Manhattan. The data center and art gallery complex explores computers, digital technology, and architectural space to provide a medium for human-machine interaction. The structure's diagrid design created an open area without columns, allowing data servers to be suspended from the ceiling. The spacious area without floor slabs generates a magnificent impression, evoking monuments and monolithic. By rotating, mirroring, and symmetrizing a module with several faces, the building's shape is endless. The data center was hung on the riverbed so data drops could travel straight into the pool for cooling. The first layer was a perforated panel, and the air holes above dissipate data-drop heat. From the site's landscape design to the data center's internal and external spaces, the design tried to combine science and art, focus on visitors' immersive experiences, and break the traditional data storage method.

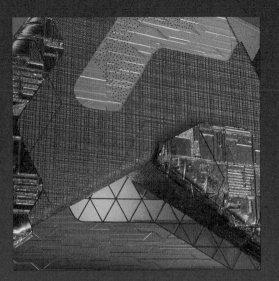

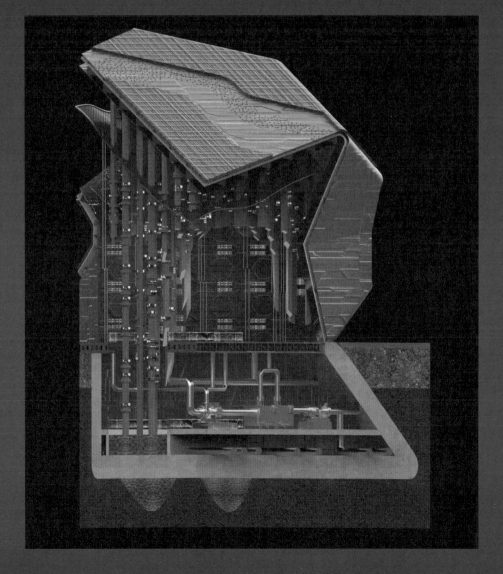

METADATA:
MEDIA TEMPLE IN THE
DESERT OF THE REAL
Joseph Depre &
Michael Willhoit

Metadata is a conceptual data center for the storage of the Metaverse, a parallel digital universe of human creation. It is a Cathedral creating a bridge between the tangible and the immaterial, the real and the hyper-real, The Simulation. The datacenter is the sole material reality of the virtual simulation. This makes the structure housing the datacenter a sacred space that requires being fortified against hostile environments and intents. As the Metaverse becomes more ubiquitous in our daily lives entire populations will abandon reality for their subjective realities manifested online. The vacuum of space found in the absence of daily interpersonal interaction will create a literal desert of the real. People will need to be lured away from the simulation through sensual experience. Metadata response to the sociological condition through programmatic intervention. Media Spectacle and the promise of luxury sensual experience are deployed as modalities of seduction. The thermal bath house in the cavernous sublevels of Metadata are heated through a thermal exchange with the data servers exploiting a cyclical economy of carbon reduction through sensual experience.

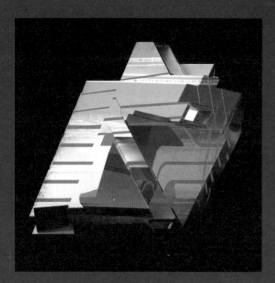

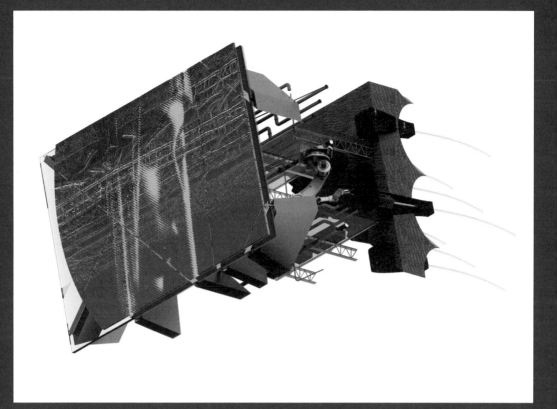

Advanced 704   Studio Overview

Advanced 704: Advanced Design Research Studio

Coordinator: Ferda Kolatan

The 704 Design Research Studios are an in-depth examination and exploration of critical architectural topics through rigorous conceptual thinking and advanced design methodologies. These elective studios are taught by a selection of leading professionals in the field who share and further develop their own research expertise with the students over the course of the semester. All studio topics and project briefs are devised in ways to support the various objectives of each research subject.

The primary goal of the final studio of the Master of Architecture program is to equip all outgoing students with a multi-faceted and robust knowledge base (encompassing design, theory, and technical skills) necessary to participate in the field of architecture at the highest level. The ability to formulate, develop, and conclude a design research project based on a set of specific parameters is a crucial step for achieving this goal.

The definition of design research has expanded significantly in recent times. The global effects of economic markets, the environmental realities of the Anthropocene, and the socio-political and DEI related challenges of our day are profoundly reshaping the discipline. The design research studios examine such conditions and envision and develop architectural responses that reflect our contemporary circumstances in sensible and productive ways.

In addition, digital and media technologies are providing us with unprecedented tools, new types of knowledge, and increasingly complex technical skills. The cultural, societal, and aesthetic ramifications of these ever-accelerating technological developments need to be examined and explored just as rigorously as their performative and material properties. Only in the synergy of the two can we articulate constructive and sustainable design solutions.

Our unique disciplinary ability to express physically and conceptually the dynamics of our world, to analyze and synthesize, to evoke and provoke, to seize the past and to imagine the future, is largely contingent on the successful integration of research-oriented thinking into everyday practice. In this spirit, the 704 Design Research Studios promote a progressive and experimental approach to architectural thinking and making.

Faculty:

Advanced 704:
MACHINIC DESERT:
Architecture in the Age of Anthropocene

Faculty: Ferda Kolatan
Teaching Assistant: Megan York

It has become an incontrovertible fact that one of the most foundational dichotomies on which Western modern culture is built no longer applies in the age of the Anthropocene. This dichotomy emerged roughly during the times of Humanism and divided the world into two distinct spheres of reality: one was governed by human thoughts and actions (such as technology and art) and the other included everything else (what we casually refer to as "nature"). As a consequence, nature was no longer viewed as a holistic and enchanted place, as it was in premodern times, but rather as a demystified object that can be observed, manipulated, and altered for material, spiritual, or aesthetic gains.

But the discovery of the Anthropocene, its presence as a fact, has exposed the strict categorical distinctions between culture, technology, and nature as pure fiction. "Reality" in the Anthropocene, as it turns out, is manifested by complex planetary ecologies where human and nonhuman objects, forces, and protocols mesh into new types of hybrids. In this new reality, the old rules and classifications through which we customarily viewed, engaged, and "designed" the world need radical rethinking and retooling.

Machinic Desert is an attempt at such rethinking. By designing large-scale solar facilities in the deserts of Nevada, the studio examined what possible rules of engagement could be drafted for designing in the Anthropocene. The desert regions in the American Southwest with their long histories as cultural and technological testing grounds, as well as their deep roots with American mythmaking (the "Frontier"), render them particularly interesting venues to ponder and address these questions.

Featured Student Work:

Advanced 704:
Synthetic Nature // Highrise Mexico City

Faculty: Winka Dubbeldam & Richard Garber
Teaching Assistant: Merrick Castillo

This semester, our work will seek to reconcile two sometimes conflicting goals within a hybrid ecology and the literal site that has been impacted adversely by environmental consequences of human-centric urban development. Our work will focus on a site within the Centro Historico area of Mexico City, an area of both much speculation as well as deep cultural heritage.

Home to 21 million people, who consume nearly 287 billion gallons of water each year, the city has sunk more than 32 feet in the last 60 years because 70 percent of the water people rely on is extracted from the aquifer below the city. Most of the street building facades in the historic Centro show signs of a serious problem, the constant sinking of the subsoil due to depletion of the aquifer below the city. Mexico City buildings are seriously leaning because of the land subsidence.

The goal of the Studio is to create HYBRIDS, to develop an architectural intervention to intervene with the increasingly defunct infrastructures; it's time to re-calibrate. We are not so much interested in the study of landscapes—many biologists are working on this—but more in how these architectural interventions/inventions would integrate into the Urban, and how they merge with the biological, economic, and cultural. This studio creates provocations and rigorous research in structures that create an architecture that not only houses humans and non humans, but also cleans water and air, and produces energy.

Featured Student Work:

Spring 704 studio would like to thank Pilar Echezarreta and Northeast Precast.
Pilar Echezarreta, who is a colleague teaching at the Universidad Iberoamericana,
who arranged travel to Mexico City and scheduled a fantastic trip for Winka and I, as well
as our ARCH 704 students in spring 2022. Northeast Precast (NEP), specifically John
Ruga, President, and Mark Gorgas, General Manger, graciously supported our students in
ARCH 704 as well. In our studio we did some experimental casting prior to our Mexico
City trip.

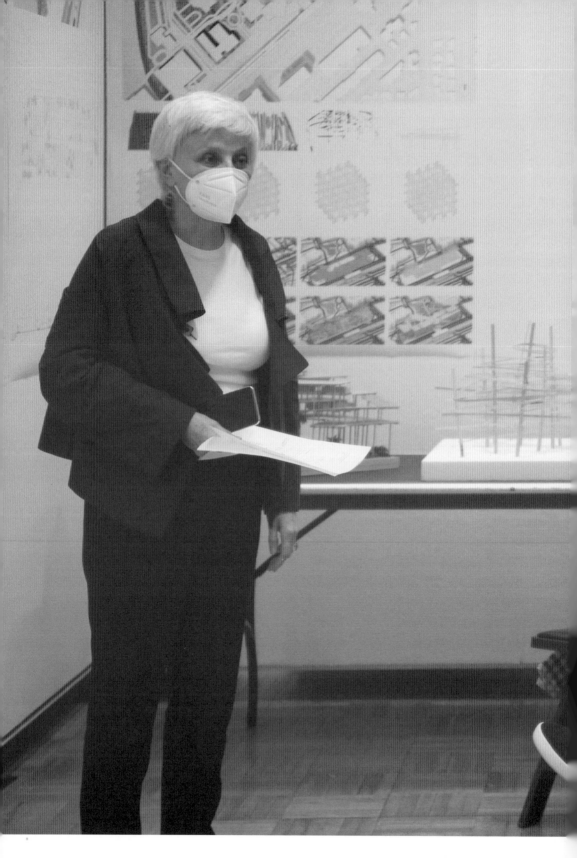

Advanced 704:
QUASI THINGS OF ARCHITECTURE
Miami: Inversions of Urban Fields/Lands

Faculty: Homa Farjadi
Co-Faculty: Chang Yuan Max

We continue our research into Quasi Things of Architecture in order to consider alternative strategies for framing agency of the architectural objects. Against the normative authority afforded to the architect/designer as the subject in relation to the objects of architecture operative since the enlightenment, the concept of Quasi Thing reconfigures and diffuses agency of the author in order to find methodologies for creating new formation of architectural objects that privileges the experiential encounter through quasi things. T. Griffero and others have referred to such work as the production of engaged atmospheres, in terms of the irrelational conditions to their sites and users. Michelle Serres called Quasi Things, "those mediating between subject and object." She gave the example of gifts, totems, and finally, the simple ball, as in football, where the ball promts new configurational spaces between players and the field through the game. Effect of such mediating object in a diffusion of objectual limits is an opening up of the world of experience or atmospheres. It has also been called the affective turn in aesthetics, to do with the heightened work of the senses rather than abstract logic.

As usual in our studio methodology we focus on the analysis of operations within two texts for the production of our project in the name of Quasi thing of air Architecture: Text one is that of Tonino Griffero's Quasi thing: the paradigm of atmospheres' where he points to the prelogical experience of the world constructing 'others' in design while considering affective conditions of space. Text two is a trilogy of artist works. The three works explore three modalities of performance in what we see as architecture of material air.

Featured Student Work:

Advanced 704:
Contemporary Aesthetics of Concealment for Baltistan

Faculty: Ali Rahim
Teaching Assistant: Cindy Zheng

Malala Yousufzai, when 15, was shot in the head by the Taliban because she stood up for her right to be educated in Baltistan. She took her actions and made them an international movement, distinguishing her as the youngest Nobel laureate ever. Her advocacy for young women's rights and their education has had major impacts globally. Her heroism, standing up to the Taliban in 2012, has altered the lives of many girls in the region, as her adversity shed light on the brutalities that were taking place under the Taliban. Due to the sudden international focus of the Taliban's brutalities, they were neutralized but have re-appeared since the US military forces withdrew from Afghanistan in September 2021.

Currently, there is still tension in the region with girls' education due to the renewed elevation of the Taliban installed as the Government in Afghanistan. The Taliban's power in the region is on the rise again, and architecture can play a role in subverting their intentions of restricting girl's education.

The most prominent charity in the area, run by Pakistani Industrialists, has asked for a design for a girls dormitory across the street from a girls' day school in the Hunza Valley located in Baltistan. In the region, the necessity for a girls' dormitory is critical as their daily commute to school is threatened by the Taliban who oppose and attempt to threaten their education. To combat this threat and protect these girls, the dormitory is proposed to be concealed within an alternate programmatic system brought forward by each student group.

Featured Student Work:

Advanced 704   Marion Weiss

Advanced 704:
The Bridge and The Box
Visions beyond the Dawson Jail and the East / West Divide

Faculty: Marion Weiss
Teaching Assistant: Nicole Bronola

Dallas is a city of paradoxes. As an urban center defined by a dramatic skyline and the slalom of infrastructure, it has also been tied to the fates of the Trinity River that has been reconfigured and relocated over the last century to protect the city from flooding. Now, a levee system protects the city from the river, surrounded by an ambiguous limbo of parking lots, on and off ramps, and bridges that span the river yet do little to connect the citizens of Dallas that reside on both sides of the river.

The studio will propose new strategies to transform the existing Dawson Jail and Commerce Street Bridge. Rendering the research case studies—multitasking infrastructures—operative in the design projects, students will propose new programs and design relationships that transcend boundaries between land and water, interior and exterior, above and below, that together can inform a territorial strategy for the Bridge and the Box. Together, these artifacts create the framework and "DNA" for a focused architectural project—a new form of multi-tasking connector—that will transform the engagement of the former jail to the river and the river to the two sides of the city of Dallas.

Without predetermined answers, the transformation of the bridge and jail raise critical questions: How can outmoded structures for incarceration be recast to create a yet-to-be-defined social ecosystem? What bridging strategies, incorporating new ecological and social aspirations, can translate into new infrastructural paradigms? How can recasting these artifacts of incarceration and highspeed infrastructure generate new infrastructures that reveal architecture's capacity to transform reality.

Featured Student Work:

Advanced 704:
Studio+: Public Schools as Equity Infrastructure

Faculty: Eduardo Rega Calvo, Ernel Martinez,
    & Abdallah Tabet

Studio + opens a space to speculate, design, and rehearse a self-organized interdisciplinary agency for design justice in real-world design-build projects and in partnership with civic organizations. Studio + is at once a space to define a radical form of spatial practice, a vehicle to imagine other possible worlds, and a means of operating concretely and immediately on this one. Studio + makes strategic alliances with diverse players including youth to advance projects for social justice spatially from large system/institutional/structural scale to the neighborhood to the built furniture/artifact within and beyond a school building. Material implementation of Studio + design projects will take place during the late spring and summer, led by interested students hired and supported as PennPraxis Design Fellows.

    Studio + is a new and permanent initiative of the Weitzman School focused on community-engaged design, planning, art, and preservation, conceived as a vehicle for interdisciplinary action on the part of Penn faculty and students to increase equity and reduce systemic racism embedded in processes, uneven distributions of public resources, underachieving buildings and spaces, and erasures in the city. This annual studio, led by PennPraxis and supported by the Dean and the school's five departments, will cultivate long-term dialogue between communities of color and the university to shape new agendas and partnerships that deliver concrete benefit. Over a period of three years, the first Studio + will advance the potential of Philadelphia public schools as equity infrastructure.

Featured Student Work:

Advanced 704   E. Rega Calvo, E. Martinez, A. Tabet

THE CLOUD
Reem Abi Samra &
Lauren Hanson

We believe solar-panel fields will span enormous desert areas like farmland in the Midwest. Our idea emphasizes the desert as a site of scientific and artistic exploration and sees the emergence of solar facility fields as part of a painterly environment. This project's aesthetics are based on our personal sense of amazement in the desert, pulling from recollections and flashes of awareness of its hues, topographies, rock formations, supernatural scales, and human interventions.

By completing these experiments and modifying the terrain, we seek to create a transformative area that may look unusual but highlights the craziness already found in the desert's landscapes and rock formations. This landscape will never be the same. It will alter throughout the day due to the sun's brightness and as these trials progress. While watching the sun set over the Valley of Fire during travel week, we found this to be the most magnificent portion of the desert. We propose major geological changes to the terrain, yet we want nature to paint the desert over time.

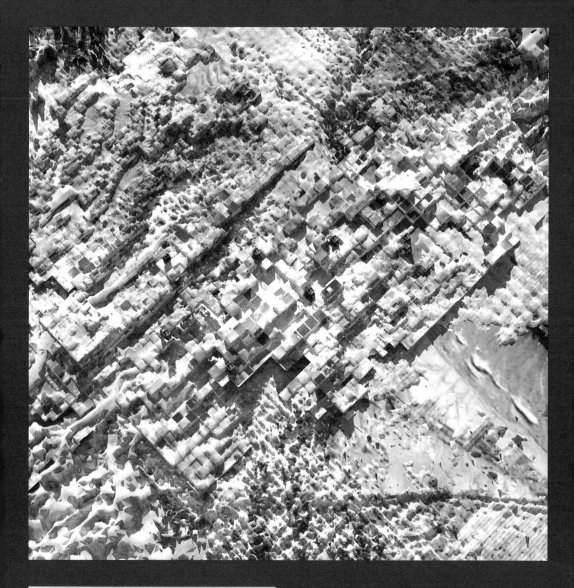

Advanced 704   Ferda Kolatan

OVERTON SPRINGS
Hongbang Chen &
Dario Sabidussi

Our project aims to create a sustainable and self-sufficient ecology in an area facing challenges such as water scarcity and environmental degradation. It is based on three solar facilities that generate electricity and desalinate lake water, producing brine and pure water as resources for this goal. The project introduces new and existing solar technologies to create solar energy and grow salt-inducive plants, which can thrive in harsh desert conditions and preserve the native species in the area.

The solar facilities are integrated into the landscape in a way that complements the surrounding environment and preserves the natural beauty of the area. The use of solar energy also helps to reduce dependence on fossil fuels and promote sustainable energy practices. The project also focuses on promoting conservation efforts for the native species in the area by growing salt-inducive plants. These plants can thrive in the harsh desert conditions and can help to preserve the biodiversity of the area.

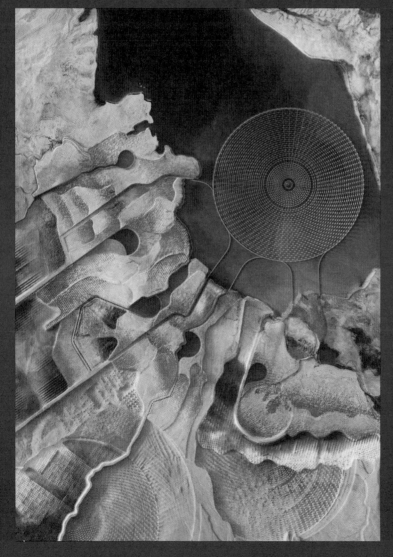

Advanced 704   Ferda Kolatan

MINERAL WELLSPRING
Riley Engelberger & Eric Fries

Our proposal attempts to address Mexico City's historic water management issues by building a water and mineral ecology. During the rainy season, the project gathers and treats water for usage and redistribution during the dry season, when Mexico City has limited access to water. The structure functions as a local stabilizer, balancing the city's water availability extremes, and it also produces a hydro-saline oasis by incorporating salt from the Lake Texcoco salt marshes. The structure includes salt baths, swimming pools, and other recreational and therapeutic spaces affected by the mineral and geological aspects of the location. A vertical watery environment is formed by the water present throughout the tower in public bath, spa, and park spaces. The tower also has living spaces that are interlaced with and in constant communication with the waters. Water is recycled throughout the building, partially utilizing sand and other minerals, especially during the months when there is little rain. Overall, the vertical landscape of minerals and water produces a wide range of experiential impacts, resulting in a water, salt, and mineral oasis that improves water management while also providing recreational and therapeutic options to visitors and residents.

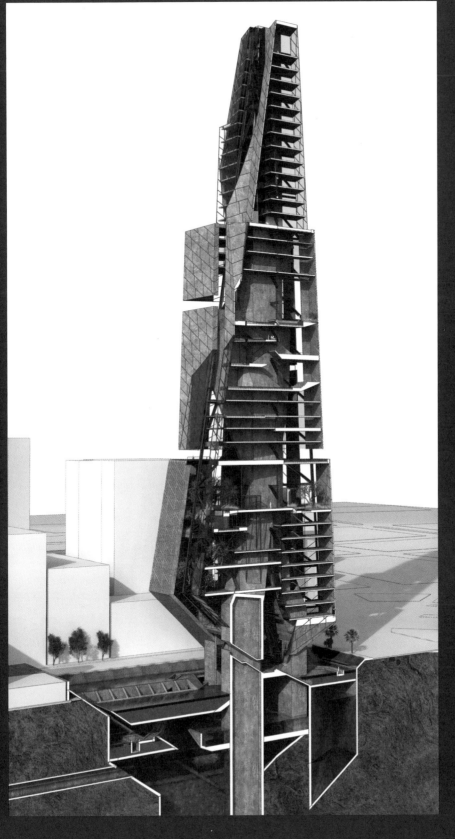

HYDRO-ROOT
Elisabeth Machielse &
Juliet McCooey

The Hydro-Root project aims to address the environmental and human hazards that have resulted from the draining of Lake Texcoco in Mexico City. These hazards include flooding, droughts, sinking of soil, and destruction of habitats. Hydro-Root addresses these issues by harnessing the power of a new water cycle that integrates human-built and natural systems, generates electricity as a battery for the city, and acts as an urban stabilizer. The main turbines occupy the ground zone and create a humid, tropical-like environment that stays constant throughout the year. The building's systems take flood water from rainfall, wastewater from residents, and groundwater into a hydropower generator that creates electricity for the building's functions and to charge electric buses and vehicles. The water from the hydro turbine is then purified and passed back to the apartments for further use. Visitors and occupants can gather, study, and experience the space together and become a part of the massive systems powering the building. The project aims to create healthy and sustainable preparations for the future of the population by managing water flows, generating electricity, and promoting stability in the urban environment.

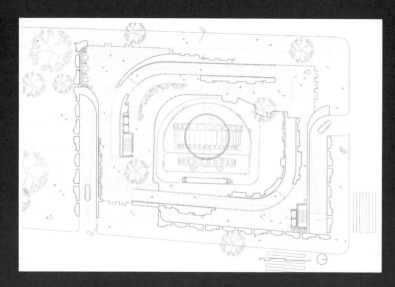

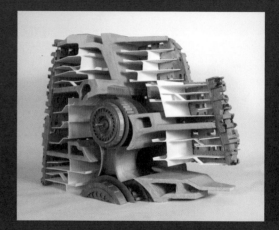

WIND AND FELT-BODY
Yiyi Luo & Yuxuan Xiong

The project began with an investigation into the Quasi thing issues of Wind and Felt-body, as well as how to make these aspects of the design tangible to the user. We found a weaving methodology that can frame the energy of strength by creating various porosity between the vertical and horizontal elements by chances regarding the body scale of human beings and allowing chances of occupancy by recreating Martin Puryear's quasi-object Contemporary Basket. This was accomplished by recreating the work of Martin Puryear. The project will be placed at a ground parking lot next to the underline and the University of Miami. It will include open and semi-enclosed places for parking, student activities, and classes. We are developing chances of occupancy in various porosities by combining two separate grid systems, universal and syncopated. This relates back to our quasi-topics of wind and felt-body.

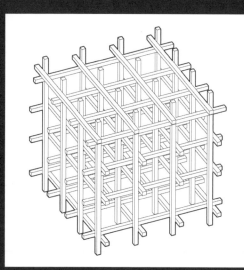
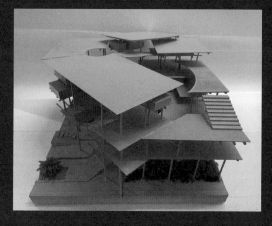

DIFFUSIVE ACCUMULATION
Jin-Seung Lee & Hayoung Nho

The recent construction of extra-large monolithic skyscrapers alters the urbanism of Miami using dichotomous terms, solid and emptiness. When geographical uncertainty extends beyond the binary, the likelihood of an unforeseen event or relationship increases. Beyond binary, the project investigates quasi-objective entities with spatial uncertainties.

The disorderly modification of the structure generates an unfixed atmospheric condition that is dynamically altered by the varying proportion, orientation, and positioning of the structural components. The system creates informal space operation. Sometimes it becomes a floor and sometimes a roof. It evolved into architecture, a structure, or the environment. The scale has been incorporated into the system.

By accumulative displacement, the project diffuses the objective boundaries and generates diverse atmospheric conditions. Due to the spatial properties of flexible density, the space's transparency and opacity vary in a dynamic manner. The quasi-built environment functions not as a representational object, but rather as a pursuit of the space's perceptual and emotional content.

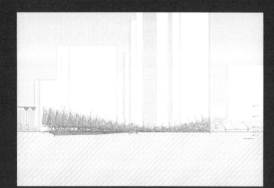

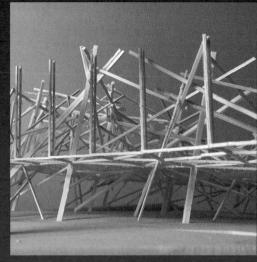

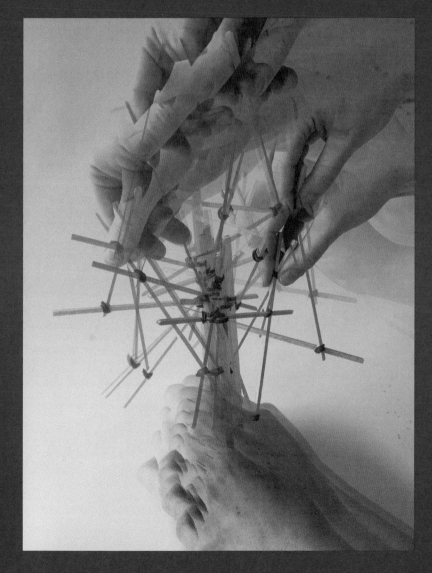

MOSQUERADE
Maria Sofia Garcia &
Bingyu Guo

The project aims to raise awareness about the issue of child marriage and lack of education for girls in the culture of Baltistan, where one out of seven children are working and only 30 percent of girls have access to education. It aims to empower women by elevating them to the top of the male-dominated textile manufacturing industry in Pakistan, which is one of the largest exporters of textiles in Asia and employs 40 percent of the labor force. It will do this by reimagining the manufacturing process using advanced technology, such as AI and software automation, to be managed entirely by women. The design is inspired by the motif of Muqarnas and explores the idea of flat vs. volumetric detail. The building is located on the river edge, and the design incorporates the idea of concealment to suggest a relationship with religious building typology. The building appears to be majestic, but inaccessible to the public.

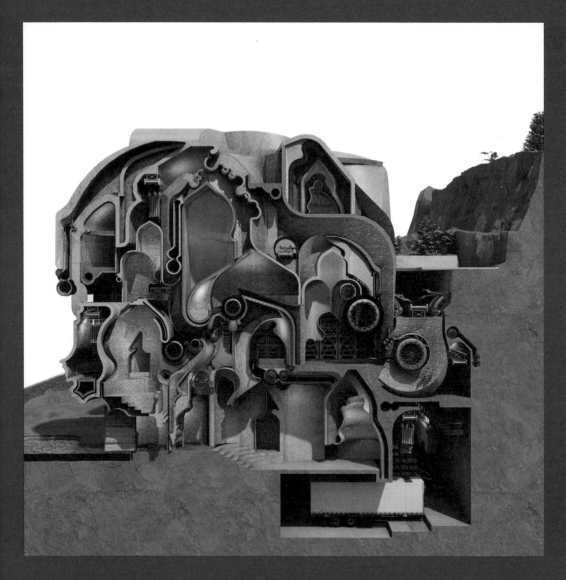

Advanced 704   Ali Rahim

Advanced 704   Ali Rahim

SYNTHETIC MINING
Miguel Matos & Beikel Rivas

The region of Gilgit-Baltistan in Pakistan is facing issues with illegal digging of natural minerals and heavy deforestation by external companies, leading to extensive environmental damage and detrimental conditions for miners. Our project aims to provide an alternative solution by introducing synthetic mining as an empowerment tool for women. The goal is to devalue the jewelry market and shift the male-dominated industry in favor of women. This not only preserves the local ecology, but also gives women control over the economy and ownership of natural resources. Additionally, the project aims to address the issue of traditional practices in the region that deny 80 percent of women their rightful inheritance, often leading to forced marriages. The design of the project incorporates cultural elements of the area, with the exterior concealing the high-tech conditions of the interior and circulation designed to conceal the production areas and dormitories for the safety of women. The project intends to help women to develop new tools to shift control of the economy in their favor.

INTERCHANGING RHYTHM
Shifei Xu & Mengdi Jia

To begin this project, DNA was extracted from the Sydney Opera House by John Utzon and the Algiers by Le Corbusier. The former has a recognizable silhouette with a hard and safe basis underneath, while the latter portrays a lovely geography with curving inhabitable infrastructure. Dallas' interchanging roadway systems make the project rapid and efficient. Dawson Jail and the Trinity River bridge are dormant and have a grim past. Dallas and the site lack slowness, interchange, and vegetation. Thus, to activate the site as the connecting tissue for east and west Dallas and create a sustainable design that allows for multiple dialogues between architecture, landscape, bridge, and water, a conservatory and farmer's market inside the existing structure and plant territories and landscape for the bridge and water are the solutions. Adaptive reuse is also sought. For the box, only the structure of the previous jail is kept and the new façade is maximized with openness and transparency. Planting areas and walks are added to the bridge construction. The conservatory cells and greenery interact yet do not impede the bridge, creating a lyrical journey and opposing rhythms.

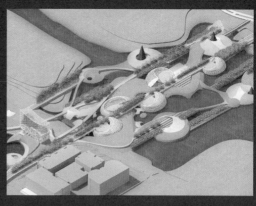

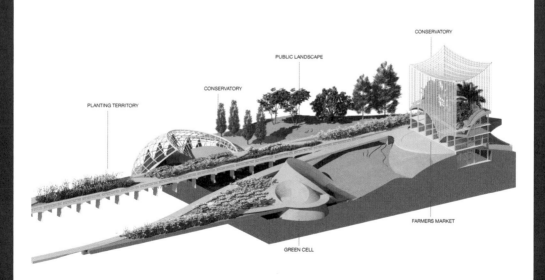

PLANTING TERRITORY

CONSERVATORY

PUBLIC LANDSCAPE

CONSERVATORY

GREEN CELL

FARMERS MARKET

PLAYSCAPE: URBAN RECREATION
John Dai & Tuo Chen

The city of Dallas has a low civic participation in recreation due to a lack of spaces and facilities compared to other cities. The city has recently published a plan to create more parks and amenities in the next decade. This project aims to recreate the landscape alongside the Trinity River for urban recreation, parks, and playgrounds to stimulate human interaction, physical community, and social engagement, and to make the case that childhood environments matter more than we think. The goal is to create outdoor spaces that are for all ages, that provide "play affordance," that are unique and memorable, and most importantly, that are fun. This is an effort to fight the scarcity of urban playgrounds and the negative impact of the current lifestyle on future generations.

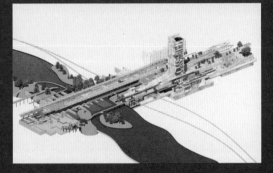

PUBLIC SCHOOLS AS EQUITY INFRASTRUCTURE STUDIO +

The Design Strategies group, one of three groups comprising the interdisciplinary design studio that brought together faculty and students from all departments at the School of Design, focused on translating the collective imaginaries of our participatory design workshops into components of a design-build project destined for a public school in West Philadelphia. The studio used maps, diagrams, and other forms of spatial visualization to communicate various scales of socio-spatial research focused on the school district, corporate forces, private interests, and the history of classist and racist public policies in the neighborhood. The work critiqued structures of power that have contributed to the disinvestment and closures of public schools in West Philadelphia, while it offered tools and methods for their dismantling. It focused on the presence of cooperative networks of mutual aid and resource redistribution to avoid the design project becoming yet another tool for gentrification.

Studio+ has created a space that combines diverse skills, interests, and cultural and disciplinary backgrounds: a space that collectively draws counter-hegemonic political imaginaries and future design projections, that learns from social justice movements how to practice design differently, that operates both within and beyond the institution of the university, and that engages public schools in West Philadelphia in education justice.

POSSIBILIST PORCH AND GREENHOUSE
Ziying Huang, Pedro Medrano, Jackson Plumlee, Marissa Marie Sayers, & Youzi (Olivia) Xu

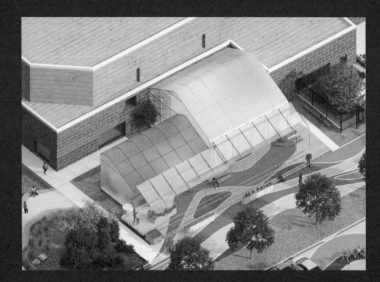

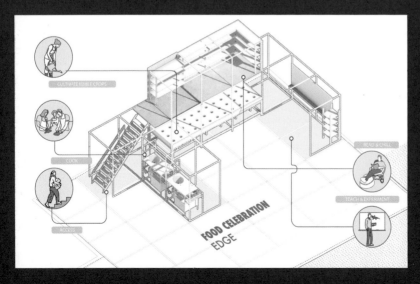

GARDEN DESIGN
Siran Chen, Kathryn Dunn,
Elizabeth Servito, &
Catherine Valverde

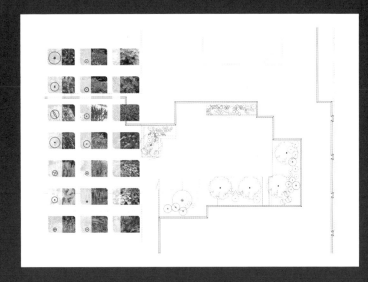

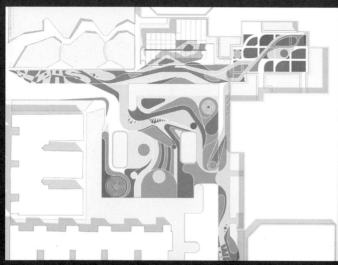

FURNITURE
Hadi El Kebbi,
Daniel Flinchbaugh, &
Jamaica Reese-Julien

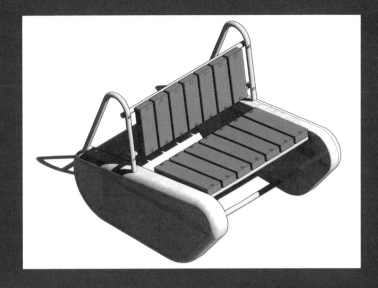

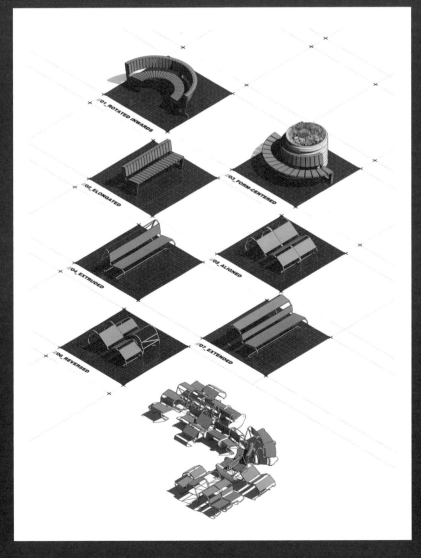

//01. ROTATED INWARDS

//02. ELONGATED

//03. FORM-CENTERED

//04. EXTRUDED

//05. ALIGNED

//06. REVERSED

//07. EXTENDED

Thesis   Studio Overview

Thesis

Coordinator: Annette Fierro

The thesis project at Penn is conceptualized as an open work, that is, its scope is limited only by the parameters of the questions that emerge. Necessarily a challenge to the discipline, each thesis topic/question establishes a relationship to ideas identified as architectural, whether belonging to the realm of building or the multiple discourses embraced within architectural study. Yet the thesis is also the site of invention and innovation, where students perforate the periphery of definitions and practices after becoming conversant in the issues involved. Each year a small group of honors students elects to pursue the thesis to undertake critical and speculative exploration of their own devising. Building an independent topic or set of questions, they work closely with an advisor and group of students and faculty over the course of the entire academic year. For students completing dual degrees—with Landscape Architecture, City Planning, or Historic Preservation—this periphery exists as cross-disciplinary study hybridizing into a third subject. Throughout the year-long thesis process, topics/questions are concurrently researched, elaborated, edited, and finally manifested in a work of architectural dimension.

A thesis project is a work of craft, a building of a set of ideas into a final statement and set of design conclusions.

The thesis project is also essentially timely: questions are posed to address current issues and crises in which architecture is implicated, even while often drawing on historical matter. In 2020–21, 11 thesis projects addressed the extremes of contemporary subject matter, springing from deeply ethical questions of the moment. Eleanor Garside, interested in the intersection of neuroscience and architecture, investigated typologies of housing of dementia/Alzheimer's patients. Veronica Rosado (featured) extensively researched building material reuse, first through the industrial processes and factors, and then redesigned an abandoned sugar cane factory in Puerto Rico. Working also in Puerto Rico, Hillary Morales Robles strategized through measures for resiliency in the face of natural disasters and colonialist histories, redeploying existing public school buildings as collective appropriations. Yasmine McBride developed techniques of community engagement to reposition concepts of the American Dream in housing and public space in the US. Ana Celdran (featured) worked on the "solar" housing typology in Havana, Cuba, investigating vernacular ornamentation through descriptive geometry as a way of fortifying decaying colonial buildings, which are highly desirable but politically repressed. Anna Lim similarly investigated ornamentation and typology as a contestation of colonial repression in Chinese modernist architecture in her fictional twin embassies in Beijing and Washington. At the other end of the time spectrum, Nicholas Houser took on the provocation of Timothy Morton's Hyperobject at a monumental scale, refiguring waste sites of massive proportions of e-waste in distant landscapes. Laura Elliot proposed a world of collectively owned automobiles, redesigning American urban and suburban typologies as they would be affected/liberated. Liam Lasting delved into form finding prompted by highly specific building materials conceived and tested at scale for extra-terrestrial use, on Mars. Finally, Danny Ortega (featured) wrote and demonstrated an application that would allow communities to "sketch" dream forms in actual, real-time sites as performances with bodily participation.

These issues lie at the periphery of the discipline but assert architecture's role in reimagining solutions for pressing, ever-changing issues. The 2021–22 Thesis Program involved these students, and their faculty advisors, from across the departments of the Weitzman School of Design and the University of Pennsylvania.

ILLOGICAL SCENES
Ana Celdran

This series of drawings describe Cuba, the solar and the hidden rooms as a unified image where the overlapping of flattened images and volumetric studies collapse in search of pictorial depth.

This research takes representational techniques as starting point to develop abstract thinking, and form finding. The basis of descriptive geometry allows us to understand an object's projection on a plane or a surface and how much it differs from its true shape and dimensions. These techniques represent objects through rotation, folding, overlapping, and discontinuity highlighting their pictorial qualities.

Using these representations and a typical colonial envelope, I created a catalog of 3D parts. These 3D pieces of a colonial building will be flattened and projected onto a plane with the purpose of creating 3D artifacts from their 2D composition. The combination of 2D views starts informing profiles as well as their volumetric qualities.

The project produced from this research will be a hidden room for Cuban Black market. Unlike other countries where this type of market involves drug dealing and prostitution, in Cuba, it is where household items, clothing, food, and electronics are sold. Illegal trading activities really took off in Cuba during the 1990s after the Soviet Union collapsed. Shortages on all kinds of goods followed.

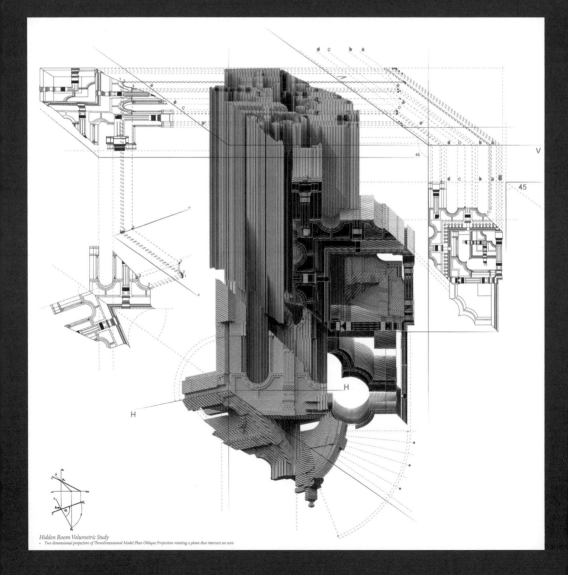

Hidden Room Volumetric Study
· *Two dimensional projection of Threedimensional Model Plan Oblique Projection rotating a plane that intersect an axis*

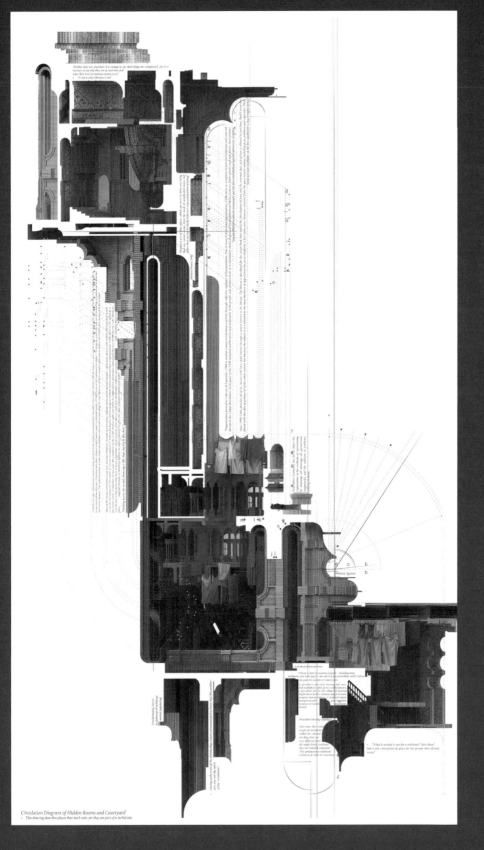

Circulation Diagram of Hidden Rooms and Courtyard
· This drawing describes that don't exist, yet they are part of a turbid site.

IN BETWEEN REALMS: BUILDING WORLDS AND REALITIES
Danny Ortega

This thesis explores how new platforms for imaging redefine architecture's role in achieving alternative modes of critical thinking. Through recent history, architecture's role has historically been defined through the act of drawing. With recent advancements with real-time digital technologies, we must take time to consider architecture that expands upon and makes use of simulation, animation, automation, synchronization, and other visualization technologies. By considering new acts of critical thinking through these technologies, designers must investigate their agency regarding autonomy, commodification, and audience within their respective medium, much like drawing has been used in the past. In order to fully understand this premise, it became inevitable that this project must be centered around creating and developing software. This software then aimed to be a decentralized and community-funded platform that acts as a generative tool for users to create and collaborate architectural experiences within Philadelphia's Callowhill/Chinatown community all while using mixed reality and one's phone. Through simple steps guided through one's device, alternative modes of critique and conversation can be set in place in their respective neighborhoods, all while experiencing a novel form of architectural exhibition that is no longer centered around a white-room gallery.

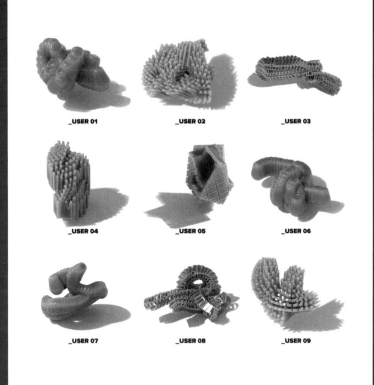

_USER 01 _USER 02 _USER 03

_USER 04 _USER 05 _USER 06

_USER 07 _USER 08 _USER 09

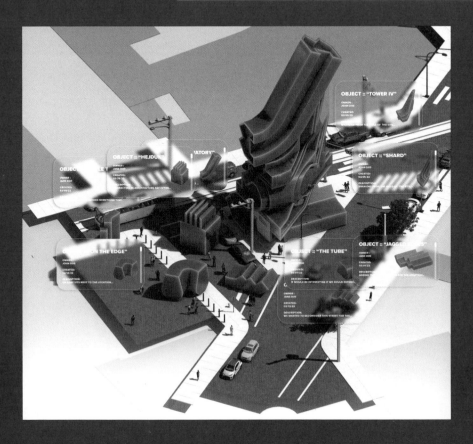

DISASSEMBLING BY DESIGN
Veronica Rosado

This thesis project is based on the argument about waste generated from building construction and demolition practices. It explores methods in which architectural design can contribute to more circular building construction, proposing recycled materials, components, and assemblages as primary tools for re-conceiving how we inhabit, rehabilitate, and occupy space in the context of climate change and rapid urbanization.

This argument is fundamental for several themes within architectural design: adaptive reuse, preservation, rehabili-tation, sustainable construc-tion, building retrofits, and embodied energy. Secondly, architects cannot claim to be doing sustainable architec-ture in a conceptual realm while designing buildings programmed to be demol-ished and become waste in a linear assembly line. Further-more, the idea that architec-ture will always be built from raw and newly fabricated materials is obsolete and unsustainable in today's

environmentally deprived context. The UN established that by 2050, 70 percent of the world's population is expected to live in urban areas. About 60 percent of the land pro-jected to become urban by 2030 is yet to be built. As cities and population grow, the demand for space and con-struction increases, requiring more energy and material extraction and consequently impacting the environment and natural resources in irreversible ways.

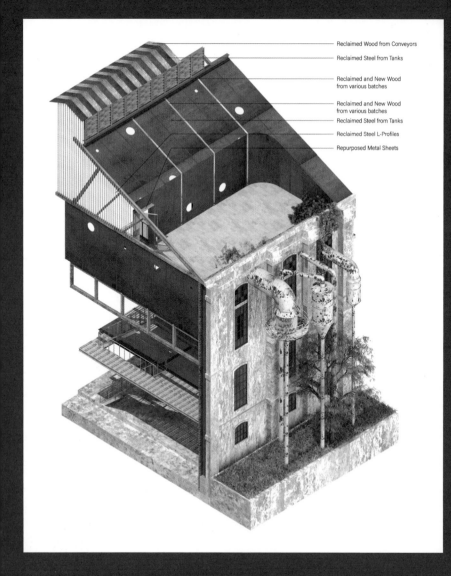

Reclaimed Wood from Conveyors

Reclaimed Steel from Tanks

Reclaimed and New Wood from various batches

Reclaimed and New Wood from various batches

Reclaimed Steel from Tanks

Reclaimed Steel L-Profiles

Repurposed Metal Sheets

Required Courses

ARCH 512
History and Theory II
Faculty: Sophie Hochhäusl

How do architecture, urbanism, and the environment reflect the dominant social, economic, and political changes of the 20th and 21st centuries, and how did their vast geopolitical shifts such as Imperialism, Fascism, the Cold War, Neoliberalism, the "War on Terror," and Nationalism reshape architecture culture? How might architecture culture respond and help construct its resistant variants, anti-fascism, anti-imperialism, decolonization, and making "quieter places" in Donna Haraway's sense? How do critical frameworks to rethink positivism, efficiency, standardization, and even utopian thinking become revised through the lenses of queer, postcolonial, critical-race, and eco-feminist theory in postwar architectural production? And how do these frameworks allow us to conceive of more equitable ways of being in the world while thinking with varied pasts? This course provides 12 discursive and theoretical frameworks to rethink architectural history in the 20th and 21st. Through 12 lectures the course traces critical questions confronting architectural modernity from the violence of settler colonialism to the possibilities of making kin. While we will trace instances of architecture, city planning, landscape, and infrastructural developments that corresponded to dominant ways of conceiving modernity and its analog progress narratives, the course is mainly interested in considering resistant paradigms that elide attempts to speak of a unified or homogenous notion of modernity.

The course will be active and interactive and will include building a collaborative dictionary of architectural terms.

ARCH 522
Visual Studies II,
Master of Architecture
Faculty: Nate Hume,
Daniel Markiewicz, Brian
DeLuna, & Olivia Vien

The coursework of Visual Studies will introduce a range of new tools, skills, and strategies useful for the development and representation of design work. Drawing and modeling strategies will be investigated for ways in which they can generate ideas and forms rather than be used solely as production tools. Control and the ability to model in an intentional manner will be highlighted. Likewise, drawing exercises will stress the construction of content over the acceptance

The World Health Organization recommends widespread use of the first malaria vaccine.

NASA successfully launches the James Webb Telescope into space where it will conduct infrared astronomy.

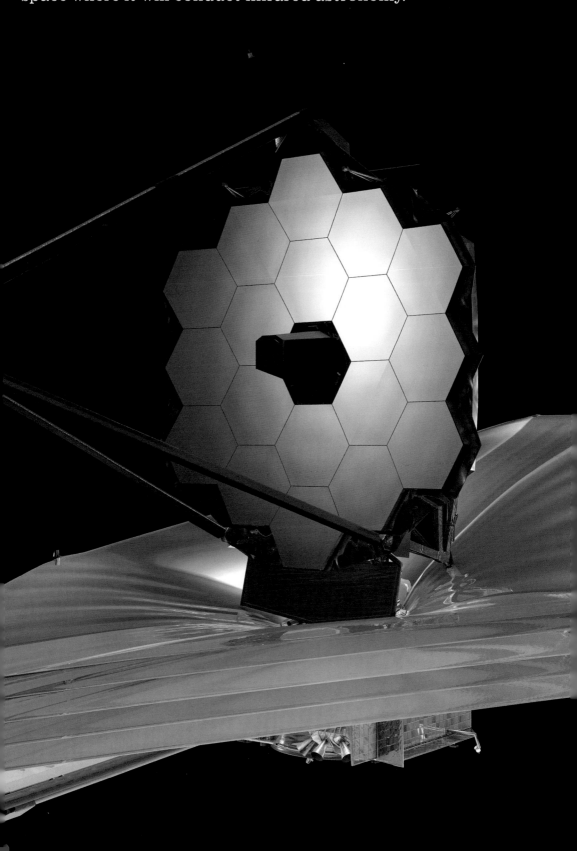

of digital defaults in order to more accurately represent a project's ideas. Documents will be produced that strive to build on and question drawing conventions in order to more precisely convey the unique character of each project. The workflow will embrace a range of software to open up possibilities to achieve intended results and resist constraint of a single program's abilities.

The course will be separated into three phases, each focusing on a different set of topics that are related to the work in studio. These phases will be in a sequential consolidation of techniques and methods. Each exercise must therefore be complete before progressing to the next. The exercises will have specific requirements and be presented by the students, as well as submitted for grading, before the next exercise is introduced.

ARCH 532
Construction II
Faculty: Franca Trubiano

Construction Technology II is an advanced course in building technology that informs, instructs, and demonstrates the extent to which industrialized building systems and innovative building technologies impact and guide the architect's design process. The course focuses on multistory buildings whose complexities require the adoption of varying material, constructional, and informational technologies; all which, are never standard, typical, or obvious.

ARCH 536
Structures II
Faculty: Masoud Akbarzadeh
& Richard Farley

A continuation of the equilibrium analysis of structures covered in Structures I.

The study of static and hyperstatic systems and design of their elements. Flexural theory, elastic and plastic. Design for combined stresses; prestressing. The study of graphic statics and the design of trusses. The course comprises both lectures and a weekly laboratory in which various structural elements, systems, materials, and technical principles are explored.

ARCH 685
Environmental Readings
Faculty: Frederick Steiner

A long, deep green thread exists in American literature from Ralph Waldo Emerson and Walt Whitman through Herman Melville and William Carlos Williams on to Terry Tempest Williams and Wendell Berry. This literature has influenced how we perceive our environments and, in the process, many planners, designers, and conservationists such as Frederick Law Olmsted, Jane Addams, Aldo Leopold, Lewis Mumford, Ian McHarg, and Anne Whiston Spirn. In this seminar, we will explore this green thread and analyze its influence on how we shape our environments through design and planning. The course has three parts. Throughout, the influence of literature on design and planning theory will be explored. The first part will focus on the three most important theorists in environmental planning and landscape architecture: Frederick Law Olmsted Sr., Charles Eliot, and Ian McHarg. The senior Olmsted pretty much created the field of landscape architecture, adapting the English landscape aesthetic for the rapidly urbanizing North American continent to address pressing urban issues. Arguably, the planning

profession in the United States also began with the senior Olmsted. Charles Eliot was a protégé of Olmsted's. Eliot pioneered the use of comprehensive, scientific landscape inventories; originated the concept of land trusts; and designed the first metropolitan regional open-space plan. Educated in landscape architecture and city planning, Ian McHarg influenced both fields in the late-20th century. He urged us to better understand natural processes and how people use space. The second part of the course will critically explore current theories in environmental planning and landscape architecture. The topics will include: frameworks for cultural landscape studies, the future of the vernacular, ecological design and planning, sustainable and regenerative design, the languages of landscapes, and evolving views of landscape aesthetics and ethics. In the third part of the course, students will build on the readings to develop their own theory for ecological planning or, alternatively, landscape architecture. While literacy and critical inquiry are addressed throughout the course, critical thinking is especially important for this final section.

ARCH 599
500 Technology Lab
Faculty: Richard Farley,
Patrick Morgan, Masoud
Akbarzadeh, & Ryan Palider

A required lab/workshop to accompany the core technology sequence in the MArch program. This ungraded course will offer additional instruction, workshops, lab time, and other support to the first-year technology courses (Structures I & II and Construction I & II).

All students enrolled in any of those courses must also enroll in the 500 Technology Lab.

ARCH 634
Environmental Systems II
Faculty: Efrie Escott

In the spring portion of Environmental Systems, we consider the environmental systems of larger, more complex buildings. Contemporary buildings are characterized by the use of systems for ventilation, heating, cooling, dehumidification, lighting, communications, and controls, which not only have their own complexity but also interact dynamically with one another. Their relationship to the classic architectural questions about building size and shape is even more complex. With the introduction of sophisticated feedback and control systems, architects are faced with conditions that are virtually animate and coextensive at many scales with the natural and manmade environments in which they are placed.

The task of the semester is to establish an understanding of how the concept of "high performance" shapes the design of modern buildings, building on the basic concepts of energy transfer and thermodynamics covered in Environmental Systems I. Through case studies, we will interrogate approaches to building enclosure, dynamic interaction between active and passive systems, air quality, acoustics, and material performance.

ARCH 636
Material Formations
Faculty: Ezio Blasetti
& Robert Stuart-Smith

Material Formations introduces robotic production and material dynamics as active agents in design rationalization and expression.

The course investigates opportunities for designers to synthesize multiple performance criteria within architecture. Theory, Case-Studies, and practical tutorials will focus on the incorporation of analytical, simulation, generative computation, and robot fabrication concerns within design. While production is traditionally viewed as an explicit and final act of execution, the course explores the potential for all aspects of building production and use to participate within the creative design process, potentially producing performance and affect. Students will develop skills and experience in computer programming, physics-based simulation, and robot motion planning. A design research project will be undertaken through a number of discrete assignments that require the synthetization or structural performance along with material and robotic production constraints. The course will explore design as the outcome of materially formative processes of computation and production. Structure: the course will commence with weekly lectures and computer-based tutorials, and culminate in a series of intensive incremental learning, and prepare groups to work on a final assignment which involves the robotic fabrication of a small design prototype.

ARCH 671
Professional Practice I
Faculty: Philip Ryan

The course consists of a series of workshops that introduce students to a diverse range of practices. The course goal is to gain an understanding of the profession by using the project process as a framework. The course comprises a survey of the architectural profession—its licensing and legal requirements; its evolving types of practice, fees, and compensation; its adherence to the constraints of codes and regulatory agencies, client desires, and budgets; and its place among competing and allied professions and financial interests. The workshops are a critical forum for discussion to understand the forces that at times both impede and encourage innovation and leadership. Students learn how architects develop the skills necessary to effectively communicate to clients, colleagues, and user groups. Trends such as globalization, ethics, entrepreneurship, sustainability issues, and technology shifts are analyzed in their capacity to affect the practice of an architect.

ARCH 699
600 Technology Lab
Faculty: Erfie Escott

A required lab/workshop to accompany the core technology sequence in the MArch program. This ungraded course will offer additional instruction, workshops, lab time, and other support to the second-year technology courses including Environmental Systems (I and II), Case Studies, and Material Formations. All students enrolled in any of those courses must also enroll in the 600 Technology Lab.

Electives

ARCH 712
Topics in Arch Theory II:
Visual Research:
Architecture and
Media after WWII
Faculty: Taryn Mudge

This course will question
how architects have engaged
in visual research of the
built environment within the
process of architectural
design. In particular, we will
consider the media and
methods architects have
used to observe and to
record building sites and
how visual information has
influenced design thinking
and informed architectural
proposals in the postwar
period. The visual material
under investigation in
this course will include,
but is not limited to, photography (aerial, documentary,
street, etc.), film, sketches,
painting, collage, mapping,
as well as magazines and
advertisements.

ARCH 712
Topics in Arch Theory II:
Architectural Envelopes:
Technology and Expression
Faculty: Ariel Genadt

Since the mid-19th century,
architectural envelopes have
become the prime subject
of experimentations and
investments, as well as
theoretical conflicts. This
seminar takes the revolution
of steel and glass technology
in the 19th century as a
starting point to examine the
relationship between con-
struction technologies and
architectural expression in
the 20th and 21st centuries.
It explores the interdependence of theory and practice
in case studies located in
various cultures and climates
around the world, and built in
a range of techniques and
materials. The lectures are
organized thematically,
looking at the different ways
by which technology can be

instrumental in selectively
revealing and concealing
structural logic, material
properties, fabrication,
digital tools, climate control,
sensorial perception,
image-making, symbolism,
and atmosphere. The seminar
develops students' critical
thinking towards contemporary practice, where glo-
balized technology and large
capital often hinder the
creation of architecture with
local cultural pertinence.
Understanding the reciproci-
ties between building,
technology, and expression
is essential for creatively
tackling architecture's impact
on the environment and
sustaining its civic agency.

ARCH 712
Topics in Arch Theory II:
Baroque Parameters
Faculty: Andrew Saunders

This course will provide
an overview of the debate

surrounding the term Baroque and its contemporary implications. The term Baroque is the subject of many debates ranging from its etymological origin, to disputes on the emergence of an aesthetic "style" post – Council of Trent in the 17th century by historians such as Heinrich Wölfflin, and the more current and most broad application of the term as a recursive philosophical concept suggested by Gilles Deleuze to "Fold" through time. Although illusive and as dynamic as the work itself, students will become familiar with how the term Baroque has been associated with specific characteristics, attitudes, and effects or more specifically the architectural consequences it has produced.

ARCH 712
Topic in Arch Theory II: Architecture, Gender, Theory
Faculty: Sophie Hochhausl

In this course, we will engage the writing of architectural histories that ask how feminism and gender theory (from eco-feminism and intersectional feminism to queer and trans theory) can spearhead new methods of research, objects of study, and ways of seeing and analyzing spaces, buildings, cities, and human alliances within them. The course is decidedly focused on forms of organizing around women's and LGBTQ+ rights in cities —from informal activist groups to institution building. The seminar highlights these group efforts as main sites for creative, critical, and political intervention in questioning heteronormative forms of living, care, and kinship. As such, the seminar emphasizes scholarship on gender theory that has helped reframe architectural history

since the 1960s and investigates how these ideas have informed and begun to alter the discipline.

ARCH 718
History and Theory of Architecture and Climate
Faculty: Kiel Moe

Climate change is upon us. This course discusses the history of thinking about climate in architecture. We confront the geographic and epistemic challenges of climate change and other environmental threats, and reconsider the forces seen to condition the development of modern architecture. The course will explore the history of buildings as mechanisms of climate management, and the theoretical and conceptual frameworks that pertain. As many of the arguments and innovations in the climate discourse were made through visual means, the images produced by architects and others interested in understanding the relationship between "man" and "climate" will be a central arena of exploration. We will treat these images as evidence of material innovations in energy-efficient architectural design technologies and also as evidence of new ways of thinking about ecological, political, cultural, and economic relationships. These narratives, images, and methods—and the broader understanding of environmental systems that emerged since the immediate post-war period—also suggest a complex relationship to the present. Rather than examine instrumental aspects of these methods and their histories, we will explore different historiographic and conceptual means for the archival analysis of climate, technology, and architecture. Recent texts concerned with

theories of historical change, of new ideas about the human, and with the cultural anxieties associated with the Anthropocene will be read to this end.

ARCH 720
Visual Literacy and Its Culture
Faculty: Brian De Luna

The digital turn in the creative fields resulted in profound transformations of techniques, aesthetics, and underlying concepts in the development of contemporary visual culture. The dissemination and consumption of information through images through all types of media platforms influence and re-define (for better or worse) all aspects of our culture and reality. It is vital to develop a deep knowledge of the current visual concepts and techniques in arts, photography, cinema, product design, and architecture to claim a critical stance through which we can positively contribute to the evolution of contemporary culture. The discipline of architecture has been deeply influenced by the digital shift in modes of design and visualization which yielded a wide array of directions within the architectural discourse, especially with questions and problems regarding representation. One clear outcome of this transformational period is the diversity of new representational strategies to seek alternative modes of visualization. It is clear that no one representational medium can be defined as the locus of architectural thought and architecture, as a cultural practice, can no longer be defined through the output of a single medium. The reality of our discipline is that we work through collective mediums and conventions of drawings, models, images,

Poet Maya Angelou becomes the first Black woman to be featured on a U.S. quarter.

Global vaccine-sharing programme COVAX reaches a
milestone of 1 billion doses.

CEPI   Gavi   unicef   World Health Organization

simulations, texts, prototypes, and buildings to visualize architectural concepts. These mediums all require degrees of expertise in techniques that are necessary for their execution: they all involve conceptual depth that define their disciplinary positions; they all require translations across each other to enable subjective work-flows; they all require aesthetic attitudes to influence the development of visual culture in architecture. This course will introduce the AAD majors to contemporary topics of visualization in arts, photography, cinema, and architecture. They will explore multiple mediums of representation to help them gain the vital visual literacy to excel in the program. Students will be introduced to discursive background and contemporary concepts of line drawing, fabricated object, and constructed image as they work through three distinct projects during the semester. Each exercise will be initiated by a topical lecture and be followed by weekly pin ups to advance student projects.

ARCH 726
Furniture Design as
Strategic Process
Faculty: Mikael Avery
& Brad Ascalon

Like architecture, furniture exists at the intersection of idea and physical form. Due to the specific scale that furniture occupies, however, this physical form relates not only to the environment in which the furniture is set, but also intimately to the physical bodies that interact with and around it. Additionally, as a manufactured product, often specified in large quantities, furniture must also address not only poetic considerations, but practical and economic ones as well. Instead of being seen

as one-off objects, the furniture created in this seminar focuses on furniture development as a strategic design process where the designer's role is to understand the various responsibilities to each stakeholder (client/manufacturer, market/customer, environment) and the additional considerations (materials, processes, manufacturability, etc.), and ultimately translate these points into a potentially successful product. In order to approach furniture in this manner, the course will be structured around specific design briefs and clustered into three distinct but continuous stages. First, through focused research into stakeholder needs and potential market opportunities, students will craft tailored design proposals and development concepts accordingly. Next, students will work toward visualizing a concept, complete with sketches, small mock-ups, scale-model prototypes, technical drawings, and connections and other pertinent details in order to refine their proposals and secure a real-world understanding of the manufacturing processes and the potential obstacles created by their decisions. From insights gained and feedback from these steps, students will ultimately develop a final design proposal for a piece, collection, or system of furniture that successfully leverages their understanding of a thoughtful and deliberate design strategy.

ARCH 732
Tech-Designated Elective:
Enclosures: Selection,
Affinities, & Integration
Faculty: Charles Berman

Details should be considered in the traditional sense, as

assemblages of constituent elements. Not as a mere collection of parts, rather as an "assemblage," the act of assembling under a guiding principle; the relationship to a whole. Frascari defines the detail as the union of construction—having the dual role of ruling both the construction and construing of architecture. This obligation of the relationship of the parts to the whole and the whole to the parts is the essence of the revelatory detail in service of architecture. This seminar seeks to establish a framework of understanding enclosures in this sense of the revelatory detail. We will seek to counterpoint the numerical (external) facts of what is accepted as facade design (criteria, codes, loads, forces, and consumptions) with an understanding of the generative processes underlying these physical criteria. The aim of this seminar is to arm the student with a guided understanding of the materials and assemblies available to them to form enclosures. The underlying intent is twofold. In a generative role as architects, the course intends not for an encyclopedic overview of the elements and calculative methodologies of envelope design. Rather we will endeavor to investigate concepts of enclosure through assemblage of elements, mediated by details, in the service of the architectural intentions of the student. In an execution role as architects in practice, the investigation into methodologies of deployment and execution of enclosure, materials, and assemblies is intended to arm the students to engage proactively in their future practices with the succession of consulting engineers, specialty facade consultants, manufacturers, and facade contractors that they will encounter during the execution of their work.

ARCH 732
Tech-Designated Elective:
Beyond the Binary
Faculty: Simon Kim
& Mark Yim

This seminar will examine the design methods of dynamic relationships in design and performance for stage and audience. The class will be one-part research and one-part development of prototype for performance with the Mendelssohn Choir. As such, a heavy emphasis will be placed in producing a working prototype for the final performance. This means that the design and engineering needs to be 'stage-proofed' so that it is robust in its parts and performance.

ARCH 732
Tech-Designated Elective:
Deployable Structures
Faculty:
Mohamad Al Khayer

The objective of this course is to introduce the rapidly growing field of deployable structures through hands-on experiments conducted in workshop environments. Students develop skills in making deployable structures.

ARCH 732
Tech-Designated
Elective: Daylighting
Faculty: Janki Vyas

This course aims to introduce fundamental daylighting concepts and tools to analyze daylighting design. The wide range of topics to be studied includes site planning, building-envelope and shading optimization, passive solar design, daylight delivery methods, daylight analysis structure and results interpretation, and a brief daylighting and lighting design integration.

ARCH 732
Tech-Designated
Elective: Principles of
Digital Fabrication
Faculty: Mikael Avery

Through the almost seamless ability to output digital designs to physical objects, digital fabrication has transformed the way designers work. To begin this course we will review these 'traditional' digital fabrication techniques in order to establish a baseline skill set to work from. We will then utilize a series of exercises in order to explore hybrid approaches to digital fabrication in which multiple techniques are utilized within the same work. With the advent of 3D printing technology in the late 1980s and the current wave of widespread adoption as a design tool—found in design schools and offices across the world—the immediate testing of complex digital models has never been quicker, clearer, or more immediate. Despite this formal freedom to test and print, the installations and buildings generated from these complex digital models rely on much more traditional building techniques for their construction. By combining various digital fabrication approaches, we seek to challenge and reframe the often reductive geometries that currently support much of this work and bring with it a new way of approaching aesthetics, structure, and construction based on the possibilities inherent in these digital tools and techniques.

ARCH 732
Tech-Designated Elective:
Heavy Architecture
Faculty: Philip Ryan

Heavy Architecture is a seminar that will examine buildings that, through their tectonics or formal expression, connote a feeling of weight, permanence, or "heaviness." Analysis of these buildings and methods of construction stand in relation to the proliferation of thin, formally exuberant, and, by virtue of their use or commodified nature, transient buildings. The course is not a rejection or formal critique of "thin" architecture, but instead an analysis of the benefits and drawbacks of the "heavy" building type in terms of a building's financial, environmental, symbolic or conceptual, and functional goals. The course will parse the alleged nostalgic or habitual reputation of "heavy" architecture within the context of architecture's ongoing struggle to be the vanguard of the built environment even while its relevancy and voice is challenged by economic, stylistic, and social forces.

ARCH 732
Envisioning Climate:
A Virtual Reality Seminar
Faculty: Vanessa Keith
& Andrew Homick

How can we mobilize to change the future for the better? Climate change unquestionably represents the biggest challenge to the continued presence of humankind—or any other species—on this planet. Managing and attempting to limit the effects of global warming should be our biggest project, prompting us to marshal our collective will, energy, and creativity to design a livable solution to the inevitable shifts in weather and habitat. Urgent timelines alone, however, are not enough to prompt action. This seminar aims to make the invisible visible and tangible by harnessing virtual reality as an empathy machine. Taking inspiration from VR artists and creatives like Participant Media and Condition One (This Is Climate Change), Marshmallow Laser Feast (In the Eyes of the Animal, Ocean of Air), Winslow Porter and Milica Zec (Tree), Tamiko Thiel (Evolution of Fish, Unexpected Growth), the Yale University Hackathon (The Reality of Global Climate Change), among others, we will bring to life the latest climate data on the city's potential future(s) in VR with the aim of creating immersive experiences that can spur us to positive change in the here and now.

ARCH 732
Tech-Designated Elective: Inquiry into Biomaterial Architectures
Faculty: Laia Mogas-Soldevila

Traditional building materials are environmentally and economically expensive to extract, process, transport, or recycle; their damage is non-trivial to repair; and have limited ability to respond to changes in their immediate surroundings. Biological materials like wood, coral, silk, skin, or bone outperform man-made materials in that they can be grown where needed, self-repair when damaged, and respond to changes in their surroundings. Their inclusion in architectural practice could have great benefits in wellbeing and the environment defining new tools and strategies towards the future of sustainable construction. Crucial projects describing future biomaterial architectures are emerging in the field. In this seminar, students will review their potential through lectures followed by case studies and propose future developments through a guided research project with special attention to functional, industrial, environmental, and aesthetic

dimensions. The course is structured to foster fundamental scientific literacy, cross-disciplinary thinking, creativity, and innovation in biomaterials in design.

ARCH 736
Tech-Designated Elective: Building Acoustics
Faculty: Joe Solway

This course covers the fundamentals of architectural acoustics and the interdependence between acoustics and architectural design. The course explores the effects of building massing, room shape and form, and architectural finishes on a project site's soundscape and the user's acoustic experience. It will include fundamentals on sound, sound isolation, room acoustics, and building systems noise control; a lecture on the history and future of performance space design; a virtual visit to the Arup SoundLab; and two assignments.

ARCH 736
Tech-Designated Elective: Virtual Construction & Detailing with BIM
Faculty: Patrick Morgan

Building Information Modeling (BIM) has become the standard of building construction, design, and operation. During the past decade significant changes have taken place in the nature of design and construction practices that have transformed the very nature of architectural representation. Architects no longer draw 2D deceptions of what they intend others to build, but they instead model, code, simulate, and integrate the final built product virtually, alongside their colleagues and collaborators, architects, engineers, and builders. The production of an information-rich BIM is the ground

upon which all construction activities for advanced and complex buildings take place. BIM is also the origin of contemporary innovations in Integrated Design, the creation of collaborative platforms that aim to maximize the sustainable outcomes in the project delivery of buildings. Moreover, being able to collaboratively produce, share, and query a BIM model makes possible the global practice of design and construction. The course will familiarize students to this important field of architectural practice.

ARCH 736
Tech-Designated Elective: Healthy Buildings: Science & Application
Faculty: Jie Zhao

This course examines the scientific evidence of how different elements of the indoor environment impact human health and well-being, and discusses practical design and technology examples for offices, homes, schools, and other living spaces.

ARCH 736
Tech-Designated Elective: Seeing Architecture: Technology, Ecology, Practice
Faculty: Richard Garber

The course will ask students to consider how we see architecture from both a technological and ecological basis—that is how we understand buildings within the larger global environment we co-habit, as well as how we can learn from both our past as well as the earth itself —from "the ever nonobjective to which we are subject" to "an object that stands before us and can be seen" (Heidegger, *The Origin of the Work of Art*, 1950), the implications of design, and more specifically the future work of architects. Through a series of lectures and readings, students will have the opportunity to consider building, both as a subjective act and an objective consequence of architectural workflows within the larger framework of built ecologies and ecologies of thought.

ARCH 733
New Materials and Methods Research
Faculty: Laia Mogas-Soldevila

There is today a renewed interest in materiality and materialization in architecture that is fueled by rapidly advancing fields in materials engineering combined with newly available cutting-edge digital design and fabrication environments. Mastering the fundamentals of material-driven decision making from the perspective of design is crucial to integrate productive dialogue with all agents in the building construction arena, and specifically relevant in advanced architecture projects exploring new materials and fabrication methods influenced by progress in science and engineering.

The primary goal of this course is to help students formulate a robust research proposal for their culminating design studio in digital large-scale fabrication and robotics manufacturing using new materials. The course provides a forum for critical discussion of contemporary design practices that is exploratory and speculative in nature. In addition to collaborative thinking and debate, student groups will develop their own research interests to formulate contemporary positions through the research of materials, fabrication methods, and their application in experimental architectural design projects.

ARCH 734
Ecological Architecture: Contemporary Practices
Faculty: Todd Woodward

Architecture is an inherently exploitive act—we utilize resources from the earth and produce waste and pollution to create and occupy buildings. We have learned that buildings are responsible for 40 percent of greenhouse gas emissions, 15 percent of water use, and 30 percent of landfill debris. This growing realization has led building designers to look for ways to minimize negative environmental impacts. Green building design practices are seemingly becoming mainstream. Green building certification programs and building performance metrics are no longer considered fringe ideas. This course will investigate these trends and the underlying theory with a critical eye. Is "mainstream green" really delivering the earth-saving architecture it claims? As green building practices become more widespread, there remains something unsatisfying about a design approach that focuses on limits, checklists, negative impacts and being "less bad." Can we aspire to something more? If so, what would that be? How can or should the act of design change to accommodate an ecological approach?

ARCH 742
The Function of Fashion in Architecture
Faculty: Danielle Willems

The Function of Fashion in Architecture will survey the history of fashion and the architectural parallels starting from Ancient Civilization to Present. The focus will be on the relevance of garment design, methods, and techniques and their potential to redefine current

architecture elements such as envelope, structure, seams, tectonics, and details. The functional, tectonic, and structural properties of garment design will be explored as generative platforms to conceptualize very specific architectural elements. One of the challenges in the course is the re-invention of a means of assessment, the development of notations and techniques that will document the forces and the production of difference in the spatial manifestations of the generative systems.

ARCH 744
Image, Object, Architecture
Faculty: Ferda Kolatan

Architecture is intrinsically linked to objects and images. Since the earliest days of prehistoric monuments and painted caves, architecture has developed an inherently iconographic function. This function can be described as follows: Immaterial ideas about the world are physically embodied through material practices such as drawing, painting, and form-making. Or in other words, architecture is a means of expressing cultural predilections, interests, and desires. This representational quality was traditionally aided by integrating painting and sculpting directly into architecture. The confluence of these different mediums and their specific techniques and technologies was viewed as a critical component of manifesting ideas in matter. In modern times however the iconographic function of architecture shifted toward abstraction and an emphasis was placed on separating mediums dealing with image, object, and architecture rather than further integrating them. The seminar will re-examine the combinatorial

Biotechnology company Moderna and IAVI announce the start of clinical trials for an HIV vaccine.

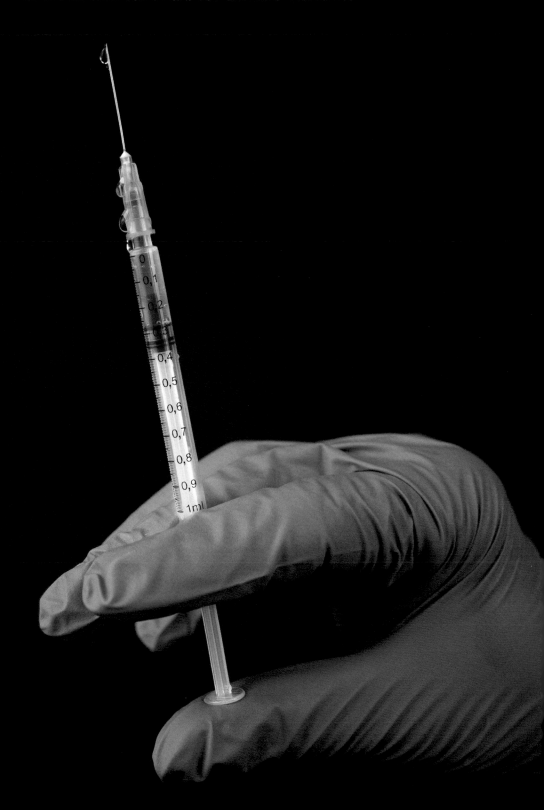

Guardianship over 523 acres of California redwood forest is returned to a coalition of Native American tribes. The forest will take the new name "Tc'ih-Léh-Dûñ" or "fish run place" in the Sinkyone language.

alliance of image, object, and architecture in the context of contemporary cultural ideas and technologies by designing artifacts that produce novel architectural effects and iconographies.

ARCH 748
Architecture and the
New Elegance
Faculty: Hina Jamelle

The seminar will define and elaborate on the following topics for the digital discourse—diagrammatic relations, technique, and aesthetic principles. Technological innovations establish new status quos and updated platforms from which to operate and launch further innovations. Design research practices continually reinvent themselves and the techniques they use to stay ahead of such developments. Mastery of techniques remains important and underpins the use of digital technologies in the design and manufacturing of elegant buildings. But, ultimately, a highly sophisticated formal language propels aesthetics. The seminar seeks to reframe the questions facing architectural design, setting the intellectual framework for an increasingly expansive set of design solutions. The goal is to narrow the gap between aesthetics, design research, and practice.

ARCH 754
Perform Design Workshop
Faculty: Jihun Kim

Environmental systems have been developed and applied in buildings to improve thermal comfort and to reduce energy use. The workshop examines the design and performance of the systems, focusing on their climatic effects on occupants while providing technical and analytic skills. Environmental

systems of interest include the Trombe wall, double-skin façade, external thermal mass, integrated shading, stack ventilation, and passive downdraft cooling. Computational fluid dynamics and building energy simulation are incorporated for quantitative analysis along with the physical model and energy tracing diagram for qualitative analysis. The course further provides technical skills that serve the ARCH 709 EBD Research Studio offered in the same semester. Meetings include lectures, workshops, and desk-crits. Students must have completed ARCH 753 Introduction to Building Performance Simulation as a prerequisite.

ARCH 762
Design and Development
Faculty: Alan Razak

This newly reconstituted course will introduce designers and planners to practical methods of design and development for major real estate product types. Topics will include product archetypes, site selection and obtaining entitlements, basic site planning, programming, and conceptual and basic design principles. Project types will include, among others, infill and suburban office parks, all retail forms, and campus and institutional projects. Two-person teams of developers and architects will present and discuss actual development projects.

ARCH 765
Project Management
Faculty: Charles Capaldi

This course is an introduction to techniques and tools of managing the design and construction of large, and small, construction projects. Topics include project delivery systems, management tools, cost-control and

budgeting systems, and professional roles. Case studies serve to illustrate applications. Cost and schedule control systems are described. Case studies illustrate the application of techniques in the field.

ARCH 768
Real Estate Development
Faculty: Asuka Nakahara

This course focuses on "ground-up" development as well as re-development, and acquisition investments. We will examine traditional real estate product types including office, R&D, retail, warehouses, lodging, single-family and multi-family residential, mixed use, and land. "Specialty" uses like golf courses, resorts, timeshares, and senior assisted living will be analyzed. You will learn the development process from market analysis, site acquisition, zoning, entitlements, approvals, site planning, building design, construction, financing, and leasing to ongoing management and disposition. Additional topics—workouts, leadership, and running an entrepreneurial company—will be discussed. Throughout, we will focus on risk management, as minimizing risk first results in maximizing long run profits and net-worth accumulation.

Jan 2022

02 03 04 05 06 07 08
09 10 11 12 13 14 15
16 17 18 19 20 21 22
23 24 25 (26) 27 28 29
30 31

Jan 26: Weitzman School of Design Lecture Series: Nader Tehrani: Timely Anachronisms

Timely Anachronisms speaks to the longue durée of architecture, and how we might become relevant to an age beyond that in which we live. In part, this is a commitment to a future that outlasts the problems we seek to solve today, but also it seeks to speak to discourses that precede us and produce conversations across history. In this capacity, we may even realize that what we do today may seem out of synch with our times, but temporally in focus with a larger discursive ambition. For his contributions to architecture as an art, Nader Tehrani was the recipient of the 2020 Arnold W. Brunner Memorial Prize from The American Academy of Arts and Letters, to which he was also elected as a Member in 2021, the highest form of recognition of artistic merit in The United States. Nader Tehrani is founding principal of NADAAA, a practice dedicated to the advancement of design innovation, interdisciplinary collaboration, and an intensive dialogue with the construction industry. He is also Dean of The Irwin S. Chanin School of Architecture at The Cooper Union. Tehrani's work has been recognized with notable awards, including the Cooper Hewitt National Design Award in Architecture, the United States Artists Fellowship in Architecture and Design, and the American Academy of Arts and Letters Award in Architecture. He has also received the Harleston Parker Award and the Hobson Award. Throughout his career, Tehrani has received 18 Progressive Architecture Awards as well as numerous national and international design awards. He served as the Frank O. Gehry International Visiting Chair in Architectural Design at the University of Toronto and the inaugural Paul Helmle Fellow at California State Polytechnic University, Pomona. He has also recently served as the William A. Bernoudy Architect in Residence at the American Academy in Rome. For the past seven years in a row, NADAAA has ranked in the top 11 design firms in Architect Magazine's Top 50 Firms in the United States, ranking at number one three years in a row.

Feb 2022

01 02 03 04 05
06 07 08 09 10 11 12
13 14 15 (16) 17 18 19
20 21 22 23 24 25 26
27 28

Feb 16: Weitzman School of Design Lecture Series: Laurie Hawkinson: Public Works + Private Practice

Laurie Hawkinson is an architect and founding partner of the New York–based firm Smith-Miller + Hawkinson Architects, focusing on work in the public realm and committed to equity, issues of climate change, and service to the public with projects of varying scales, from temporary public art projects such as the Freedom of Expression National Monument, to a new Ferry building at Wall Street, Strategic Open Space Study for Lower Manhattan, 87 units of housing in midtown Manhattan, and the Energy Advancement Innovation Center at the Ohio State University. Laurie is also a professor at Columbia University's Graduate School of Architecture Planning and Preservation and a Commissioner for New York City's Public Design Commission.

Queen Elizabeth becomes the first British Monarch to celebrate a Platinum Jubilee, marking 70 years of service.

A medical first, CRISPR injected into the blood treats
genetic diseases.

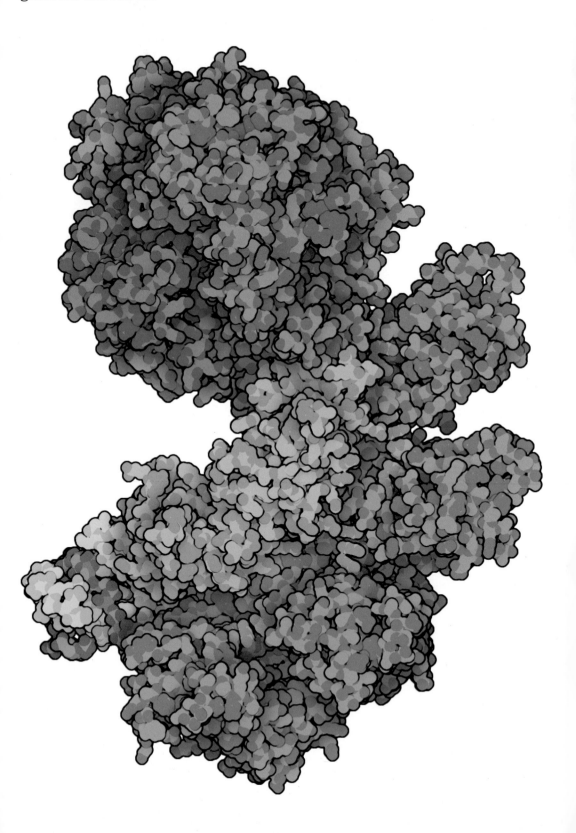

Mar 2022

01 02 03 04 05
06 07 08 09 10 11 12
13 14 15 (16) 17 18 19
20 21 22 23 24 25 26
27 28 29 (30) (31)

Mar 16: The KPF Lecture: Nanako Umemoto & Jesse Reiser on the Kaohsiung Port Terminal in Taiwan

The Department of Architecture welcomes Nanako Umemoto and Jesse Reiser, principals of the RUR Architecture DPC, who will give the lecture titled Just Architecture.

Reiser + Umemoto, RUR Architecture DPC, is an internationally recognized multidisciplinary design firm, which has built projects at a wide range of scales: from furniture design, to residential and commercial structures, up to the scale of landscape, urban design, and infrastructure. In 2010, the firm was awarded first prize for the Taipei Music Center and the Kaohsiung Port Terminal in Taiwan, both of which began construction in 2013. The Kaohsiung Port Terminal received the 2014 Progressive Architecture

Award. The firm celebrated the grand opening of Taipei Music Center in Taiwan in 2020. Their O-14 tower, a 22-story exoskeletal office building in Dubai completed in 2012, has received numerous international honors, including an AIA Design Award, the Concrete Industry Board's 2009 Award of Merit and the American Council of Engineering Companies' 2009 Diamond Award. A comprehensive monograph of the building, entitled *O-14: Projection and Reception*, was released in 2013 in collaboration with AA Publications.

Jesse Reiser and Nanako Umemoto have received numerous awards for their speculative work and built projects, including the Chrysler Award for Excellence in Design, the Academy Award in Architecture by the American Academy of Arts and Letters, the Presidential Citation and John Hejduk Award from the Cooper Union, and the USA Booth Fellowship from United States Artists for Architecture & Design. They published the Atlas of Novel Tectonics in 2006, and released the Japanese version in 2008. The firm's first comprehensive monograph, *Projects and Their Consequences*, was published in 2019 and traces 30 years of innovative, multidisciplinary investigations of form, structure, technique, and planning.

Mar 30: Dales Traveling Fellowship Winners Announced, and Architecture Faculty PechaKucha

Join us for this exciting event as we announce the winners of the E. Lewis Dales Traveling Fellowship, followed by a night of PechaKucha presentations by Weitzman Architecture faculty members.

Learn more about the research and ideas of our faculty members in the PechaKucha format. This event will be hosted by Associate Professor Ferda Kolatan and will feature presentations from Chair of Architecture Winka Dubbeldam, Rashida Ng, Robert Stuart-Smith, Laia Mogas-Soldevila, Nate Hume, Andrew Saunders, Richard Farley, Masoud Akbarzadeh, Kevin Cannon, Danielle Willems, Annette Fierro, Gisela Baurmann, Brian DeLuna, and Daniel Markiewicz. PechaKucha is a storytelling format where the presenter talks through 20 slides for 20 seconds each.

The E. Lewis Dales Traveling Fellowships are awarded each year to select students of the second-year class in the Master of Architecture program for travel abroad in the summer before their final year of study. Students are selected for the Fellowship through an anonymous portfolio competition judged during the first week of the spring semester by a committee comprised of standing and core studio faculty. The Fellowship enables the Department to encourage students to begin the documentation and presentation of their work, a process that is integral to the development of a design ethic and to interviewing for a job.

Mar 31: The Cunningham Lecture: John Tuomey, A Celebration of David Leatherbarrow

In 2020, David Leatherbarrow was awarded the Topaz Medallion, the highest award given by the AIA and ASCA for excellence in architectural education, and in 2021, he achieved the rank of professor emeritus. The program includes a series of tributes by architecture faculty followed by a lecture by his longtime friend John Tuomey.

Leatherbarrow has taught theory and design at Penn since 1984, and before that at Cambridge University and the University of Westminster (formerly PCL) in England. He lectures throughout the world and has held honorary professorships in Denmark, Brazil, and China. In prior years, he was also the recipient of the Visiting Scholar Fellowship from the Canadian Center of Architecture (1997–98) and two Fulbright Fellowships. His books include: *Building time: architecture, event, and experience; 20th Century Architecture*; *Three Cultural Ecologies* (with R. Wesley), *Architecture Oriented Otherwise; Topographical Stories, Surface Architecture* (with Mohsen Mostafavi); *Uncommon Ground; Roots of Architectural Invention;* and *On Weathering: The Life of Buildings in Time*. His research focuses on history and theory of architecture, gardens, and the city.

John Tuomey was managing director of Group 91 Architects, an architects' collaborative who designed the masterplan for the regeneration of Temple Bar as Dublin's cultural quarter. O'Donnell + Tuomey designed two buildings within the quarter, completed in 1996.

He has had a leading involvement in architectural education, teaching in the studios at UCD Architecture from 1980–2019. He was the inaugural Professor of Architectural Design at UCD from 2008–19. He was chair of external examiners at the Architectural Association London for many years as well as at the Universities of Cambridge and East London. He has taught and lectured widely in European schools of architecture and at North American universities.

Apr 2022

					01	02
03	04	05	06	07	08	09
10	11	12	13	14	15	16
17	(18)	19	20	21	(22	23)
24	25	26	27	28	29	30

Apr 18: Dr. Hitoshi Abe: March 11th, 2011...Community and Architecture

In collaboration with The Center for East Asian Studies, the Department of Architecture welcomes Dr. Hitoshi Abe.

Eleven years have passed since the Great East Japan Earthquake. The coastal areas of Tohoku were devastated by the massive earthquake, tsunami, and nuclear power plant accident, and so many efforts and resources were poured into the area to reconstruct its community in the past 11 years. This talk will review the reconstruction process from an architect's eye and discuss architects' role in the process, especially its relationship with the community through the speaker's own experience and works.

Hitoshi Abe is a professor and former Chair in the Department of Architecture and Urban Design at UCLA and the Director of the UCLA Paul I. and Hisako Terasaki Center for Japanese Studies. He also holds the Terasaki Chair for Contemporary Japanese Study. Since 1992, when Dr. Abe won first prize in the Miyagi Stadium Competition and established Atelier Hitoshi Abe, he has maintained an active international design practice based in Sendai, Japan. As a successful designer and educator who continuously lectures and publishes throughout his career, Hitoshi Abe has earned a position among the leaders in the field of architecture and urban design for his ability to initiate productive interdisciplinary collaborations and establish professional partnerships with various constituencies.

Apr 22–23: Precarity: Conference on Architectural Research at the limits of technology, project-making with PhD Chair F. Trubiano

'Precarity' is a difficult-to-overlook condition of life in the 21st century. Almost as if by design, the circumstances of global capital—whose extractive industries and financial arrangements imperil labor, material supply chains, and all who engage with the built environment—have rendered architecture highly vulnerable in the face of material and data waste, and the accelerated specter of environmental collapse. While such actualities pose difficulties for those who practice, there is perhaps no more urgent a moment to reckon with inherited Enlightenment epistemologies that have led to this point, and to imagine alternative models of architectural research and scholarship. 'Precarity' can begin to trace the outlines of a new framework that address architecture's extended milieu and the outcomes it produces. This conference hosted by the PhD Program in Architecture of the Weitzman School of Design encourages the exploration of ideas aligned with the theme of 'Precarity.' It features papers that examine the theme of Precarity from the perspectives of technology, project-making, and history/theory. The conference represents an opportunity to question the boundaries of architecture, as well as to seek interdisciplinary contributions that interrogate multiple perspectives.

May 2022

01 02 03 04 05 06 07
08 09 10 11 12 13 14
15 16 17 18 (19 20) 21
22 23 24 25 26 27 28
29 30 31

May 19–20: CONSTRUCTIONS AND LOCATIONS: Festschrift in Honor of David Leatherbarrow

Presented by the Stuart Weitzman School of Design of the University of Pennsylvania, the Department of Architecture, and the PhD Program in Architecture.

It is with much pleasure that the Weitzman School of Design invites you to a Festschrift in honor of Professor David Leatherbarrow, our colleague, teacher, and ACSA TOPAZ Medal winner (2020). Over two days, Constructions and Locations will celebrate the many highlights of an illustrious career dedicated to architectural education. It will offer its participants many opportunities to share in each other's company and to engage in spirited dialogue on the practice of architectural theory. Invited speakers include Joseph Rykwert, Carlos Eduardo Comas, John Dixon Hunt, Marion Weiss, James Corner, Billie Tsien, Grace La, and others.

News

Jan 2022: Winners of the Albert F. Schenck-Henry Gillette Woodman Prize for First-Year MArch Students Announced

This year's theme, Fresh Air, prompted students to redesign an intersection within a provided map to feature two eateries, while considering the sidewalk and the streets in between.

The goal of the project was to provide the community with a function it may not even be aware that it needs, with consideration to why a business needs an expanded street presence, and how that expanded street presence can make a meaningful contribution to the urban experience of the neighborhood.

This year's winners include:

Team #5: Bohan Lang, Ross Mackenzie, Qin Wen
Team #17: Danny Jarabek, Tobie Soumekh, Owen Wang
Team #19: Francisco Anaya, Telmen Bayasgalan, Zihan Li
Team #6: Jinyi Huang, Ravina Puri, Valerie Tse
Team #20: Chongyan Chen, Yuanyuan Lin, Kelvin Vu
Team #23: Shengnan Gao, Maxwell Lent, Shiyi Qi
Team #32: Rachel Seto, Khang Truong, Yanjie Zhang

Honorable Mentions:

Team #9: Zhixuan Song, Sophie Wojtalewicz, Grace Infante
Team #18: Jessica Wong, Siyu Gao, Weijun Peng
Team #22: Hedi Mao, Shenyi Zhang, Xiayu Zhao
Team #24: Liujie Lu, Diego Martin, Jun Yue
Team #29: Daniel Lutze, Boyu Xiao, Rongxuan Zhou

The rainbow-colored *Cirrhilabrus finifenmaa*, also known as the Rose-Veiled Fairy Wrasse, is discovered in the reefs of the Maldives.

Researchers find explorer Ernest Shackleton's *Endurance*, one of the greatest lost shipwrecks, which sank in 1915 during his explorations of the Antarctic.

Feb 2022: Weitzman Students Win the 2022 HOK Futures Competition

Three teams of Master of Architecture students were awarded all three top honors in the 2022 HOK Futures Competition:

First Place: "Jumbled Synergies" by David Perrine (MArch'23) and Kyle Troyer (MArch'23). The project refers to a delicate, yet untidy mixed aggregation of programmatic and spatial synergies. Unpredictable relationships in a jumbled landscape question the original model of the winery, offering a synergy between making, entrepreneurship, and community.

Second Place: "Frizzante" by Rachel Seto (MArch'24) and Sharlene Yulita (MArch'24). Faced with the imminent threat of flooding due to climate change, this urban winery and incubator space acts as a catalyst for social connection, creating an ecosystem that bridges Manayunk's past, present, and future.

Third Place: "The Leaf on the Bank" by Chen Su (MArch'24) and Yuhang Tao (MArch'24). Manayunk is historically known for its textile industry, and in recent decades the former factory area has become a petri dish for the development of small businesses. The new building can be elevated to reduce the damage caused by the flood season, taking into account the actual situation of the site, and adding to the groundedness of the project.

Mar 2022: Architecture Students Win the BLTa Student Design Competition

2022 BLT a Design Competition, Building A New History, challenged contestant teams to tackle an adaptive reuse and addition to one of BLT's historically designated buildings, The International House. Three teams of first-year Architecture students won the competition. Designs were judged by the clarity of the overall concept, connectivity to the surrounding community, core skills in design, and an oral presentation.

First Place: Wenliu Tu and Luxin Zhong with The Hug. This project respects the historical brutalist building, and adds a new vibe to it by having elements "hugging" the original building.

Second Place: Ming Chen (MArch'24) and Vicky Zheng (MArch'24) with International Housing. The old building was manipulated into a new style. All design methods are to create a balance between old and new, artificial and natural, and to respond to the existing brutalist architecture.

Third Place: Maria Jose and Maitrey Prajapati with Reimagining Connectivity: Cluster Communities. As international students ourselves, our proposal envisions this building as a living history. The enlarged program features thematic affordable-housing clusters nested in shared spaces, allowing for ample co-living spaces and semi-public zones for community development.

Apr 2022: Weitzman Students Chosen for Metropolis magazine's "Metropolis Future 100"

Six Weitzman Master of Architecture students were among the 19 graduate awardees selected for Metropolis magazine's second-ever "Future 100" showcase. Sponsored by CannonDesign, Daltile, Formica, Interface, Keilhauer, Rapt, Sherwin-Williams, and SOM, the Metropolis Future 100 is conceived as a showcase of the most-talented students in the Class of 2022. Submissions came from top schools in North America, which Metropolis notes were a "diverse group—with many identifying as female, BIPOC, LGBTQIA+, or neurodiverse—[and] they are leaders on their campuses, advocating for equity and inclusion through their work and extracurriculars." The Metropolis team selected 56 interior design and 44 architecture students. Nominated by Andrew Saunders, associate professor of architecture and director of MArch program at Weitzman, the featured students include Dongqi Chen (MArch'22), Umar Mahmood (MArch'22), Danny Ortega (MArch'22), Dario Sabidussi (MArch'22), Peik Shelton (MArch'22), and Yuxuan Xiong (MArch'22). Metropolis commented that these honors "speak loudly of [the Weitzman Master of Architecture] program and the quality of the work students are generating." The winning student portfolios are featured on the Metropolis website and their work appears in the March/April issue of the print edition.

May 2022: Weitzman professor Simon Kim co-creates "Beyond the Binary: A Meditation on Humans and Machines"

The Mendelssohn Chorus of Philadelphia (MCP) presented "Beyond the Binary," a new choral cantata, and a choral work about artificial intelligence, by composer Andrea Clearfield, libretto by Ellen Frankel, and newly designed percussion and electronic instruments by David Kontak. As part of this production, MCP collaborated with students from the University of Pennsylvania GRASP Lab and Weitzman Architecture, led by Mark Yim and Simon Kim, to showcase working robot prototypes. In an innovative partnership, audience members will have opportunities to interact with robotic sculptures and wearables both on-stage and placed throughout the venue. These custom-fabricated prototypes are being designed and built by students of the world-famous University of Pennsylvania's GRASP Lab and the Weitzman School of Design's department of architecture. "The piece starts out with this duality – the pros and cons of robots," Clearfield said. "As the piece goes on it starts to nod to other possibilities: What if we went beyond yes and no, on or off, one and zero, black and white, male and female, to an expanded way of thinking?"

May 2022: Laia Mogas-Soldevila "Bio Quotidian" wins 2022 The Sachs Program for Arts Innovation Grant

Now in its fifth year, The Sachs Program for Arts Innovation announced its 2022 cycle of grantees, contributing to a total of $288,000 in funding for the year and 49 grants. The Sachs Program launched in 2017 thanks to a $15 million donation from Keith and Kathy Sachs, who are Penn alumni.

Faculty and staff had four projects awarded this year under the Independent Creative Production Grants category, with up to $8,000 awarded for a project. As one of these project grantees, Laia Mogas-Soldevila will develop "Bio Quotidian," a collection of everyday objects made with innovative biomaterials like shrimp shells, fungi roots, algae cell walls, and other biodegradable materials that don't damage the environment. The idea is to bridge the arts and sciences while also introducing a new bio-aesthetic culture.

Jun 2022: UPenn Set to Receive $2.4M in Funding to Research Turning Buildings into Carbon Storage Structures

The University of Pennsylvania has been selected to receive $2.4 million in funding from the US Department of Energy Advanced Research Projects Agency-Energy (ARPA-E). The funding is part of the ARPA-E HESTIA program, which prioritizes overcoming barriers associated with carbon-storing buildings, including scarce, expensive, and geographically limited building materials. The goal of the HESTIA program is to increase the total amount of carbon stored in buildings to create carbon sinks, which absorb more carbon from the atmosphere than released during the construction process.

The University of Pennsylvania, in collaboration with Texas A&M University, The City College of New York, Kieran Timberlake, and Sika, will design carbon-negative, medium-sized building structures by developing a high-performance structural system for carbon absorption and storage over buildings' lifespans.

The team will use a novel carbon-absorbing concrete mixture as a building material, and design and assemble a high-performance structural system with minimized mass and construction waste, and maximized surface area. The parts will be prefabricated using robotic 3D printing technology.

The project team includes: Masoud Akbarzadeh (PI), director of the Polyhedral Structures Laboratory and assistant professor of architecture, University of Pennsylvania; Dorit Aviv (co-PI), director of the Thermal Architecture Lab and assistant professor of architecture, University of Pennsylvania; Shu Yang (co-PI), Joseph Bordogna Professor of Engineering and Applied Science and chair of the Department of Materials Science and Engineering, University of Pennsylvania; Peter Psarras, research assistant professor in chemical and biomolecular engineering, University of Pennsylvania; Zheng O'Neil (co-PI), associate professor of mechanical engineering, Texas A&M University; Mohammad Bolhassani (co-PI), assistant professor, The City College of New York; Billie Faircloth (co-PI), partner and research director, KieranTimberlake, and Ryan Welch, principal, KieranTimberlake; and Didier Lootens, head of research and development, Sika Switzerland.

MSD and PhD Programs

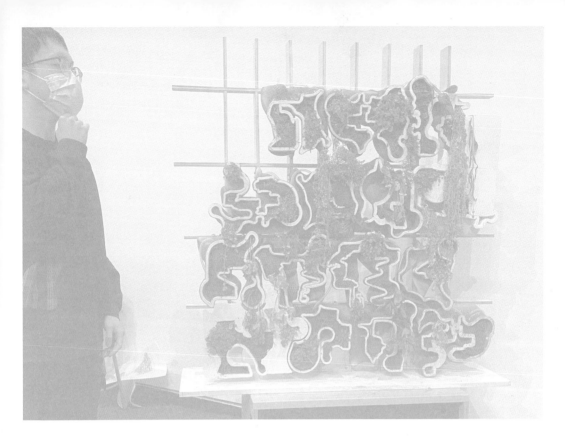

MSD in Advanced Architectural Design

Director:
Ali Rahim

The Master of Science in Design: Advanced Architectural Design is a three-semester post-graduate program that is focused on design innovation and material practice grounded in real-world application. The discipline of architecture is foregrounded, and issues including building assembly, structure, and organization are fore-fronted and combined with the latest technology and techniques to rethink architectural precedent. Technology has matured within architecture over the last 25 years. Through the process of maturation, key issues of the discipline were neglected in favor of creativity enhancing abstraction. Abstract experiments were fundamental to rethinking the design process, and material form was sidelined for virtual analogs. This was counter intuitive, as the centrality of buildings and their construction in the discipline was left behind.

The AAD program recenters the building in architectural pedagogy. Contemporary Theory focuses on theory starting with the digital turn in architecture in the early 1990s, considering a broad spectrum of conditions including labor, as, for instance, studied through the floor plan and section of Zaha Hadid's BMW factory and office building in Leipzig, Germany.

Design Innovation explores the narrow use of Artificial Intelligence directed at material assembly and building facades. Visual Literacy makes a bridge between architecture and representation techniques within contemporary culture, foregrounding their usefulness in addressing disciplinary issues.

Reinvigoration through narrow applications of technology has the potential to continually open up the discipline to contemporary culture, allowing it to affect and inflect the techniques that we use in more critical ways. This enables a richer and more rigorous architecture engaged with intersectional cultural issues including climate change, racial justice, and the non-human. The robust nature of the program empowers students to think creatively and gives them the tools and knowledge necessary to make incisive buildings with material impact.

Faculty:

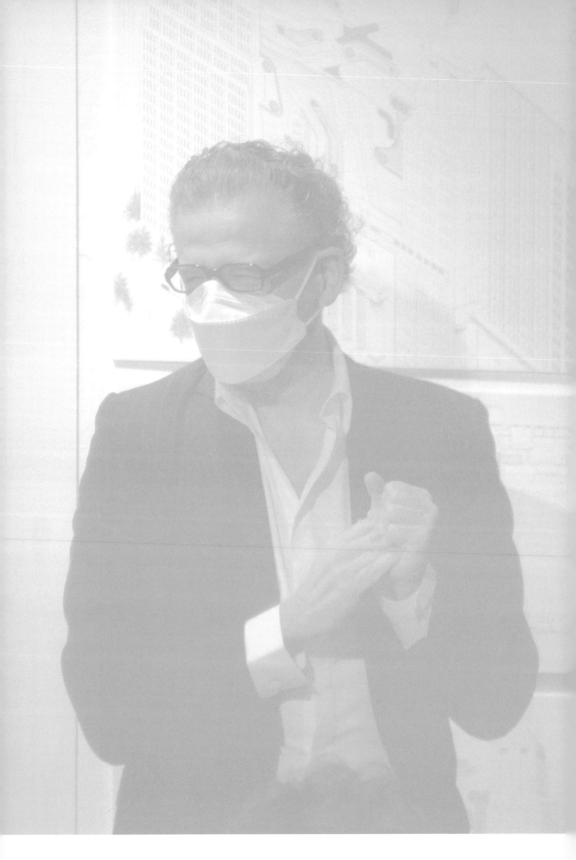

MSD in Advanced Architectural Design:
COINNEXT: The Future of the NY Stock Exchange

Faculty: Ali Rahim
Teaching Assistant: Caleb White

This studio speculates that a new typology can help sustain New York City's financial global leadership in the world. New York cannot solely rely on import and export economies with the uncertainty of political pressures that affect the prices of goods and services. New York and other cities need to re-invent existing networks to be able to compete with trade barriers that are cumbersome and willfully destroying the growth of the global economy while having ramifications on New York City.

   The MSD-AAD studio speculates upon New York City continuing its financial leadership in the world and simultaneously having the the local economy of the city thrive. The center of the US and global economy is the stock market which started as an exchange for goods and developed into a marketplace that exchanged shares of American companies. The stock market over time has amassed international companies which have been attracted because of increased liquidity, diversified investors, more analyst coverage and the shares trade in US currency, and gain access to 27 percent of the world's consumers. Due to uncertainty in global relations, some foreign governments are pressuring their own companies to de-list from the New York Stock Exchange to add volatility to the financial market. The uncertainty affects stock prices, and the amount of capital companies have access to for growth and Research and Development. In the long term the withdrawal of these substantial global companies will affect the NYSE adversely. To continue its global leadership the NYSE needs to expand its core business.

Featured Student Work:

MSD in Advanced Architectural Design:
Envelope Stuffing

Faculty: Nate Hume
Teaching Assistant: Matthew White

The studio explored stuffing envelopes as a means to subvert traditional ideas about the binary of the inside and outside at several registers within architecture. One of the fundamental understandings of buildings is that through enclosure they provide a barrier from the outside. That includes not just the space on the other side of the wall, but the perceived divide created between public and private domains and the constructed environment from the natural environment.

In the 20th century, building envelopes continually shrunk until at mid-century they were thin glass sheets. This ultimately proved harmful to the environment because of the systems necessary to maintain comfort as well as the jump in energy costs especially following the '70s oil crisis. By the '90s there started to be experiments with double envelopes and this rethickening continues with strategies such as superinsulation. The studio was interested in engaging with these thickened assemblies not just for mechanical systems and efficiency but also their spatial and programmatic potential.

In recent years, the binary between building materials that come from the "outside" and those from the "inside" has become far more nuanced and ambiguous. Historically, building materials have either been natural materials sourced from raw, organic matter or artificial materials being produced from chemical or factory processing. Today's material culture exists largely in a liminal territory between the two states: the studio was interested in working with these hybridizations as well as rethinking traditional building materials and their assemblies through organization, scale, and chromatic and textural qualities. Specifically, the projects worked with clay and robotics to mix old and new technologies in forming their envelope systems. The students developed full-scale facade mockups to develop these ideas.

MSD in Advanced Architectural Design:
Reduced-Waste Assembly

Faculty: Masoud Akbarzedah
Teaching Assistant: Yuxuan Wang

The architecture and construction industry are indeed responsible for serious waste problems. The construction process leaves significant waste and debris, including the process of demolishing structures to construct new buildings at the end of the life cycle and the waste and debris resulting from the material processing and preparation for new construction. They all contribute significantly to the waste problems globally. To address this problem and eliminate waste, the continual use and reuse of resources should be at the core of the design process. Consequently, an architect should carefully select the construction material and analyze the method of construction and preparation of the materials to minimize the waste and allow for re-usability in the future. Moreover, the building design and use characteristics should also be involved in this process. Only then, a circular design process may be established, which would be at the intersection of the material properties and building design and use.

This studio aims to investigate innovative methods of design, assembly, and disassembly of prefabricated parts that meet the functional requirements of a mid-rise building. The assembly method should evolve progressively to ensure the structural integrity of the building and consider environmental factors of the site. The overarching objective of the studio is to: (i) learn from the ancient local methods of assembly; (ii) propose innovative, site-specific prefabricated methods of construction and labor; (iii) minimize waste in both pre-production and post-production; (iv) facilitate reusability of the parts in the future; and (v) value the cultural factors that form the architectural function.

Featured Student Work:

MSD in Advanced Architectural Design:
The Contemporary Arabesque.
A New Agha Khan Museum of Islamic
and Contemporary Art for Dubai

Faculty: Hina Jamelle
Teaching Assistant: Caleb White

This studio will examine eastern Islamic and Contemporary Art
and its relation to the formulation of architecture by using
digital techniques in an opportunistic fashion for the generation of growth and evaluation of patterns in the development
of form. Digital techniques allow us to deal with the full complexity of material systems that lead to effects that are greater
than the sum of their parts. Through an exploration of two-
dimensional patterns, two-and-a-half-dimensional techniques,
and then 3D spatial exploration, students will develop layered
and complex formations that address disciplinary questions of
flatness, relief, and complex three dimensionality.

   The program for the studio is the design of the new Aga
Khan Museum of Islamic and Contemporary Art in Dubai.
U.A.E. His Highness Aga Khan, spiritual leader of Shia Ismaili
Muslims, has planned to build a number of major museums
around the world for Islamic art, artifacts, and contemporary
art that align with the Ismaili community's mission to offer
new perspectives into Islamic civilizations by weaving together
cross-cultural threads throughout history. The Aga Khan
Museum offers visitors a window into worlds unknown or
unfamiliar: the artistic, intellectual, and scientific heritage
of Muslim civilizations across the centuries, from the Iberian
Peninsula to China. Its mission is to foster a greater understanding and appreciation of the contribution that Muslim
civilizations have made to world heritage.

Featured Student Work:

MSD in Advanced Architectural Design:
Fragments

Faculty: Florencia Pita
Assistant Faculty: Katarina Marjanovic

This studio focused on the topic of 'Fragments' or parts, through the smallest of architectural elements, namely the brick. The concept being that the brick is but a fragment of architecture, it carries such a rich and profound history, and therefore represents a powerful potential, for space, material, and landscape. We researched its history and also advanced it to its future, and found design innovations that sprung from this ancient object.

The focus on the terra-cotta brick references Argentina's long history with this material. Brick construction is one of the most-used building systems in Argentina; from the most humble of dwellings to the tallest of buildings, this material can be found in every city throughout the country. Researching a myriad of case studies, from historical to current work, the studio learned the craft by creating detail section models and drawings, informing the formal attributes of the project at large.

Featured Student Work:

MSD in Advanced Architectural Design:
Desert Reliefs

Faculty: Andrew Saunders
Co-Instructor: Sharvari Mharte

The second studio in the MSD-AAD is charged to take on the architectural detail. Desert Reliefs approaches detail through the lens of relief. Adolf Hildebrand describes three types of relief in the Problem of Form (1907): bas (low) relief that is more 2D based, high relief that is more 3D, and figural relief that is fully figural. Although traditional relief is typically achieved through a subtractive process of carving stone, 20th artist Louise Nevelson demonstrated throughout her career that the construction of relief can also occur through an additive process of composting and compiling found objects and painting them uniform to focus on shade and shadow to build depth through shadows creating object-on-object reliefs in all three categories.

The studio begins by modeling and combining a range of artifact objects from desert culture of the American Southwest. As a novel way of rethinking figure/ground relationships through figure/figure reliefs the studio deploys convolutional neural networks to merge newly constructed reliefs with the topography of the desert. Features from both the artifact reliefs and desert landscape are redistributed and hybridized as a new ground condition to motive both site and building strategies for a desert resort.

The studio analyzes recent development of desert resorts and speculates on how this trend can situate itself in the American desert. The studio traveled and toured major National parks and land art sites while surveying the unique topography through drone-based photogrammetry. The resultant resorts proposals posit unique forms of retreat through the hybridization of indigenous factors including environment and material culture. Multiscale details of desert relief operate as the primary vehicle of novel architectural expression.

Featured Student Work:

NEW YORK STOCK EXCHANGE
Hui Mi & Xiaohan Zhao

The New York Stock Exchange of the future is imagined as a mechanical system where the machinery is treated as exhibits and the space as an exhibition hall for people to experience and perceive the relationship between the machine and the body. The design features a tilting system with different materials and textures used for different functions, with a surface connecting the façade and roof that contrasts with the mechanical space and inhabitable space. The volume of the surface is for circulation and the materials are distributed separately for people to interact with the surrounding mechanical systems. Escalators connect the independent inhabitant space and the mechanical space, allowing passengers to move from one system to another, such as from a mining system to a cooling tower and then to a server. The building structures are designed for different functions and the façade and top of the building are continuous, creating a continuous and 3D space.

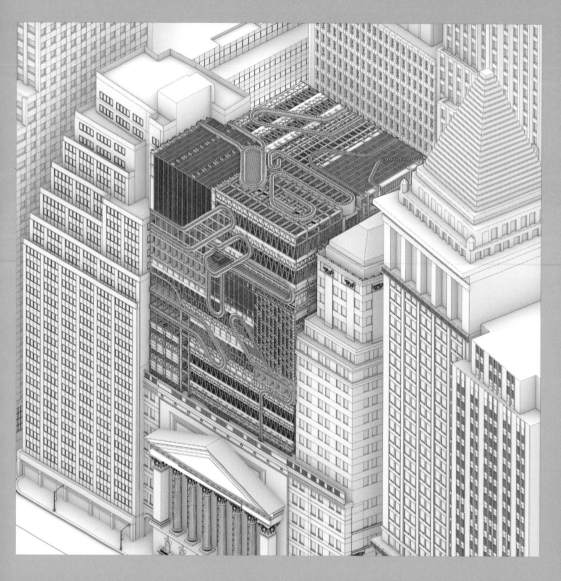

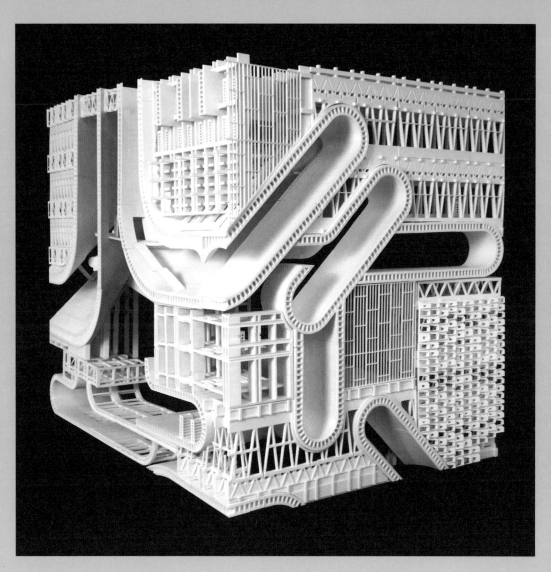

NYSE NFT
Zhaohui Wang & Shiyu Jin

Through the utilization of various architectural styles, the NYSE NFT Museum project intends to present information to visitors regarding the sophisticated technology that underpins the NFT system. The architecture of the museum investigates the possibility of using seams and vaults as means to navigate the structure and aesthetics of the building. Either the vaults are revealed to be human-occupiable rooms, or they are kept hidden as mechanical spaces for things like air circulation and server storage. The exterior of the building contains a variety of patterns as well as apertures for vents and air ducts. Human spaces, server spaces, and ventilation service areas make up the interior layout of the structure. These three categories of space are separated from one another throughout the building. All of the programs are held together by the continuous seams, which also facilitate linkages between the programs. The structure is supported by four pillars, which results in the creation of a public area as well as open access to the interior.

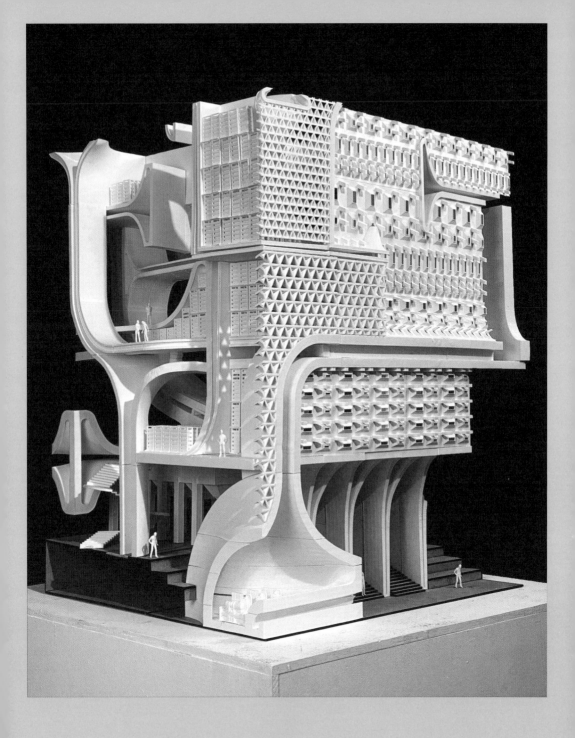

ENVELOPE STUFFING
Yiming Zhao & Zheyuan Fu

In our project, pockets of space within the thick walls are redefined as new zones for plants and people, letting the exterior space extend into the interior, thereby blurring the boundary between what is the inside and the outside. We developed different geometric profiles and composed them to develop spatial figures at the scale of the wall and the detail of the planter. Through fabrication methods utilizing the robotic lab, we investigated how the shape and texture of these ceramic planters could be manipulated and form the blurred boundary condition.

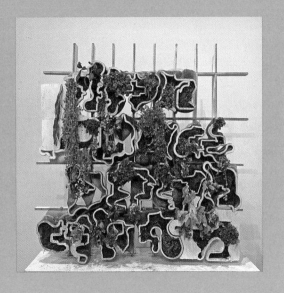

ENVELOPE STUFFING
Han Chan & Zihao Jin

Using the robotic arm to print
clay, the design developed
a hydroponic wall system for
a new agricultural center
in Philadelphia. The design
developed in a series of
H-shaped clay containers
which compose a façade for the
center. The design investigated
different glazing effects to
accentuate the unique geometry of the planters. The physical
wall detail model presents
how containers are attached to
the wall frame and how the
hydroponic technique works.

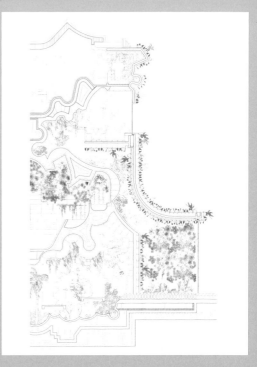

REDUCED-WASTE ASSEMBLY
Joonhyuk Yun & Lichen Zhu

Located next to a migrant worker's dormitory in the northern suburbs of Singapore, the project aims to provide an environment for migrant workers with a wealth of recreational, cultural, and educational opportunities to communicate with residents, thereby enhancing social justice. The design adopts a prefabricated strategy. Learning from the ancient Chinese Dougong system, a branch-shaped structure was developed that gradually changed the structure's scale in height. We take advantage of CLT's easy extension and structural strength, simultaneously creating a cantilever system on the periphery and atrium spaces in the center. The scale change improves the structure's efficiency, reduces waste, and forms inhabitable spaces of different dimensions.

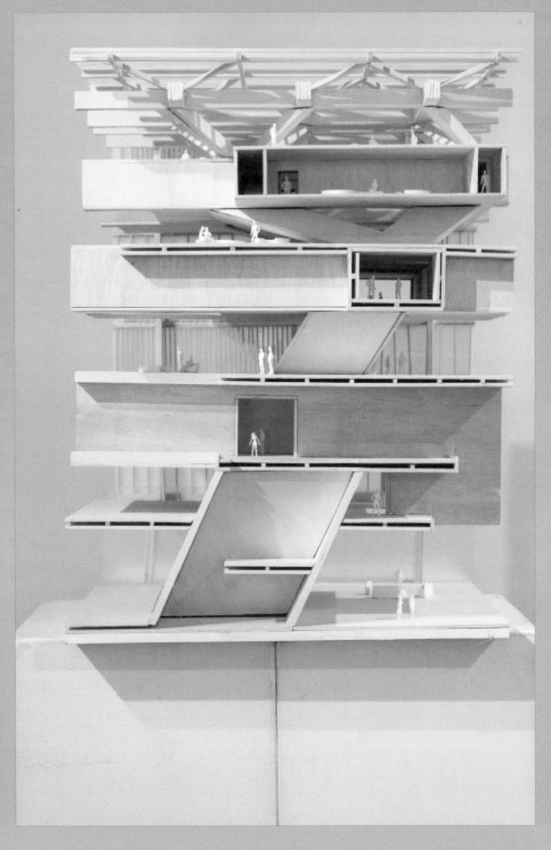

MSD: AAD   Masoud Akbarzedah

REDUCED-WASTE
ASSEMBLY
Ruili Wang & Dayu Long

structure combining
hogan's stacking logic
and Muqarnas' geometry.

The design explored the
marriage of two ancient
construction methods.
The initial investigation was
based on the hogan construction method, a sacred home
for Navajo people. A particular way of stacking forms
the roof structure of hogan.
The secondary inspiration
comes from Muqarnas in Iran,
typically applied to domes'
undersides as a structural
ornament. The project
proposes an architectural

NEW AGA KHAN MUSEUM
OF ISLAMIC AND
CONTEMPORARY ART
Zijie Wei & Yaxin Sun

By analyzing an historical
arabesque artwork through
analysis, diagramming, and
machine-learning tools,
a series of shapes of geometry
and prototype of space can
be established. The black
edge as the dominant element
uses pure-black marble, and
other materials present
different levels of concrete
and textured stone from dark
gray to light gray to white
according to light and shadow,
so as to increase the atmosphere of different depths of
the interior space. Spaces are
then generated from the
harmonious prototype and
organized with a rethinking of
a museum programming and
interior spaces. The relationship between interior and
exterior is controlled by the
similar logic underlining
the arabesque artwork which
makes the experience inside
the building dynamic. The
material of the building is
inspired by the vernacular
architecture, which uses three
different materials to establish the transition of the
building and environment.
The result is a rethinking of
the role of the museum in
presenting, displaying, and
experiencing contemporary
art for a global audience.

NEW AGA KHAN MUSEUM OF ISLAMIC AND CONTEMPORARY ART
Zihang Wang & Pinguo Wang

By analyzing an historical arabesque artwork through analysis, diagraming and machine learning tools, a series of shapes of geometry and prototype of space can be established. Spaces are then generated from the harmonious prototype and organized with a rethinking of a museum programming and interior spaces. The relationship between interior and exterior is controlled by the similar logic underlining the arabesque artwork which makes the experience inside the building dynamic. The material of the building is inspired by the vernacular architecture, which uses three different materials to establish the transition of the building and environment. The result is a rethinking of the role of the museum in presenting, displaying, and experiencing contemporary art for a global audience.

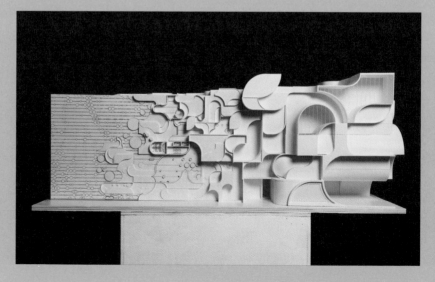

ANTIQUE WAVE
Tianyi Yin & Jiahui Shi

This work uses two basic traditional brick-making materials and one basic brick shape as the entry point for the preliminary material exploration. While retaining the bare terracotta and gray clay, resin is introduced as a third material. Clear resin bricks let more light pass into the interior. Mixing gray clay and terracotta with resin creates a third material that has the color of the original brick dust and the solid and smooth qualities of resin.

The first shape inspiration came from semi-circular bricks often used as windows and walls in classical Chinese gardens, which are stable standing up and rotated 90 degrees to the side. They are translucent standing up and opaque on the side. We then introduced two more types of bricks: hole square and double-hole rectangular, whose modulus is the same as semi-circular bricks. It also uses up to 10 combinations of colors, sizes, and shapes of the three types of bricks to form a surface texture with wave-like dynamic curves.

The scheme introduces curved concrete floor slabs, forming a wave effect from layer to layer. It allows the brick to climb and extend between layers. The concrete also assists the brick in reinforcing the 3D curved effect. In the section cut, each house has its personality. Brick walls integrate into residents' lives as partition walls or roofs with curved shapes. The semi-permeable brick wall can also be used as a fulcrum for climbing plants, bringing more life to the residents.

FRAGMENT POSSIBILITIES
Dongjun Wang &
Ranran Zhang

The concept of the Fragments Possibilities project is transforming the smallest architectural element, brick, into various functions. For example, this project transformed bricks into structures, apertures, balconies, seats, planters, and landscape patterns. In addition, the project creates different connections between each architectural element, like floors and brick walls, walls and columns, building and landscapes. As a result, the buildings' pieces are 'knitted' to each other. The project contains three communal spaces. There is a gym, a communal kitchen and an outdoor barbeque space on the second floor; a small vegetable garden on the sixth floor; and a large roof garden. Each room inside this building has its characteristics. Therefore, there are various types of life inside this building.

The physical model contains 8,500 bricks. The bricks were cast with resin and different gradient colors of mica powder. In addition, the model made opacity contrast; for example, transparent, translucent, and opaque.

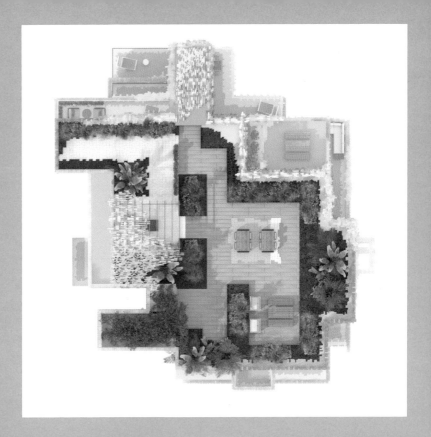

OASIS
Yujing Jiao & Ling Lin

We want to focus on hidden desert areas, that kind of experience of discovering, like finding a secret oasis in the desert. Our conceptual model is hidden in the desert, embedded in a valley with rocks, layers, and gaps that generate secret spaces. Our CNN research shows organic surfaces in the foreground, and gaps, grids, steps, all kinds of geometries in the background. We created a conceptual relief model that floats, creating a space underneath. Then we transformed our conceptual model into architecture. We took desert crystal and desert rose as raw material for their inherent construction and structural logic. Then we assembled this piece of façade, and it can be seen as both a skin and a structure itself. Then we transformed this into other architectural components, like facade, stairs, parapets, and on the interior, the furniture. The CNN relief model motivated us from the conceptual framework, all the way to a bed in the suite! During this process, we also extracted techniques from CNN images, such as the folding, stepping, overlapping geometries, to create a series of spaces in the chunk model—people enter the entrance from below, then layers of lobbies and gardens lead people to get through a series of spaces to the final garden on the top. This experience is all about wandering around and discovering oasis.

DESERT CHASM
Zhaohui Wang & Jessica Lyn

Our study starts with the US western desert, its cultural artifacts, and topography. We investigate three reliefs: the bas relief, the high relief, and the figural relief. We then developed a hybrid prototype model and next architectural tectonics and detail in different scales. The resort "Desert Chasm" is located less than 10 miles away from Page, AZ, and it serves as a destination of spiritual pilgrimage that aligns with the Antelope Canyon nearby. The resort features two grids: orthogonal grid and 45-degree oblique. The oblique grid with a strong figural directionality is designed as a sunken canyon pool that aims to resemble the geographical characteristics of the Antelope Canyon. The canyon pool provides an immersive experience for the visitors, while the orthogonal grid uses "fringe" relief, as it introduces merging and splitting between surfaces that produce nuance in depth and shadow. The vortex in the fringe relief lets fringe elements transitions into the oblique elements. The fuzziness of the fringe becomes a vehicle for dissolving the edges of the architecture into the surrounding landscape.

Besides programs of typical resorts like suites and pools, the resort also features an amphitheater, meditation rooms, and a workshop for craftsmanship. We apply the idea of sand-painting from the Navajo tradition, which is used as a living sacred entity, enabling mental and physical transformation. The modified material is 3D-printed GFRC panels that have texture and color of sand-movement.

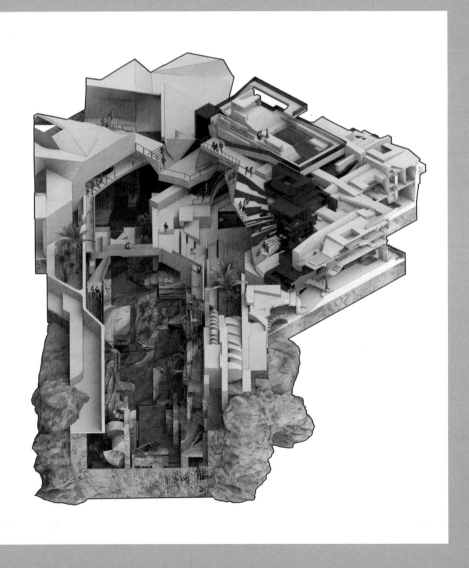

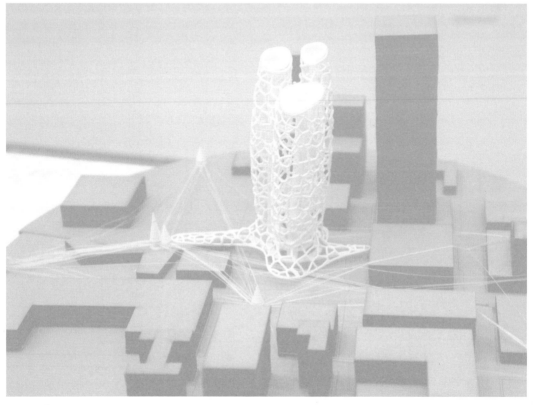

MSD in Environmental Building Design

Director: Bill Braham

The global pandemic has made clear that spatial arrangements and the cultural practices embedded in them are directly related to environmental impact. It has been clear for decades that to confront the pressing task of reducing carbon emissions, environmental building design must be integrated in the disciplinary practices of architecture. The MEBD & MSD-EBD are post-professional degree programs created to teach architects to innovate in the field of energy and environmental design, training them for a low-carbon economy.

The program's pedagogy is based on theories of ecology and sustainability, building science and performance analysis, and their integration into design workflows. The challenges of low-carbon construction demand practices and/or practitioners that can reconcile the divide between design and engineering, recognizing that architecture has to directly address environmental problems and also make the results visible and intelligible to its occupants. Five guiding principles organize the program: 1) make visible the invisible; 2) many simple models, not one complex simulation; 3) design for comfort and specific climates, not energy; 4) find the architectural narrative, not the energy score; and 5) innovate through modeling and prototyping.

The program has a two-design-studio sequence, the first on Bioclimatic Design and the second a Research Studio. The Bioclimatic studio begins with passive strategies in multiple climates, but also seeks to explore the impact of the many novel techniques that are being deployed in progressive buildings, from thermal air movement and evaporative cooling to double glass walls, diurnal and seasonal thermal storage, solar recharged desiccants, and radiant night-sky cooling. The Research studio continues that work with direct modeling and experimentation.

Faculty:

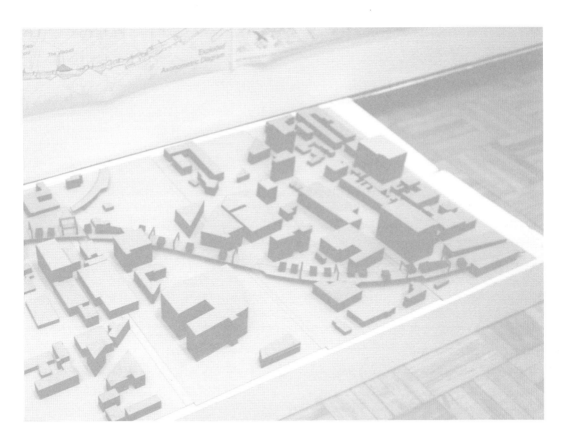

MSD in Environmental Building Design:
What Do We Know From Here?

Faculty: Billie Faircloth

A window is a need and a right; an asset and a liability. It lets in light, air, and view and lets out heat, cold, and pressure. A window is often an exception—it is a transparent figure in an otherwise opaque wall that marks the passage of time. Or it exists without comparison, having become a window-wall, a curtain-wall, that privileges expanse over enclosure. A window's shape, layers, and assembly signify the convergence of specialist knowledge. It is at once the concern of the thermodynamicist, manufacturer, engineer, and architect, as it is the physician, environmental psychologist, counselor, and anthropologist. Our understanding of a window should be technical and social; spatial and temporal; functional and ethical. The potential of a window is ever-evolving as it now signifies the interface to an otherworld for the quarantined, lonely, and at-home learner.

The 2021 EBD Research Studio will build upon the projects and findings from the 2020 EBD Research Studio and explore the demands on a window, and the total potential there-in for it to do and be more both environmentally and culturally. Studio teams will make one proposal demonstrating the comprehensive rethinking of a window informed by a program of research, assessment, design, and prototyping.

Featured Student Work:

MSD in Environmental Building Design:
2022 Bioclimatic Design Studio: Climate-Adaptive
Design for the Data Center of the Future

Faculty: Dorit Aviv
Teaching Consultant: Saeran Vasanthakumar
Teaching Assistants: Jiewei Li & Jun Xiao
CFD studies conducted in collaboration with Dr. Jihun Kim

The data center is a building typology proliferating through the past decades in an unprecedented rate to provide the ever-growing demand of cloud computing services. They are amongst the most energy-intensive building typologies, with energy demand up to 50 times that of an office building. About 40 percent of that energy load is spent on cooling and ventilation systems necessary to reject the heat produced by the servers. In order to minimize data centers' carbon footprint, this studio asks the following questions:

What would be a sustainable model for the design of the data center of the future? Is it possible to reduce reliance on mechanical systems through the use of climate-adaptive strategies? How can we envision an architecture that provides our world's growing computing needs while managing their environmental impact?

Programmatically, the data center posits a fascinating building type for architects to explore because much of the building's volume is dedicated to sheltering and providing the thermal needs of machines rather than of human beings, while people still inhabit sections of the building as well as its immediate surroundings. The studio examines the potential synergies between human and machine spaces such as co-beneficial thermodynamic cycles and other types of exchanges between them. As data centers are becoming increasingly widespread in cities and not just in remote locations, the environmental and social impact of these buildings on their immediate context are important factors to consider when reimagining their role within the urban environment.

Featured Student Work:

LIVING LAB FOR THERAPEUTIC DESIGN

Jeiwei Li, Allen Johannes, & Qi Yan

A window should be a building interface allowing end-users to take control over what they want to see and experience. The window enables end-users to orchestrate and adjust the microclimate of their space by the different layers created in the interface. It should foster a constant feedback loop and therapeutic atmospheric space. Moreover, the window should enhance an organic environment and promote a healing space.

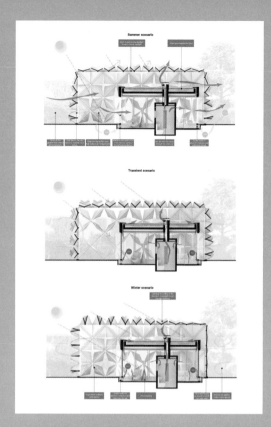

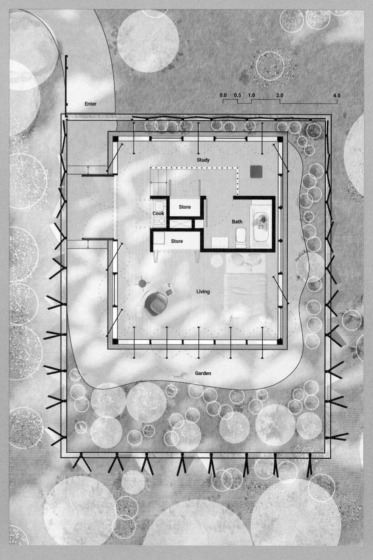

URBAN LIVING LAB
Jiayu Dong, Chenyang Li, &
Jun Xiao

A window in an urban environment should be a filter that provides control and comfort to an inhabitant. If a window can selectively filter environmental information, we can create a more comfortable indoor urban environment.

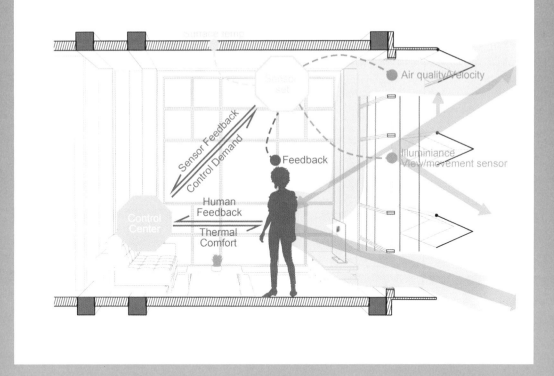

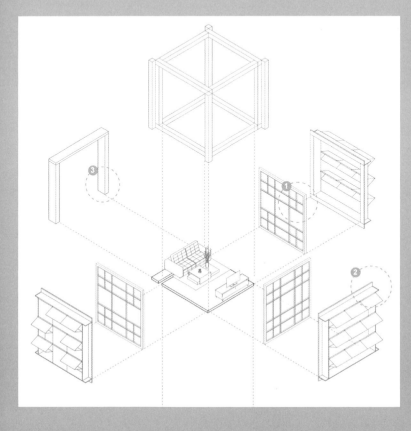

DELIRIOUS NEW YORK
Xiaoxiao Peng, Zhen Lei, & Xinru Chen

The data center is located in downtown Manhattan near the East River. The project aims to build a sustainable high-rise building in the high-density metropolitan center area. The tower massing is derived from the wind simulation of the site, and the scheme utilizes natural ventilation and buoyancy effects as the main passive cooling strategy of the building. Energy loads are further reduced through dynamic façade shading systems and a vertical landscape. The shape of the building is generated by the rotation of two main volumes enclosing a vast atrium. At the bottom is an open entrance as a plaza facing the urban context, and each transition level in the middle acts as a sky garden. The top has an overhead layer as an open viewing platform. The server rooms and offices are cross-staggered to optimize energy transfer and additional waste heat in the cold seasons is distributed to the surrounding residential buildings.

From the perspective of the urban environment, it will be an open building close to the river and park, a bioclimatic data center, and a huge green machine. So will it be a new landmark? While programmatic adjacencies of Delirious New York are unified with a curtain-wall facade, this building takes a bioclimatic approach to the building skin and internal arrangements to create a synergetic system of seemingly disparate programs. Deem it as a manifesto for a future eco-architecture, a hybrid building within the high-density vertical city.

SKY GARDEN
Yingbo Liu, Yiyan Jiang, & Shihan Shan

The data center is located in Des Moines, Iowa, in a climate with major temperature differences between cold winters and hot summers. The cooling strategy for the data center typology is critical. We are committed to maximizing the advantages of climate-adaptive properties, which can help us achieve passive cooling, as well as the use of waste heat from the data center as an energy source for heating up adjacent spaces. We first maximize the use of natural ventilation through façade openings and solar chimneys, and optimize the shading system to reduce the solar gain. Next, we consider how to reuse the waste heat generated by the servers. We use the stack effect in the chimneys at the cores of each of the tower sections to guide the heat generated by the servers to be transferred to the upper office and green house areas, in order to reduce the heating loads in the winter. The polygonal structural system is used to support the server stacks: except for the core, there is no need for additional columns inside the main body of the building.

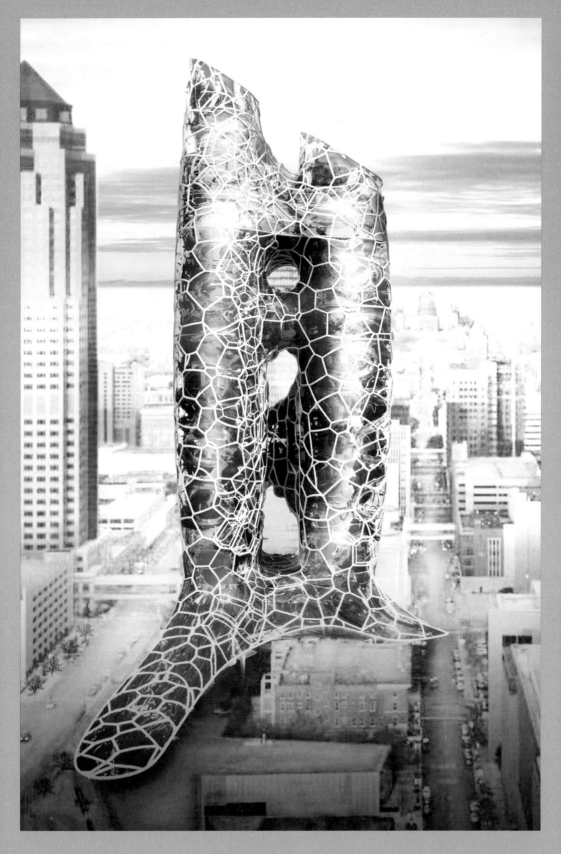

MSD: EBD   Dorit Aviv

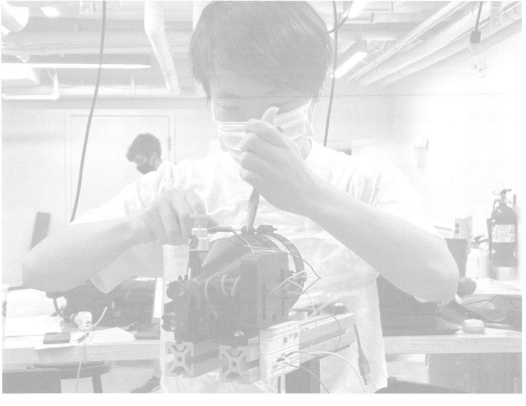

MSD in Robotics and Autonomous Systems

Director: Robert Stuart-Smith

The Master of Science in Design: Robotics and Autonomous Systems (MSD-RAS) is a one-year, post-professional degree program. The MSD-RAS is a relatively new addition to the Department of Architecture's MSD programs, with the exceptional projects presented here already leading to exciting career opportunities for our second year of graduates! The MSD-RAS aims to develop novel approaches to the design, manufacture, use, and life-cycle of architecture through creative engagement with robotics, material systems, and design-computation. The program has launched in a period where the building industry is adopting robotic approaches to prefabrication and on-site construction at an accelerating rate. Industry is motivated by the opportunities these technologies afford in improving abysmal productivity and quality levels compared to other manufacturing sectors, while reducing the time, cost, and safety hazards of building work, also addressing a skilled-labor shortage in construction workers. These greater levels of automation are also creeping into architectural software and practice, challenging established means of design production, while offering opportunities for us to think differently about the way we conceive, develop, and materialize architecture. The MSD-RAS aims to address this shifting and increasingly automated approach to architecture and construction through a fusion of creative, practical, and speculative means of design that aim to expand the agency of architecture and the architect to develop innovative and alternative means of engagement with the world at large.

The degree fosters integrative design thinking, allowing students to gain skills in advanced forms of robotic fabrication, simulation, and artificial intelligence, to develop methods for design that harness production or live adaption as a creative opportunity. Going beyond automation, the MSD-RAS explores how varying degrees of autonomy can offer sensitive, situated, and adaptive relations between design, production, and our experience of the built environment, that enable designers to re-think social, environmental, and ethical considerations not only within design outcomes, but also in the conception and making of architecture. The MSD-RAS runs over two semesters. In the Fall semester students participate in two half-semester design studios each supported by a technology course (in algorithmic design and cyber-physical systems), a theory course taught by MOMA-curator Evangelos Kotsioris, and an elective within either the design or engineering school. In Spring, students focus on the production of a single project developed within semester-length courses including a design studio, industrialization, materials and tooling course, advanced RAS programming (coding for AR/VR and real-time robotics), and a course in scientific research and writing. Throughout both semesters, design is explored primarily through the hands-on production of experimental robotically fabricated prototypes, and the synthesis of knowledge gained in theoretical and technical courses. This year, three of the four Spring-semester project teams opted to submit research papers to world-leading conferences, with two accepted for publication in ACADIA 2022 and the third for SiGRADI 2023. These publications demonstrate that MSD-RAS student projects are competitive with world-leading research undertaken by full-time faculty and PhD students, yet these projects were undertaken in a single spring semester! We are excited to see the diverse, technically challenging, and ambitious research-led-design projects our students have achieved being shared with the broader academic and professional communities, and to see our graduates transition to alumni as they embark on careers in innovative design, fabrication, and technology-driven industries and practice!

Faculty:

MSD in Robotics and Autonomous Systems:
Material Agencies: Robotics & Design Lab II

Faculty: Robert Stuart-Smith
Teaching Assistant: David Forero
Collaborators: Via Domani, TCR Composites, Lemond Carbon,
    & Dropbox

In Material Agencies, speculative design proposals are developed through fabricated prototypes, and the parallel development of a design-to-production workflow that is explored and demonstrated through computer simulation, modeling, and robotic workflows. As such, Material Agencies seeks to engage with robotic fabrication and material production as generative contributors to creative design outcomes, enabling design agencies to also operate through materials and robot platforms. Qualitative design character is curated through the parallel development of custom approaches to conceiving, manipulating, and responding to matter. Successful design outcomes aim to exhibit bespoke character intrinsic to their design and production workflow.

This year, in a project undertaken across all Spring-semester courses, students developed a full-scale prototype of a multipart ceramic assembly for a façade screen together with a larger-scale digital building-scale façade design. Projects were developed outside of a traditional architectural brief or site constraints, operating primarily through research and development of a material manufacturing process, and strategies for robot programming and generative/computational design that facilitated the realization of each prototypical design proposal. These prototypical proposals speculate and demonstrate diverse opportunities related to facade performance, fabrication, use, and aesthetics.

Featured Student Work:

MSD in Robotics and Autonomous Systems: Material Agencies

Faculty: Andrew Saunders
Teaching Assistants: Riley Studebaker and Matthew White
Collaborators: Via Domani, TCR Composites, Lemond Carbon,
  & Dropbox

Material Agencies Section 1 is the half-semester introductory studio to the Master of Science in Design: Robotics and Autonomous Systems (MSD-RAS) program at the University of Pennsylvania Stuart Weitzman School of Design. This course will introduce students to the Robotic Lab through a software/hardware routine to engage the ABB IRB4600-60 six-axes industrial robot with a hot-wire foam cutting end-effector. The studio focuses exclusively on working with an industrial robotic arm and a large-scale hot-wire cutter end-effector to cut foam. This relatively simple robotic extension quickly introduces students to the robotic lab, robot interface, and ultimately produces tangible results quickly, yet also highlights the designer's need to develop designs within geometrical constraints that are tightly related to specific manufacturing processes—in this case, the hot-wire cutter's production of ruled surface geometries. Operating through ruled surface geometries enables the designer to have maximum control over the manufactured output whilst removing the need for post-design geometric rationalization or value engineering activities. The architectural project for the studio is a speculative ceilingscape re-design for one of the large galleries in Meyerson Hall that currently features a ubiquitous hung acoustical tile system.

Featured Student Work:

MSD in Robotics and Autonomous Systems: Material Agencies

Faculty: Ezio Blasetti
Collaborators: Via Domani, TCR Composites, Lemond Carbon, & Dropbox

The second half of the semester, the Material Agencies Studio focuses on robotic fabrication of composite fiber materials and generative algorithmic methods in architectural design. The students investigate non-linear systems at both a methodological and tectonic level. The exploration takes the form of design research, which is tested through an architectural proposal.

The project of the studio is the design of a hybrid programmable structure that supports an Autonomous Public Garden. The project manifests as a lightweight endoskeleton providing envelope and support for the growth of an organic structural and ephemeral system. This semi-structural composite scaffold supports the internal growth of the garden: synthetic environments of high definition. Over time the two systems—organic and inorganic—merge into a single ecology.

Participants learn to apply principles of computational thinking into an architectural proposal. They develop their own generative evolutionary design strategy through algorithmic techniques for the analysis and generation of form. They explore and document the relationship of material behavior and digital simulation. Participants synthesize this knowledge into a robotically fabricated adaptive architectural proposal that responds to environmental and other external inputs.

The project is concerned with the relationship of art and architecture, formation and performance. Historically, the space of the Garden is a hybrid gradient of public and private, a territorial buffer that interfaces with the commons and the environment. In this studio we operate under the conceptual framework for architectural space as a form of life itself: a living nexus operating in a multiplicity of material, biological, technological, and economic domains.

Featured Student Work:

THESE THINGS SWIRL
Davis Dunaway, Layton Gwinn, & Dan Rothbart

The phase-changing nature of slip casting makes it ideal for the production of complex, standalone components; however, it currently lacks the ability to produce meaningful visual variation between components without the use of an entirely new mold. This research explores a novel technique for creating bespoke, slip-cast artifacts through the use of six-axis robotic motion to use plastic rotational molding methods in slip casting.

By incrementally injecting different ratios of colored slip into the mold while it is rotated, we are able to achieve variable color, pattern, and structure. Because of the highly precise nature of the robotic motion, this variation can be repeated with a relatively high degree of accuracy. In addition, incremental injection of slip allows a full cast to be achieved with a minimal amount of slip, entirely removing the draining process used in traditional slip casting. A prototypical façade part was developed with this slip-casting method to produce diverse marbling within

a series of tetrahedral components. Before each component is bone-dry, and still malleable, they are assembled using a custom robot pick-and-place routine that attempts to subtly squish components against each other. The orientation and placement of each element was determined within a custom-developed generative design and material physics simulation. The research aims to introduce new variables into the world of mass-manufactured slip-cast ceramics in the form of controllable color and pattern.

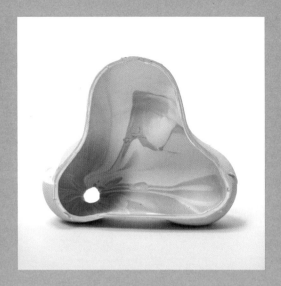

LIGHT-ING
Jingjing Yan, Siyu Dong, Xiangguo Cui, & Shunyi Yang

This research investigates different clay bodies' physio-material properties and their transmittance post-firing, together with their relationship to form, material properties, and porosity, and how these correspond to different interior and exterior lighting effects. Glazed architectural ceramic components are fabricated using a custom robotic manufacturing and tooling method that forms clay into variable panel configurations through iterative manipulations that do not require costly and materially wasteful molds. A real-time adaptive perforation control and tooling method allows components to incorporate a distributed field of variably orientated holes to achieve a specified lighting transmissiveness in relation to computer vision and sensor data in addition to 3D design criteria. A semi-autonomous process manufactures panels that are partially designed within a computational approach to 3D building performance analysis metrics and façade design, and partially during fabrication where a desired light transmittance level arises from the manipulation and perforation of each panel in relation to live sensor data feedback. The research approach exploits the malleability and translucency of porcelain ceramics within an industrially scalable bespoke process and is realized in a partial facade assemblage that demonstrates a variable panel geometry, light transmittance, and material aesthetic.

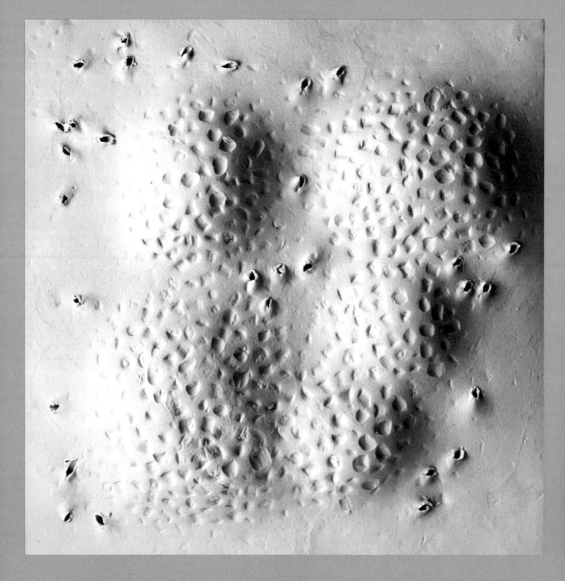

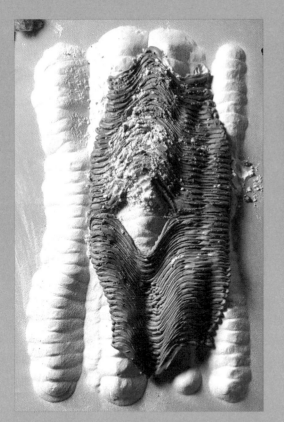

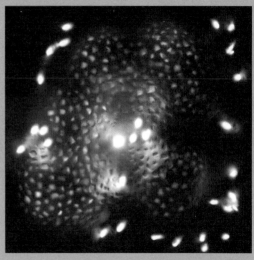

RULED PEAKS AND NOZZLE-SCAPE

Xianggou Cui, Jingjing Yan, Davis Dunaway, & Siyu Dong

To familiarize ourselves with the process of creating ruled surfaces we studied the sculpture of Nuam Gabo's Linear Construction in Space No. 2. We then gave images of reconstructed models to a CNN. The goal of the process was to have a Convolutional Neural Network identify features from the images and propagate them in a much larger area in ways that were interesting and unexpected.

When multiple features are brought together, the tooling links up to create winding paths and spirals that traverse the whole ceiling. The smooth surface of each protrusion stands out in stark contrast to the rest of its surroundings. After seeing this contrast we decided to lean into this by turning each of the smooth protrusions into a unique light fixture that cast dynamic shadows around them.

For a proof of concept for the entire ceiling we settled on a grouping of three cells totaling 17 pieces. It was important for us to produce

more than a single cell, as the interactions in the ceiling where cells' boundaries met produced the most interesting overall results.

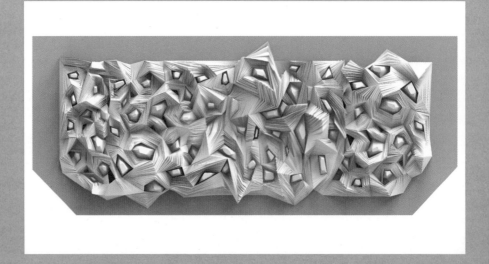

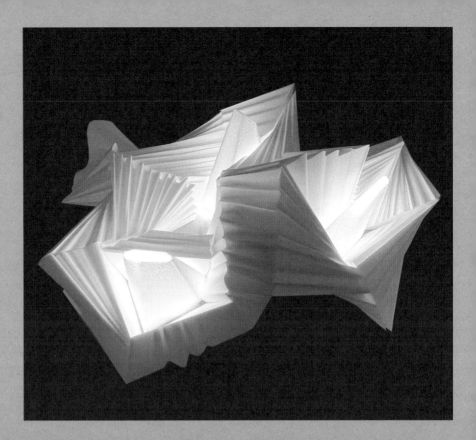

LUMINESCENT POLAR-SCAPE
Zilong Han, Yuxuan Wang, Chenxiao Li, & Mingyang Yuan

We tried to preserve the harmony of both constructivist sculptures by adding surface micro reliefs to enhance the quality and aesthetics of the cutting surface. Thus, after a thorough understanding of how hyperbolic surface rails come together, we applied the Convolutional Neural Network style transfer process to it. We applied the human-in-the-loop theory to the CNN's process, and by combining humans' aesthetic judging ability with CNN's generating ability we can achieve some unexpected but exciting results. We let the CNN generate a series of results from a series of inputs, and selected the most promising result by team discussion. We took the form out of the style and base images and turned it into the overall design. Then we reorganized and recomposed the form to create a more distinctive character which consists of four different types of modules. The participation of robots allows the entire ceiling to be freed from the current limitations in terms of space, material, and form. The advanced production techniques made it possible to achieve mass customization and further allowed for new ideologies and sculptural forms to be derived in real construction projects.

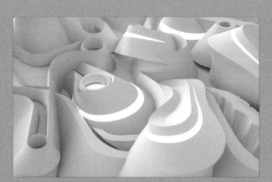

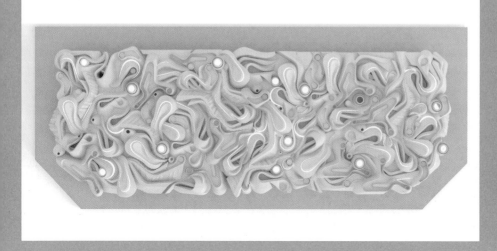

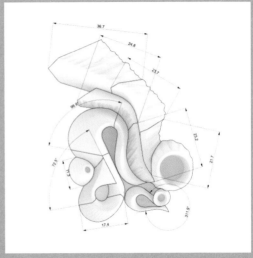

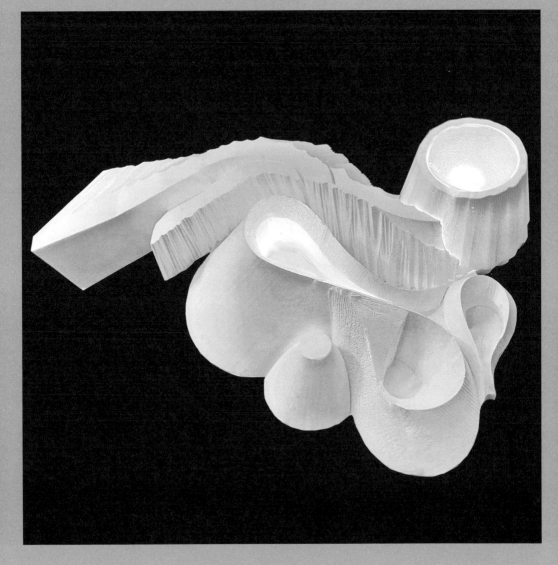

MSD: RAS   Andrew Saunders

TENSIONET
Jingjing Yan, Siyu Dong, Davis Dunaway, & Xiangguo Cui

The project Tensionet is an adaptive carbon-fibre pavilion project based on wind environment in the past semester, in which we calculated the optimal force shape of the pavilion using mechanical simulation in Karamba3D. For a freeform arrangement of carbon-fibre linear members to have architectural value, we created an agent-based system where each has its magnetic field that causes adjacent agents to align themselves perpendicularly.

Additionally, amassing mesh serves as an additional attractor, the strength of which can be varied by mesh color. Over time, the agents are pulled close to the mesh and begin to encapsulate it, creating a rough surface approximation. In addition, to create a pavilion with a reasonable mechanical structure and an excellent indoor wind environment, we also set the wind sensor and motor on the windward side, and the Arduino can control the opening and closing of the surface according to the wind.

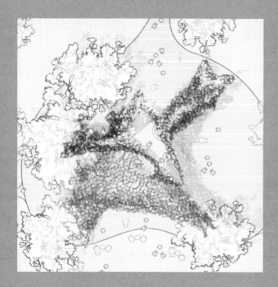

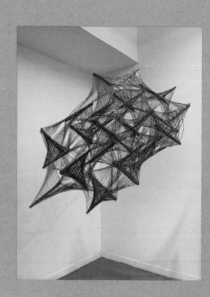

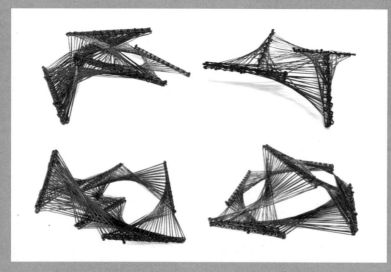

QUAY KNIT
A RECONFIGURABLE KINETIC FLOATING GARDEN BY ROBOTICALLY WOVEN CARBON FIBER

June Yuan, Chenxiao Li, Yuxuan Wang, & Zilong Han

The project is located in Fairmount Park, near the Philadelphia Museum of Art. Our goal is to build a facility to benefit animals by providing high-quality habitat for them while providing people with an appealing and unique place to visit. On the site, wetlands and forests provide habitat for animals, and the driftwoods become the place where birds would like to gather.

Inspired by the Rubric Snake geometry, we developed an algorithm for unit aggregation with agent-based logic. Incorporating the parameters such as attraction, avoidance, alignment, and cohesion, we came up with a massing that reacts to the water current and programming needs.

In order to adapt to rapid bespoke production, we designed a prefabrication and assemblage pipeline with carbon-fiber contour weaving on ABB IRB 4600. Due to the lightness of weight, these components could be easily transported to the site for custom assemblage. They will also be able to respond to different needs with the sensor and motor installed at the connections.

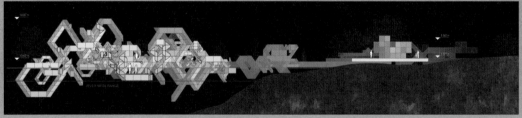

MSD: RAS   Ezio Blasetti

MSD Required Courses

ARCH 710
Contemporary Theory
Faculty: Esther Choi

Theory can be a set of principles to explain a practice, a philosophical viewpoint, a manifesto, a conceptual structure for self-reflection, an ideological argument, or a cultural project in itself. This semester-long course in architectural theory will explore the changing roles, objectives, and methodologies of architectural theory since the early aughts with the goal of instilling students with a greater sense of historical and cultural awareness, and tools for critical inquiry. Each week, we will analyze international architectural projects of the past 30 years, as well as the interpretive frameworks that architectural theorists have offered in each instance.

ARCH 715
Contemporary Aesthetics
Theory
Faculty: Daniela Fabricius

This weekly seminar will take as its object the field of aesthetics and its relationship to architecture and its contemporary social and cultural condition. Aesthetics are often sidelined in architectural discussions as dealing with mere surface, style, or subjective notions of beauty. By contrast, this course will place aesthetics at its center in order to reveal how it functions as a discourse that is deeply enmeshed in material, political, and cultural histories. The course will present a number of critical approaches to aesthetics, as well as explore different contemporary ideas around the transformative potentials of aesthetics as a form of

sensorial and cultural practice. In discussions on readings and case studies, students will explore aesthetics in relation to contemporary issues, including gender, the Anthropocene, the non-human, race, the digital, and the post-colonial.

ARCH 751
Ecology, Technology,
& Design
Faculty: Dr. William W.
Braham, FAIA

The course draws on systems ecology and the history and philosophy of technology to examine the complex task of environmental building design. Rethinking ecological design at the beginning of the 21st century means reconsidering the strong claims made about ecology and technology—utopian and dystopian—through the 20th century, as the impacts of

Cristiano Ronaldo makes FIFA history by becoming the s
leading goal scorer with a record of 807 goals.

NASA unveils the first color images from the James Webb Space Telescope.

technology on eco-systems were encountered.

The term ecology was first coined in the late-19th century to describe the complex role of the environment in the evolution of species, and has grown to become the branch of biology concerned with the organization and dynamics of the entire bio-geosphere. Since the 1930s, the reach of ecological thinking has been extended dramatically by two developments, increased awareness of the environmental effect of human actions and the refinement of systems theory.

Environmental building design is a process of discovery, of deciding what to work on, before it ever becomes a matter of design. The course begins with urban self-organization, using cities to explore the principles of systems ecology, developed by HT Odum and his colleagues. Considering the theories of self-organization, natural selection, maximum power, and energy transformation hierarchies will provide a scientific basis for the examination of energy and resource flows in buildings. The next section applies those concepts to buildings as shelters, and the final section to the products and processes that occupy buildings, from working, eating, sleeping, playing, and so on. Course work will include weekly readings, in-class exercises, and a project in three stages. Weekly class meetings will be divided between lectures, discussion, exercises, and student presentations.

ARCH 752
EBD Research Seminar
Faculty: Dr. William W. Braham, FAIA

Environmental building design is a process of discovery, of understanding what to work on, before it ever

becomes a matter of design or of performance analysis. This means tackling questions large and small, considering both technical details and architectural possibilities, and establishing a position in a continually evolving field.

The work of the seminar is to develop methods of research for this complex field, to develop tools, information, and concepts to guide design.

The course will help students establish research habits and agendas to support their work in environmental building design, both in design studios and in practice. That work will be developed in stages through the semester. Based on case studies of exemplary environmental buildings, students will explore specific topics in building science as they contribute to architectural projects, developing bibliographies of current work and a final research report, summarizing the state of the field and current tools and practices.

ARCH 753
Building Performance Simulation
Faculty: Kit Elsworth, & Saeran Vasanthakumar

WHAT IS SIMULATION? Simulation is the process of making a simplified model of a complex system to better predict or understand the behavior or the original system. This course provides students with an understanding of building design simulation methods; hands-on experience in using digital and physical simulation models; and exploration of the technologies, underlying principles, and potential applications of simulation tools in architecture through weekly lectures and hands-on simulation lab exercises. A series of analysis projects

will link design decision-making to building performance outcomes.

ARCH 803
Algorithmic Design & Robotic Fabrication
Faculty: Ezio Blasetti

Supports ARCH 801 Material Agencies I. Topics vary to suit application within the Arch 801 brief. This seminar ties the programming of robot motion to a generative design process, removing conceptual and practical barriers between design conception and project implementation. Computer and robot programming skills will be developed to support both design and robotic fabrication constraints in parallel. Working within a 3D programming environment, participants will aim to program robot production methods that in turn generate design outcomes when deployed in physical processes on Penn's Industrial Robots. Subject matter and software varies; examples include: Java, Python, Grasshopper, etc.

ARCH 805
Introduction: Micro-Controllers
Faculty: Ezio Blasetti

Supports ARCH 801 Material Agencies I. This introductory seminar covers the design and assembly of electronic circuits using sensors/actuators and micro-controllers, and their use in closed or open reactive systems. The seminar work is intended to support an ARCH801 project prototype to drive additional design affects (e.g., morphology/kinetics, lighting, porosity, translucency, etc.). The course explores control, feedback, energy, and force in relation to interactions of matter, space, and perceived activity (human or non-human), and the embedment of Internet of Things (IOT)

MSD Required Courses

technologies to drive additional design agencies.

ARCH 807
RAS Theory Seminar:
Architecture in the Age
of Thinking Machines
Faculty: Evangelos Kotsioris

Robotics, autonomous systems, advanced methods of fabrication, AI—are all terms that seem to have become common-place among architects. Yet their origins, evolution, and philosophical underpinning often remain obscure. This seminar is intended as a historical and theoretical introduction to a series of key concepts that are central to the MSD Robotics and Autonomous Systems program. Using contemporary discourse and concerns as a jumping-off point, the course (re)constructs an archaeology of interdisciplinary knowledge central to design computation, machine intelligence, and automated fabrication. The intellectual origins of these areas, and their profound consequences for architecture, are traced back to the fields of technology, communication theory, cybernetics, systems theory, developmental biology, robotics, network theory, aesthetics, psychology, and artificial intelligence, among others.

The combination of historical sources and contemporary texts provide students with a common lexicon and set of references that will allow them to articulate and critically assess their own conceptual and material explorations in robust ways. Particular emphasis will be put on the philosophical, socio-political, environmental, and ethical extensions of existing and emerging digital technologies—including the adverse effects of profiled surveillance, automated decision-making,

and algorithmic bias, among others. Weekly readings will provide the basis for discussions but also serve as interpretative lenses for the analysis of case study projects. Supplementary sources will enable students to deepen their literacy on specific topics beyond the completion of the seminar.

ARCH 802
Material Agency: Robotics &
Design Lab II
Faculty: Robert Stuart-Smith

This course will leverage knowledge gained by students in the Fall and set an ambitious aim for the experimentation, development, and demonstration of a robotically manufactured design prototype that is intrinsically related to a bespoke production process. The end product will involve a one-to-one part or whole, physically fabricated work that will be accompanied by either a live demonstration or video production. During the first half of the semester students will engage in the development of bespoke robotic tooling, sensor, and programming capabilities in order to create novel manufacturing processes that explore ideas of intelligent or autonomous manufacturing with an emphasis on responsive or manipulation-based processes. Industry processes will be leveraged yet re-cast through creative engagement with manufacturing materials, tools, and production operations. Participants will follow a brief that specifies a line of inquiry or scenario, whilst allowing some degree of self-direction. Projects will engage in a speculative and critical approach to architectural design, production, and use while leveraging robotics platforms, methods for machine vision, sensing, and learning, in addition to an

engagement with material dynamics and computer programming within design research. A successful project is expected to: demonstrate a rigorously crafted design artifact; explore novel approaches to design, material fabrication, and user engagement, questioning the role and nature of architecture's physical and cultural contribution; and explore novel forms of robotic production and representation. Some proposals will involve live or filmed demonstrator performances. All projects will require a computer simulation or animation that demonstrates a temporal consideration for design, manufacture, or use. The course introduces robot tooling, sensor-feedback procedures, one-to-one material prototyping, and building design with tectonic considerations. Examples of potentially relevant industry processes include: sheet-metal bending, incremental metal forming, and additive and subtractive manufacturing.

ARCH 804
Advanced RAS Programming
Faculty: Jeffrey Anderson

This seminar provides a theoretical context to the program, relating autonomous robotics and fabrication research to architectural discourse, philosophy, science, and technology. The course commences with a historical overview of scientific topics including cybernetics, complexity theory, emergence/self-organization, evolution/developmental biology, and behavior-based robotics. The course also critically assesses present and future societal trajectories in relation to technology, exploring socio-political, ethical, and philosophical arguments that concern a broader technological shift that has occurred

Scientists develop solar panels that can generate electricity at night.

An original print of Man Ray's *Le Violon d'Ingres* becomes the most expensive photograph ever sold at auction after it sells for USD$12.4 million at Christie's in New York City.

during the last decade which has given rise to our unquestioned reliance on algorithms within our everyday lives (social media, shopping, navigation), and similar impact from Urban OS's, Industry 4, and driverless car technologies. Readings cover philosophy, computer science, cybernetics, robotics, sociology, and psychology, and will be discussed in relation to their consideration within the domain of architectural design and building technology. Examples include: Blaise Aguera y Arcas, Maurice Conti, Norbert Weiner, Kevin Kelly, Ray Kurzweil, Ed Finn, Donna Haraway, Andre Gorz, Bruce Sterling, Daniel Kahneman, Timothy Morton, Levi Bryant. A theoretical written statement related to ARCH 801 Material Agencies I Section 1 or 2 will be produced by participants within this core seminar.

ARCH 808
Experimental Matter
Faculty: Nathan King

This course aims to extend knowledge into state-of-the-art materials, material applications, and fabrication methods and contribute research and experimental results towards ARCH 802 Material Agencies II course prototypical projects. Operating predominantly through research and controlled physical experiments, students will develop a material strategy for their ARCH 802 Material Agencies II work, investigating scientific research papers, industry publications, and precedent projects in order to develop know-how in materials and material applications. A material application method will be proposed and experimented with to evaluate and develop use within a robotic fabrication process. Submissions will incorporate

experimental test results, methods, and precedent research documentation.

ARCH 806
Experimental Tooling
Faculty: Nathan King

Experimental Tooling positions ceramic material systems as a vehicle for exploring applied research methodologies and investigations into the opportunities (and challenges) afforded by robotic fabrication techniques. More specifically, Experimental Tooling builds knowledge in robotic and material methods of production and develops applied research for industrial robot end-of-arm tooling and I/O to enhance a material production process and facilitate new design opportunities.

ARCH 812
Methods in Architectural Field Research
Faculty: Franca Trubiano

Methods in Architectural Research is an advanced research seminar aimed at PhD and MS students which introduces means, methods, types, and values typical of architectural research. This "Methods" course (which is also open to MEBD and MArch students) speaks to the 'how' and 'why' of research. It investigates how one identifies a field of enquiry; what are the questions of value to the field; the various methods, strategies, and tactics of engagement representative of the field; as well as the critical knowledge needed in communicating one's results. The architectural profession is largely predicated on studio-based practices and yet the larger discipline—as defined in post-professional programs, doctoral studies, think tanks, research centers, and labs—participates in multiple forms

of enquiry whose investigative protocols and metrics of excellence are often borrowed from both the humanities and the sciences. Why therefore, do we hardly ever engage in this form of knowledge production in professional schools of architecture? Architecture's destiny is to be a form of composite knowing, in which both qualitative and quantitative methods of enquiry are needed in delimiting its research horizons. As such, students in Methods in Architectural Research are introduced to a spectrum of methods inclusive of the arts, design, theory, history, social sciences, environmental sciences, building science, and engineering. Whether architects reflect, theorize, analyze, or test ideas; whether they construct, build artifacts, simulate environments, develop software, or cull data, they do so by implementing research processes and by communicating their results using verifiable reporting mechanisms. The seminar introduces, discusses, and reviews the full spectrum of research methods typical of the discipline with the goal of having students design the research process for their respective dissertations.

ARCH 813
Qualifying Research
Faculty: Sophie Hochhäusl, & Dorit Aviv

This is an independent study course for first-year PhD and MS students, supervised by a member of the Graduate Group in Architecture. A course of readings and advisor sessions throughout the semester will result in an independent study paper, which will also be used as the student's qualifying paper for the Qualifying Examination. This research paper will be prepared as if for scholarly publication.

ARCH 814
The Idea of the
Avant-Garde in Architecture
Faculty: Joan Ockman

No historian of architecture has written as intensely about the contradictions of architecture in late-modern society or reflected as deeply on the resulting problems and tasks of architectural historiography as Manfredo Tafuri (1935–94). For many, the Italian historian's dismissal of "hopes in design" under conditions of advanced capitalism produced a disciplinary impasse. This in turn led to call to outlier Tafuri—to move beyong his pessimistic and lacerating stance. The seminar will undertake a close reading of one of Tafuri's most complexly conceived and richly elaborated books, *The Sphere and the Labyrinth: Avant-Gardes and Architecture form Piranesi to the 1970s*. Initially published in Italian in 1980 and translated into English in 1987, the book represents the first effort to define and historicize the concept of an avant garde specifically in architecture. Its content centers on the radical formal and urban experiments of the first three decades of the 20th century. Yet Tafuri surprisingly begins his account with the 18th century inventions of Piranesi, and he concludes with an examination of the "neo-avant-garde" of his own day. In addition to traversing *The Sphere and the Labyrinth* chapter by chapter—starting with the extraordinary methodological introduction, "The Historical 'Project'" —we shall also read a number of primary and secondary sources on the historical contexts under discussion and consider a number of important intertexts that shed light on Tafuri's position. The objectives of the course are at once historical and historiographic: we shall be concerned both with actual events and with how they have been written into history. Finally, we shall reassess the role of an avant garde in architecture and compare Tafuri's conception to that advanced in other disciplines. Is the concept of an avant garde still viable today? Or should it be consigned to the dustbin of 20th century ideas? Assignment for first class: read the introduction to *The Sphere and the Labyrinth*, pp. 1–21, "The Historical 'Project.'" A copy of the book is on reserve at the library. Note: The book is out of print. For future classes please make every effort to purchase a used copy or obtain one via interlibrary loan. Copies of individual chapters will also be made available on our class website.

Ketanji Brown Jackson becomes the first Black woman to serve as a Supreme Court Justice.

Capable of processing over a quintillion calculations per second, Frontier becomes the world's first exascale supercomputer.

PhD

Chair of the Graduate Group: Franca Trubiano

Of all the disciplines associated with building, architecture has participated in advanced scholarship and research for nearly six decades. The first PhD in Architecture in the United States was established at the University of Pennsylvania in 1964. Since its inception, the program has focused on advancing academic knowledge in the discipline of architecture. As one of the few professions whose founding texts originate in 100 AD, for decades the PhD Graduate Group in Architecture has hosted advanced scholarship in the History and Theory of Architecture by carefully considering the impact that reflective and critical ideas have on the discipline. Most recently, the knowledge environment associated with architecture has continued to transform and expand at Penn with the PhD program now conducting research in environmental design, structural design and computation, and bio-materials.

The past year, the program hosted PRECARITY, the online PhD conference on architectural research at the limits of technology, project-making, and history/theory, which invited an international cadre of PhD students to present their peer-reviewed work. Discussed across three sessions, is the difficut-to-overlook condition of life in the 21st century that is the precarious condition of the built environment. Whether by design or by circumstance, global capital, extractive industries, and their financial arrangements have rendered architecture highly vulnerable in the face of the wasteful consumption of matter, energy, and data. In addition, the necessary reckoning of the discipline with questions of gender, post-colonialism, and social justice has invited a necessary questioning of architecture's limits and audience.

The past year a number of graduates have successfully defended their dissertations. These narratives offer but a partial view of the diversity of subjects and questions investigated by our doctoral candidates. difficult

THINKING, SEEING, PRACTICING ARCHITECTURE: FROM THE SMITHSONS TO SCOTT BROWN AND VENTURI
Taryn Mudge

This dissertation situates the thought, vision, and design approach of Alison and Peter Smithson in relation to that of Denise Scott Brown and Robert Venturi to reveal a shared attitude toward "the real." I argue that each couple utilized a mode of visual research that was inspired by the social sciences; each relied on straightforward photographic documentation to represent their findings; and each made similar claims to "defer judgment" and embrace reality on its own terms: "as found." Their novel attitudes were first prompted by postwar conditions and progressed during a period when the discourse of architecture was shifting away from Modernism and toward Postmodernism. During this period there was a dissolution of Utopia and an energetic embrace of the status quo. Thus, the Smithsons and Scott Brown and Venturi adopted a method of architectural observation that tended to favor realism over utopianism and tended to look outside of the traditional academic bounds for sources of design inspiration. The question at the center of this research—what are the external forces that influence an architect's mindset and design process?—is vital to the historiography of architecture and urban planning for all periods and styles. The specific contribution of this narrative, however, is the acknowledgment that an architect's method of engaging and visually analyzing a site at the onset of a project affects production and determines the value of their work. Furthermore, the attitude of reserved judgement and method of sociological observation and photographic documentation outlined in this dissertation, I believe, is noteworthy and offers important lessons for present and future practitioners and students of architecture.

Denise Scott Brown, Philadelphia, 1961

GEOMETRY & TOPOLOGY: BUILDING MACHINE-LEARNING SURROGATE MODELS WITH GRAPHIC STATICS METHOD
Hao Zheng

This dissertation aims at developing a machine-learning workflow in solving design-related problems, taking a data-driven structural design method with topological data using graphic statics as an example. It shows the advantages of building machine-learning surrogate models for learning the design topology—the relationship of design elements. It reveals a future tendency of the coexistence of the human designer and the machine, in which the machine learns the appearance and correlation between design data, while the human supervises the learning process. It proposes to use machine learning as a framework and graphic statics as a supporting method to provide training data, suggesting a new design methodology by the machine learning of the topology. Different from previous geometry-based design, in which only the design geometry is presented and considered, in this new topology-based design, the human designer employs the machine and provides training materials showing the topology of a design to train the machine. The machine finds the design rules related to the topology and applies the trained machine-learning models to generate new design cases as both the geometry and the topology.

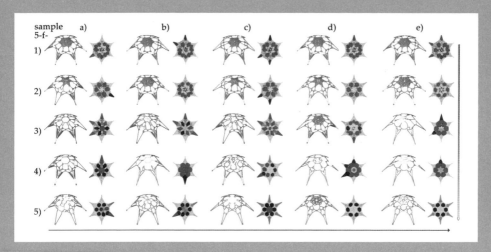

Form finding of shell structures based on machine-learning-assisted performance evaluation.

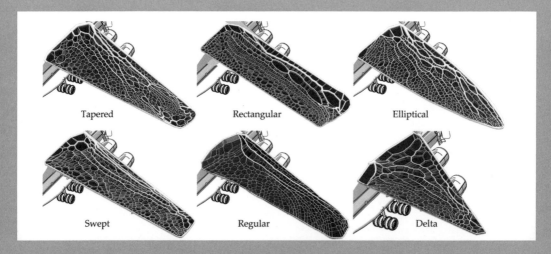

Tapered · Rectangular · Elliptical

Swept · Regular · Delta

Structural forms of airplane wings generated from machine learning of dragonfly wings.

Dr. Masoud Akbarzadeh

HANS SCHAROUN,
NEUES BAUEN, AND THE
CHINESE WERKBUND:
THE SEARCH FOR POST-
PERSPECTIVAL SPACE
Liyang Ding

The dissertation investigates
the role that Chinese architecture, urbanism, and cultural
history played in shaping
Hans Scharoun's design
thinking and postwar practice. Influenced by Hugo
Häring's organic building
agenda and profound interest
in East Asian architecture,
Scharoun engaged in the
mid-1930s with the Chinese
architectural tradition. From
October 1941 to May 1942,
Scharoun participated in
an organization called the
Chinese Werkbund initiated
by Häring. Thanks to these
meetings, and notwithstand-
ing never having visited
China, Scharoun developed
his unique understanding
of organic buildings as well
as strikingly original urbanist
ideas and spatial concepts
including Stadtlandschaft,
"a-perspectival" space,
and Raum der Mitte. All these
concepts borrowed and
adapted Chinese architecture
and town-planning principles.
This research argues that
Scharoun's turn toward
Chinese precedents—wholly
removed from European
examples tainted by the
National Socialist distortions
of the tradition—provided him
with an opportunity to rethink
the fundamentals of architectural and urban order.

Early Sketch, Hans Scharoun, Berlin Philharmonic Concert Hall, 1956.

Dr. David Leatherbarrow

Integrated Product Design

Director: Sarah Rottenberg

The Integrated Product Design Master's program brings the Weitzman School of Design together with two other world-class institutions, the School of Engineering and Applied Sciences and Wharton School of Business, to offer students an opportunity to develop a holistic understanding of the product design process. Students from design, engineering, and business backgrounds learn how to integrate the other disciplines into their process and design what's next. IPD draws upon the heritage and research strengths at Penn and teaches students how to implement fully formed product ideas. Our graduates go on to become product designers, design engineers, corporate innovation leaders, and entrepreneurs.

In addition to skills in design, business, and engineering, IPD students learn how to creatively solve problems, how to wade into ambiguity and create a path forward, and how to adapt and evolve their projects in response to new learnings and feedback. This creative agility is increasingly valuable to organizations as they realize the necessity of ongoing innovation, invention, and reinvention to their businesses. The skills that IPD students possess enable them to focus on social innovation, solving big, complex challenges and designing better digital and physical products for a better world.

In 2022, a project from IPD 799 Final Project, Maeve, was selected to be showcased in the Global Grad Show, an international graduate exhibition in Dubai featuring 100 impact innovation projects.

Faculty:

Integrated Product Design:
Final Project

Faculty: JD Albert, Chris Murray, & Sarah Rottenberg

The last two semesters of the IPD studio sequence consist of the IPD Final Project. Students choose to work on design problems that follow their passion or a real-world problem provided by our partners in academia, industry, or the non-profit world. The Final Project enables students to put the skills that they have developed in engineering, design arts, and business into practice, following the process from initial opportunity identification into the development of a working product with a complementary business plan. Interdisciplinary group work is encouraged on final projects. Working in teams offers students the opportunity to collaborate across skill sets and learn from teammates from different disciplines. Final Projects provide students with ample opportunity to learn leadership and collaboration skills that are invaluable in today's workplace.

Featured Student Work:

Integrated Product Design:
Problem Framing

Faculty: Mike Avery & Sarah Rottenberg
Teaching Assistants: Sean Barrett, Rachel Cole, & Zining Liang

This studio is structured for IPD students as an intensive, interdisciplinary exploration of Design as purposeful for Integrated Product Design. The goal of the studio is to give students a firsthand experience of various processes involved in creating successful integrated product designs. Students go through various stages of the design process including problem definition, concept development, ideation, prototyping, and idea refinement.

This year, students focused on designing A Future at the Boundary. Now more than ever, it feels that the world is at an inflection point—a boundary condition—where the future will not result from a direct and linear extension of the present. Instead, as a result of competing and often contradictory forces (transmissible respiratory illnesses, climate change, growing inequity, political dynamics, advances in technology, etc.), now is the time for a major shift in the way we, as individuals and communities, approach every aspect of our lives. As designers we have a pivotal role to play in shaping this trajectory. With this perspective in mind, students were asked to develop a physical product that would exist within and/or help make possible your envisioned future state within the topics of health and wellbeing, food systems, learning and education, or work.

Featured Student Work:

MAEVE
Rachel Cole, Zining Liang, Sarah Nowell, & Abigail Stein

Maeve is a just-in-time adaptive intervention mirror and app designed to improve mental health. Maeve works in conjunction with cognitive behavior therapy to disrupt negative behaviors in moments of need. Maeve's mission is to flip a common trigger, the mirror, into a healing tool, to support people throughout the entire recovery journey and make therapy more effective. Five million Americans will develop an eating disorder (ED) this year. Ten percent of the US population will develop an ED at some point in their lives. Mirrors are a common trigger and can be where people exhibit body checking and body avoidance, two common harmful body-related behaviors. Yet this is a space that has seen very little innovation outside of journaling apps and meditation videos. Maeve helps people regulate their mirror use during crisis moments.

VERT
Madeline Warshaw

Algae is the future. As climate change progresses, our air will become dirtier and our need for low-energy, clean food sources greater than ever before. We'll be eating less meat and needing more alternative forms of protein. We'll be looking for ways to purify the air in our homes from increasing pollutants. Algae is the answer on both accounts. Algae is a super-food, comprised of nearly 60 percent solid protein and full of essential vitamins. It relies on sunlight and carbon dioxide to survive, meaning it actively purifies the air as it grows, using the CO2 in your home as fuel.

Vert provides people with daily servings of algae while simultaneously cleaning the air in their homes. Add a bit of live spirulina to each of Vert's 54 pods, along with purified water and a drop of algae food, and turn on the air pump that oxygenates the cells. Over about two weeks, the cells will turn more and more green. The color is a cue for when to harvest; once a cell has turned dark green, it's time to remove the pod, eat the algae, and start the process over again. The Vert window unit has the air-purifying power of two 10-year-old trees or 120 indoor house plants. Vert can be customized to fit into a variety of home styles and window sizes with infinite design possibilities and patterns.